D0941678

DISCARDED

DISCARDED

TREATING ARTHRITIS

Medicine, Myth, and Magic

Illustration by Graciela Madrid,
representing an interpretation of drawings
from the cave Aux Trois Frères in France,
depicting a primitive medicine man

YOLO COUNTY LIBRARY
226 BUCKEYE STREET
WOODLAND, CA 95695-2600

TREATING ARTHRITIS

Medicine, Myth, and Magic

Félix Fernández-Madrid, M.D., Ph.D.

616.722
FER

Foreword by

Daniel J. McCarty, Jr., M.D.

INSIGHT BOOKS

Plenum Press • New York and London

Library of Congress Cataloging in Publication Data

Fernández-Madrid, Félix.
  Treating arthritis.
  Bibliography: p.
  Includes index.
  1. Arthritis—Popular works. 2. Arthritis—Treatment. 3. Quacks and quackery. I. Title. [DNLM: 1. Arthritis—therapy—popular works. 2. Folklore—popular works. 3. Magic—popular works. 4. Quackery—popular works. WE 344 F363t]
RC933.F47   1989   616.7′22   89-9140
ISBN 0-306-43185-8

© 1989 Plenum Press, New York
A Division of Plenum Publishing Corporation
233 Spring Street, New York, N.Y. 10013
An Insight Book

All rights reserved

No part of this book may be reproduced, stored in a retrieval system, or transmitted in any form or by any means, electronic, mechanical, photocopying, microfilming, recording, or otherwise, without written permission from the Publisher

Printed in the United States of America

FOREWORD

This volume by noted rheumatologist Félix Fernández-Madrid, M.D., Ph.D., is an ambitious undertaking. Dr. Madrid provides a unique approach to the massive problem of quackery in our modern "enlightened" society. He shows that beliefs in magic, sorcery, demons, and mystical "forces" were clearly found in the primitive, prescientific medicine of ancient cultures. These irrational but all-too-human beliefs persist in the "faith" healers, quacks, and charlatans of today. Most types of joint inflammation can be treated very successfully and a few can be cured (patient remaining well when the medication is stopped). Development of an irreversible deformity is always sad. When this occurs because truly effective treatment is delayed or not given at all, it is not only sad but tragic.

Dr. Madrid emphasizes the positive aspects of quackery— the laying on of hands, release of pent-up emotions, mental relaxation, and sometimes good advice on "clean living," such as avoidance of tobacco, moderation in eating, and regular exercise. These positive effects should also accompany conventional medical (drug) treatment by appropriately trained physicians. Unfortunately, some physicians treat only the disease while neglecting the patient. The quack almost always "treats" the patient's psyche. Any effects on organic disease (that which has caused pathologic changes in cells and tissues) are secondary to improvements in psychological outlook. The disease process in the tissues continues unperturbed.

The author proceeds to provide easily read commentary on diet, exercise, relaxation techniques, and other health care aspects that will answer most questions patients pose to rheumatologists. I enjoyed reading this book, particularly the imaginary trips through time and space seeking an effective treatment for arthritis. I heartily recommend it to arthritis sufferers who would like to be more informed about their disease.

Daniel J. McCarty, M.D.

Milwaukee, Wisconsin

ACKNOWLEDGMENTS

As I send this book to press, I recall with gratitude my patients who inspired this work and to whom it is dedicated.

There are many individuals to whom I am indebted. In applying the quotation from John Donne—"no man is an island"—to the question of my debts, I would like to thank the many rheumatologists with whom I have been associated over the years, for a good number of the facts and ideas in this book represent a consensus of the field or the product of multiple professional interactions. I am deeply appreciative of the tremendous help of Mrs. Patricia Kavolis, who has been personally involved in the many drafts required for preparation of the manuscript. She not only did the word processing, but also provided an ingredient that is rarely found in educational material for the public—patient input. Mrs. Kavolis should be an inspiration for the arthritic patient since she has rheumatoid arthritis.

I would also like to record my gratitude to Dr. Sherry Quiroz, who gave me critical advice on the way to focus this work on my audience. I am also grateful to Professor Daniel J. McCarty who carefully read the manuscript and made many valuable suggestions and criticisms. Special thanks go to Mrs. Ana Wand who was my nutritionist consultant and to Mrs. Rose Sullivan who also gave me valuable input.

I am also indebted to my cousin, Mrs. Graciela Madrid, and to Mr. Hubert Volkmann, two gifted artists, for contributing illustrations for this work.

Figure 1-1, Grave Stele with Isis, was a gift of Frederick K. Stearns to the Detroit Institute of Arts. The selection and interpretation of this piece of art was made possible through the help of Mr. William Peck. Figure 2-2, a reproduction of Lazarus by Rembrandt, was made possible through the kindness of the Toledo Museum of Art. Figure 4-1, a reproduction of a Greek bas-relief, was kindly authorized by the National Archaeological Museum of Athens.

Félix Fernández-Madrid

CONTENTS

INTRODUCTION

You now live in a box. The box is a disease called arthritis. Sometimes you function better than other times, but the box is always there as a reminder that you are not what you were, limiting your social life and your physical ability with pain and fatigue. Responding to "How are you?" becomes a study in self-control, for when your life is dominated by pain you just don't want to talk about it. You hate to think about waking up in the morning because you're always stiff and sore and getting up isn't much fun. When you move during your sleep you hurt yourself and the pain wakes you up. When you see your toes beginning to curl out of shape you are grateful for shoes and socks because no one else will see your deformed toes. It bothers you when people see the bumps on your elbows so you keep them covered with long sleeves. You get scared when you look at your hands because you can see them gradually deform-

1

ing. Your fingers worry you because they can no longer be straightened out and you have a hard time picking up little things like pins or pennies. You try hard not to think about your Aunt Hattie who finally could no longer move and your Aunt Esther's gnarled little body wracked with pain, but they stay tucked away in your memory to scare you. Sometimes, when the pain just won't go away, you can't avoid the thought that even death can be sweet and certainly better than hurting forever. But then, when the pain eases up, it seems as though being dead may not be such a good idea after all, and you want to be alive again. Like everyone else, you took your health for granted, but now you really appreciate the glory of not having pain.

You used to enjoy camping and roughing it in a tent with a sleeping bag on the ground. On a crisp fall day when the leaves blazed with color you used to canter through the woods on horseback as the sweet breath of the horse steamed in the cold fresh air. You used to love to walk the paths of an arboretum and occasionally spend a day at the zoo with a bunch of little kids who had never been to those places—ever in their lives—and listen to their squeals of discovery. But a day came when you could no longer do those things, because of the box. When your mother was ill she fell and gashed her head, but you couldn't pick her up. All you could do was clumsily try to cradle her head while you propped yourself close to her and said you were sorry—but she could not understand. You could not help her because of your box! You had to deal with a relative who received messages from the spirits and told you that your disease is bad karma brought with you from another life and that if you do not work it out in this life you will carry it with you into yet another for you to seek a solution. She further urged you to meditate, to go to spiritual healers (she was one), and praised various infallible holistic procedures to treat your arthritis.

You have been exposed to a mountain of books that extol the virtues of holistic approaches that employ occult methods and nonmedical techniques while scoffing at the advancements of medicine and disseminating doubt about the value of new treatments. There is a great deal of confusion about what is holistic healing and what is medical care. One of the tenets of the holistic approach is the responsibility the person has in his own healing. It may not be obvious to you that patient and family education and their participation in the treatment are essential components of the team approach to patient care. Indeed, a responsible patient's attitude is an essential component of orthodox medical treatment. Most of the old techniques used by holistic practitioners have only historical value and the compassionate treatment of the entire person rather than narrowly concentrating on only the disease itself has been used by good medical practitioners for centuries. With time, any nonmedical procedure may become medical if it is no longer supported by hearsay evidence alone but also is proved by controlled clinical trials. Some medical procedures may be old, yet continue to be in use because they have withstood the test of time, while many of the new ones may be abandoned after failing in experimental trials. The treatment of the patient's mind is just as medical as it may be holistic, and many maneuvers to relieve pain and anxiety frequently considered to be nonmedical are really medical. Medicine is a dynamic discipline that is continually changing as old methods that become obsolete are abandoned and new and promising ones are adopted. The need to stress the positive aspects of the medical treatment of arthritis was my primary motive in writing this book. Since many "cures" for arthritis involve dietary schemes, misinformation about nutrition runs rampant among arthritics. Consequently, an important part of this book is the focus on the real importance of nutrition for the arthritic.

The beliefs found in folklore about arthritis and many of the popular cures used by quacks are not modern inventions, but have their roots in ancient rituals that have been used by sorcerers for thousands of years. Faith healing, so popular among our arthritic patients, was also widely practiced during the time of ancient civilizations as the best available mode of treatment. Spiritual healing was the most effective technique available to the medicine man of primitive societies. Frequently, our arthritic patients keep searching for a better solution to their problems and eventually stumble upon and embrace unorthodox treatments. The alternative treatments draw the naive and many times the not-so-naive into the quagmire of quackery that promises a "cure" for the incurable. A myriad of false information available in popular publications, and commercial interests that hawk their products as fast relief or cure, encourage self-treatment and postpone seeking competent medical treatment.

If you accept my invitation to travel through ancient and now extinct civilizations in your quest to find relief for your pain and misery, you will be both amused and amazed as you experience the alternative cures of today from this fascinating perspective. When your travels finally return you to modern times, after you have shopped around and sampled the magic and miracles that have been offered for thousands of years, you will be wiser and more critical of any type of treatment offered to you. I hope that your journey through antiquity will improve your understanding of arthritis, stimulate your resistance to those who promise a cure for arthritis, and persuade you never to be tempted to try quack cures.

The testimony of many of my patients and the strong feelings I have about the fact that you have access to only the popular literature which glorifies magic and mystery and entices you to try "miraculous" cures also prompted the writing of this book.

Many patients unconsciously refuse to believe the reality of the situation and embrace quack treatments, delaying the beginning of effective medical therapy. If denial is the main coping strategy in your repertoire, you may not realize the urgent need to deal with the consequences of a disease that is there to stay. Although it is always possible to offer some relief, no matter how severe the destruction of the joints may be, realistically it is also true that less and less can be done for the patient when the arthritis has already caused great damage and he is totally incapacitated. This is frustrating when we know that many patients have expended critical time as they sought relief through unorthodox cures. In contrast, when a patient is seen early, a great deal can usually be done to suppress inflammation, retard the joint damage, protect the joints from future damage and, occasionally, induce a remission of the arthritis.

The beginning of many types of arthritis can be very confusing because pain and suffering may be present without deformities and with normal laboratory tests. No one likes being labeled a hypochondriac; but when your doctor doubts the reality of your complaints and your family looks at you with suspicion, you become vulnerable to the promises of quacks and you can easily be lured into their hands. It is when a person is in deep trouble, faced by the terror of the unknown, that his or her mind is more than ever laid open to the mystique of submitting to the "miracle cure." Such is your plight when you are struck by a chronic debilitating disease like arthritis. When you do not understand your disease, you can be deluded into thinking that you may as well try anything that is presented to you as long as it promises relief from your pain. It is likely that some patients may be turned off because their physician lacks the human touch that is so essential to obtaining a favorable response when pain and stiffness continue unabated. The alternative offered by the healer appears irresistible, for he not only promises a cure but he often shows the compassion that patients need. You cling to the idea that you can't be worse off than you are—but the overwhelming evidence proves that you can be—and will be—without treatment.

Mild inflammation with stiffness in early morning that disappears during the day may not be recognized as abnormal until it has persisted for a long time, and frequently joint damage has already begun when treatment is sought. If you are afflicted with "arthritis," you may have any of a large number of rheumatic diseases, some of which are chronic in nature. This means that their effects often extend throughout your lifetime. Although it is immensely beneficial for you to learn about the nature of arthritis, it is not wise to become your own diagnostician or to engage in self-treatment. Even though we cannot cure most of the chronic arthritis, medical thought does not rule out the possibility that a cure will be discovered in the future. In contrast, the holistic approach, as well as multiple quack schemes including spiritism and faith, and divine healing promise a cure for arthritis. It should be clear to you that it does not make sense to think of arthritis as though it were one disease nor is it logical to expect a single cure for many different diseases.

In the United States, almost half of the 50 million patients with arthritis are afflicted with osteoarthritis or rheumatoid arthritis, the two most common types. The cause of these arthritides, just as that of most common diseases afflicting mankind, is unknown. In spite of this, holistic practitioners as well as quacks pretend to get rid of the cause of arthritis. A rational discussion of the merits of the purported "cures" for the rheumatic diseases is long overdue. Some of these "cures" have grown out of ancient folklore and are mixtures of naiveté, ignorance, and common sense, but many have been invented by quacks to capitalize on the desperation of their victims. Following these alternative treatments can only lead to critical time lost during which irreversible destruction of the joints continues, leading to a lifelong course of pain and disability.

Inflammation of the joints is usually accompanied by pain; but pain may or may not be caused by inflammation. You should recognize that a patient with arthritis may have severe pain for reasons unrelated to the disease itself. Anxiety and stress can modify the perception of pain and elicit reactions that are excessive or abnormal. Inappropriate expression of pain can be responsible for unnecessary treatment, which can give rise to dangerous side effects. The proponents of the holistic approach would lead you to believe that medical treatment consists only in the use of drugs. Not true. You must become aware that there are many ways to combat arthritic pain. In addition to the use of drugs, dealing with important psychological factors such as relieving anxiety, decreasing stress, improving patient and family understanding, and various modalities of physical and occupational therapy and orthopedic techniques can effectively aid in relieving the arthritic pain and preventing disability.

For your expectations to be appropriate, you must have an understanding of the natural course of the disease. One of the most striking features of most types of arthritis is their characteristic flares and periods of lesser disease activity. When the arthritis improves spontaneously, denial of the reality of the problem is reinforced and will still carry over when the disease flares up again. Patients engaging in alternative treatments frequently do not understand that a "miraculous cure" may simply be a spontaneous remission. Some patients will have either a complete remission early in the disease or a mild course that will require little medical attention. In contrast, a small proportion of patients will develop relentless, crippling disease leading to severe limitation of activity, but the majority will be able to remain functional in spite of periods of decreased joint symptoms and flares of arthritis. Multiple studies reported in the last several decades suggest that earlier, more effective treatment of arthritis frequently prevents deformities and destruction of the joints, allowing the arthritic patient to enjoy an active role in society.

PART I

ANCIENT SORCERERS AND MAGICIANS—THE HARBINGERS OF THE MODERN QUACKS

CHAPTER 1

THE PRIMITIVE HEALER

This imaginary trip through the ancient civilizations will help you understand the origin of some of the existing popular "cures" for arthritis. You will soon learn that the repertoire of the primitive healer consisted of the observance of religious ceremonies as well as the practice of magic. In primitive societies special powers were attributed to those who had knowledge of the stars, medicinal plants, poisoned weapons, and those who claimed to have the means of defeating demons and pacifying angry spirits. From the earliest times there have been persons who have claimed to possess powers over nature and over the unseen. Medicine had its origin in magic and the earliest physicians were magicians; thus the earliest forms of medical treatment were magical rites. As a consequence, the first physician-magicians were those who "knew" how to predict the future by reading the stars, by interpreting natural phenomena, or by examining the viscera of animals. For thousands of years the organs of animals or of enemies that had been killed were thought to have curative powers when swallowed or rubbed on the body. Amulets simulating parts of the body are still used as a symbolic way to increase the healing power of these organs. An analogous belief held that some plants whose shapes resemble certain organs were potent remedies. Even today, the belief in the power of magic can still be found thriving in many parts of the world.

What did the primitive healer look like? You may see him depicted in the human figure in a painting on the wall of a French cave which is thought to have been created by the Cro-Magnon man who lived almost 40,000 years ago. There he was dancing, naked below his waist with an animal skin around his shoulders and a pair of deer's antlers on his head. One could speculate that the prehistoric magician considered himself to be the personification of a god, half human and half animal (see Frontispiece).

The primitive physician already knew how to influence human passions. The medicine man definitely employed psychologic support in his healing practices, using elaborate garments, sacrifices to the gods, prayer, fumigation, purification, and fasting, which were complemented by the use of amulets, the performance of exorcisms, and various symbolic rituals. The administration of medicinal drinks, massage, bloodletting, baths, and dietetic treatment were all well-known to the primitive healers. Primitive men sought to avoid the menacing influence of evil demons by hiding from their sight. This old idea is behind the origin of the masks and other rituals, some of which are still preserved in popular superstitions like the symbolic chain placed around your neck to guarantee that you will be preserved from harmful contacts, the rite of taboo and changing the name of a person in order to change his fate. Priestly medicine evolved from the primitive magical medicine. The history of religion and medicine is one and the same in very primitive times, as both essentially strive toward the same end—the protection of the individual from evil. During that time there was also an intimate link between magic and religion, and the first magicians were probably also priests.

You will recognize methods of diagnosing and treating arthritis that have been carried down from primitive times and are still in use by modern healers. Magic and healing were not only practiced by legitimate or authorized persons such as the king, the medicine man, or the priest. From very early times healing through magic was also widely practiced privately by illegitimate and unauthorized persons. The quack was born. You will see how quack practices developed and the way quacks lived and worked alongside orthodox practitioners and priests in the earliest Babylonian and Greek cultures. Although the mechanism of cheating has changed over many centuries as man became more sophisticated, you will notice that the psychology of the quack has changed very little. In ancient times, the course of the disease and the prognosis were partly revealed by the higher powers in dreams or while the healer was in a state of ecstasy, and partly by casual omens or by consultation with oracles. Much to your surprise, the ancient healers will personally interact with you on this imaginary trip as the striking similarities to modern-day quackery unfold.

Mesopotamian[1] Physicians and Sorcerers

Ancient tablets with cuneiform writing are practically the only source of information about Mesopotamian medicine. In the time of Ashurbanipal, the last great king of Assyria, the scribes were in the habit of copying and recopying ancient tablets. The bulk of medical tablets was found in the King's library, which was buried with the palace when "the divinely great city," Nineveh, was destroyed in 612 B.C.

[1]Mesopotamia, region in Asia Minor bounded by the Tigris and Euphrates rivers.

In Mesopotamian times healing was offered in two different ways. When you developed pain and swelling in your hands you could have consulted the *asu*, or physician, who had learned the art of healing with drugs. However, if you were desperate, you had the option of seeking the services of the *assipu*, or sorcerer, who used charms and incantations. The assipu can be considered one of the earliest recorded predecessors of modern-day faith healers. Both were certainly used by kings, for their correspondence with royal physicians is found along with general advice given by sorcerers. The sorcerer sometimes used drugs, and the asu occasionally used charms. When the Akkadian world declined, the sorcerer became much more important than the physician, a transient triumph of magic over medicine. That the sorcerer was a member of the clergy may have been a factor in his rise in importance. In Mesopotamia, the gods were the powers responsible for order in nature, peace and prosperity in social life. Direct contact with the higher gods was sought by the individual who was ill. Even the greatest kings assiduously solicited divine guidance.

Babylonians developed astrology, which they believed not only predicted plagues and cast horoscopes, but also revealed the prognosis of disease. They related the signs of the zodiac to certain illnesses and originated the belief that the course of the stars determines the lot of man from birth to his deathbed. Babylonians were responsible for many of the superstitions and misbeliefs which have exerted their influence on humanity for thousands of years. Many centuries later, in medieval Europe, the signs of the Zodiac were associated with certain parts of the body. For example, a surgeon would not operate on a wounded knee when the moon was in Capricorn, which was supposed to govern the knees. Babylonians believed that all events were subject to fate or the inevitability of predestination. For centuries astrologists have made a living selling horoscopes and amulets.

It is not surprising that in a civilization believed to be directly ruled by divine intervention, the assipu, as a member of the clergy, had a predominant role in the healing of bodies and souls. The two types of healers were probably collaborators rather than competitors. Moreover, the asu was probably subordinate to the priestly educated sorcerer, in whose service he may well have been a slave (Manjo, 1975). An equally important factor in the decline of the power of the asu in Akkadian medicine was probably the quality of the medicine he practiced, for he had very limited knowledge. His understanding of anatomy remained at the level of butchery, since dissection of human cadavers was taboo. His conviction that the liver harbored anger, strength was in the kidneys, and the brain was an unimportant part of the body revealed that his knowledge of physiology was almost nil. Mental disorders were thought to be caused by the magic of demons and were considered to have their origin in the heart, which was thought to be the seat of intelligence. If, during your stay in Babylonia, you wanted to consult a "cardiologist," it was probably because you suffered from a psychiatric condition!

When you arrived in Nineveh looking for the best physicians in the divine city, you first consulted the asu. Although you did not have wide experience with doctors, since your arthritis had just begun a few months earlier, you certainly did not like what you saw. It was obvious that the asu practiced a humble folk medicine, going about half-naked, with his hair shaved off, carrying a bag of herbs, a libation jar, a censer with coals ablaze, and a barber's knife (Manjo, 1975). Nevertheless, you tried some of the asu's preparations, which bore secret names. After the medicine of the sun god, the dog's tongue, and the skin of the yellow snake failed to relieve the recurring stiffness and pain in your joints, you were somewhat discouraged. Although the asu had some knowledge about the stars, the plants, and the organs of animals, you were not satisfied with his answers to your questions. His sparks of understanding were not vivid enough to discourage you from consulting the sorcerer. Since the rheumatic diseases were already common disorders, one could speculate that you and many other arthritics were eventually cared for by the assipu.

While you were in Nineveh the talk of the town was a "breakthrough" in the treatment of arthritis. Indeed, all the royal teeth had recently been removed to alleviate King Ashurbanipal's rheumatic pains. Since the treatment was clearly unsuccessful, you remembered this experience when this treatment was offered to you in the twentieth century to relieve your arthritis. The assipu was versed in the art of oneiromancy[2] and, in all probability, you spent one or more nights in the temple awaiting a dream-revelation from the gods concerning the cure of your arthritis. While your body was being anointed with oil and sprinkled with holy water, you could not help but compare this whimsical modus operandi with the simple and unattractive approach offered to you by the asu.

You soon learned that Mesopotamian medicine had its roots in magic. Life, sickness, and health were thought to be basically dependent upon metaphysical forces, gods, and demons. According to the Akkadian concept of disease, if you became ill it was either your own fault for having committed a sin, or you had become the victim of outside agents such as an evil spirit, a demon, a god, cold, dust, or a bad smell. Since you did not think your sins justified the punishment of arthritis, you were looking very hard for an outside agent.

The belief in the evil eye is said to have originated in Babylonia. The term has been applied to an eye believed to have the power to inflict various diseases and evils on persons by a mere glance. Although you kept thinking about it, you did not believe that anyone you knew could have done that to you. Babylonians were convinced that internal diseases, such as most arthritides, were caused by invisible malevolent spirits that entered the body with food, drink, or air. That was the solution to the riddle! With this concept of disease, it naturally followed that cure of your arthritis could have resulted from the expulsion of the evil spirit by magic or exorcism. You can clearly see that this thinking has been preserved right down to our times, as though fixed in formalin for over 3,000 years. Noting the similarity between

[2]Divination by means of dreams.

these beliefs and those promoted by some present–day faith and divine healers is unavoidable. It seems that while the asu has come a long way since King Ashurbanipal's time, the methods used by many modern faith healers and their concept of disease do not vastly differ from those of the Mesopotamian sorcerer of 3,000 to 5,000 years ago. Unhappily, in spite of the glamor of the assipu's approach to the treatment of your arthritis, when you left Mesopotamia you were still hurting as much as before.

The Yang i

In your struggle against arthritis you have now reached ancient China. Even before leaving for China you became acquainted with the principles of ancient Chinese medicine which were recorded and preserved on wooden tablets and on bamboo strips. The great medical classic, the *Huang Ti Nei Ching*, or *The Yellow Emperor's Classic on Internal Medicine*, called *Nei Ching* for short, written in the later years of the Chou dynasty more than 4,000 years ago, dealt extensively with acupuncture.

In the Nei Ching you found the first record of yin and yang, the two universal forces of Chinese philosophy. Many of your questions on the cause of arthritis, the way to treat it, and the relationship between diet and health were probably answered to your satisfaction in terms of these two principles. Yang was bright, dry, and masculine, while yin was dark, moist, and feminine. These forces were thought to be complementary, both necessary in specific proportions for proper balance. The ancient text claims that there is always yin in yang and yang in yin, and that pure yang or pure yin could not exist alone. This beautiful philosophical principle is one of the earliest expressions of the concept of harmony and proportion which lay behind many practical applications of order. The ancient Chinese thought that disease occurs when the equilibrium between the yang and the yin was disturbed. When yin was dominant, the individual suffered a yang disease, which is usually of sudden and acute onset. When yang was dominant, a yin disease resulted, usually gradual and insidious in onset. Yin diseases were thought to develop from within. When you learned these principles, it was clear to you that you suffered from a yin disease.

As an educated person, you probably read another classic available in the Chou library, the *I Ching*—or the *Book of Changes*, which stressed the value of prevention. Had your visit to China occurred many thousands of years ago, you would have consulted a physician, a priest, or a sorcerer. If you arrived in China after the fifth century B.C., you would have discovered that medicine—as in Greece—had slipped out of the hands of the priests and the sorcerers who each had separately listed duties. The evolution from religious and magical healing to medical healing must have already occurred by the time of Confucius. Around 500 B.C. he said that "a man without persistence will never make a good magician or a good physician." With few exceptions, religion and medicine then followed independent pathways for over 2,000 years until the beginning of this century, when the Pentecostal movement appeared.

The *Nei Ching* was written in the form of a conversation between Emperor Huang Ti and his prime minister, Ch'i Po, who never presented himself as a medical man but spoke as a wise logician. The Emperor once asked his prime minister why people in ancient times lived to be over a hundred years of age, yet remained active and did not become decrepit, while in their own times people reached only half that age and yet became decrepit. Ch'i Po answered: "In ancient times those people who understood Tao,[3] patterned themselves after the Yin and the Yang, and they lived in harmony with the arts of divination. There was temperance in eating and drinking. Their hours of rising and retiring were regular and not disorderly and wild. By these means the ancient kept their bodies united with their souls. Nowadays, people use wine as beverage and they adopt

[3]The way, in philosophical Taoism; that by virtue of which all things exist.

recklessness as usual behavior...they do not know how to find contentment within themselves, they are not skilled in the control of their spirits. They devote all their attention to the amusement of their minds, thus cutting themselves off from the joys of long life. Their rising and retirement are without regularity. For these reasons they reach only half of the hundred years and they degenerate." You most likely heeded these words of wisdom and found very useful the advice given by Ch'i Po to be moderate in eating and drinking, to find contentment within yourself, and to have a balance between rest and physical activity.

Although these principles were most helpful in improving your health in general, you were looking for a specific way to cure your arthritis. After all, the disease had now progressed to involve your elbows, shoulders, knees, ankles, and joints of your feet, and you experienced great difficulty in functioning. On this Ch'i Po was cold. He said: "The superior physician helps before the early budding of the disease...the inferior physician begins to help when [the disease] has already developed,...and since his help comes when the disease has already developed, it is said of him that he is ignorant." Hence, the Chinese sages did not treat those who were already ill, but they instructed those who were not yet ill in the art of staying healthy. "To administer medicines for diseases which have already developed...is comparable to the behavior of those persons who begin to dig a well after they have become thirsty, and of those who begin to cast weapons after they have already engaged in battle. Would these activities not be too late?" Since your arthritis was fairly advanced, you were somewhat disappointed with Ch'i Po's approach.

You could learn a great deal from these basic principles of Chinese philosophy. There is no question that disease prevention—when this is possible—is better than a "cure" of an established disease. Many of us could heed Ch'i Po's advice, since the intemperance in eating and drinking and the reckless behavior seen nowadays probably cannot compare to those observed by Ch'i Po in the time of the Yellow Emperor. I believe that a calm, philosophical attitude as well as temperance in what you eat and drink can support a healthier life. Modern examples of preventive medicine, among many others, are the eradication of some of the infectious diseases through vaccination and improvement of sanitation and hygienic conditions, the elimination of endemic goiter through the addition of iodine to salt, or the prevention of scurvy by the ingestion of citrus fruits and vegetables. Although we do not yet know how to prevent arthritis, even today Ch'i Po's prescription seems very reasonable.

You had heard so much about the power of acupuncture that you could not wait until you could experience its marvelous effects. You were astonished when the pain in your hands and shoulders greatly diminished after the first session. However, shortly after each treatment, disappointment quickly replaced your initial joy when the pain reappeared with regularity and your purse was empty.

Although the Chinese physician could not cure your arthritis, his reply to your question about the origin of pain was probably very useful. He declared that "when the spirit is hurt, severe pain ensues; when the body is hurt, swelling occurs. Thus, of those in whom severe pain is felt and swelling appears later, one can say that the spirit has injured the body. And of those in whom swelling appears first and severe pain is felt later, one can say that the body has injured the spirit." You could detect in his reply a deep concern about the relation of impairment of the mind to bodily ailments and vice versa. It appears that the concept of psychosomatic symptoms has been around for over 3,000 years.

Like many other arthritics, you had been desperately shopping around among physicians and healers. When you saw the Yang i, the Chinese physician, he began by investigating your social background and asking questions related to your environment. Were you rich or poor? Had you seen better times? Had there been any change in your standard of living? Was your arthritis affected by changes in the weather? Had you noticed any change in your appetite? Had you been emotionally upset?

Then, in an elaborate and lengthy ceremony, the Yang i felt the pulse in both of your wrists and compared them with his own. Although the Yang i probably obtained little diagnostic information by palpating your pulse, you surely felt comforted by this prolonged and direct contact with your physician. By feeling the pulse, the Yang i measured the meridians in which Ch'i, the inner energy, would be constantly flowing. You can see that in some ways this ritual was a precursor of the laying on of hands used in charismatic practices or of the contacts established by the mesmerist's finger magnets with the patient's mesmeric energy. The pulse ceremony of ancient Chinese medicine, however, was devoid of mystery or magic. It seems evident that the establishment of a strong doctor–patient relationship was a high priority for the early Chinese physician.

Since pain is a way of life for the arthritic, you were most interested in the stoical attitude with which the ancient Chinese withstood pain. This is epitomized in the traditional story about General Kuan Yu, whose arm had been pierced by a poisoned arrow, and was operated on by the surgeon Hua T'o. While the surgeon was scraping the bone, the General, seemingly unconcerned, played a game—and drank wine.

Chinese medicine, of all the medical systems of antiquity, came closest to being identified with philosophy. Although the Yang i did not cure your arthritis, you were extremely satisfied with your visit to ancient China because you were more serene and, from that time on, more than ever before, you felt you could better cope with the problems inflicted by the disease.

The Land of the Pharaohs

In your eternal quest to cure your arthritis, you next arrived in Egypt, attracted by the fame of the *Swnw*, the physician of the civilization that flourished along the Nile. Medicine became distinct from magic early in Egyptian history—for in the age of the pyramids, although the Swnw was still closely associated with magic and religious ritual, he was not a magician. If fame is a measure of success, the Swnw was very successful. In the Mediterranean world his healing art was unsurpassed, until it was absorbed and replaced by Greek medicine (Manjo, 1975). Although Egypt produced physicians who specialized in diseases of the eye, the head, the teeth, the abdomen, the anus, and the internal organs, you looked for a specialist in the rheumatic diseases but found none. Egyptian physicians belonged to the priesthood. Medicine, as well as the other branches of knowledge, was taught in the schools that existed in connection with the temples. The Egyptian art of healing achieved a height of national glory, outlasting the pharoahs and eventually merging with Greek medicine. We know about the Swnw from many sources including the papyri and the writings of the Greek historian, Herodotus. The first of the Egyptian medical writings appeared a little later than those of Mesopotamia. A trend toward replacing down-to-earth medicine with magic spells also developed in ancient Egypt. Throughout Egyptian history many of the functions of the priesthood were magical in character. When Egypt was dominated by Persia, medicine became a trade of sorcerers, drug vendors, and charlatans who preserved only the mysticism of the ancient medicine. You remembered that the magic of the sorcerer eventually predominated over the medicine of the primitive Akkadian physician.

Although most patients sought to be cured in the temples, the physician-priests also visited the sick in their own homes. Inasmuch as you were a visitor, you chose to go to the temple. You soon learned that the choice between drugs and magic to cure your arthritis was dependent upon the set of causes believed to be responsible for the disease. Those healers who became skilled in the preparation and use of drugs were no longer magicians; nevertheless, early physicians kept magic as a reserve force to be used in case of need. Magic was thought to have the power to eliminate the cause of the disease, while drugs were used to relieve symptoms. Since evil forces were thought to be an important cause of disease, magic was accepted as a perfectly logical treatment. Magic and incantations were the prevailing treatments for internal diseases, especially when the clinical situation was severe. I suggest that the claims made by most modern faith healers that their cures eliminate the cause of disease reflect the persistence of magic in primitive thought. Undoubtedly, your choice was magic since your condition had now progressed and you were quite disabled.

You were immediately fascinated with incantations based on the myth of Isis, the great enchantress (Fig. 1-1). The magician-goddess had two brothers, one good, Osiris, who was also her husband, and one bad, Seth. Seth became jealous of Osiris' success and power and sought to destroy him. At a feast to which both were invited, Seth succeeded in shutting him up in a chest which was then cast into the river. Isis at once looked for the chest and finally found it at Byblos in Phoenicia, hidden inside a sycamore tree which was made into a pillar for the king's palace. To Isis' despair, after she brought Osiris' body to Egypt, Seth again managed to get hold of it and proceeded to rip it into fourteen pieces which were scattered throughout Egypt. Isis, determined to bring Osiris back to life, looked for each of the lost pieces and found them all, except for the phallus, which had been eaten by a fish in the Nile. The magician-goddess probably lamented the lost part, but patiently reassembled the remaining pieces, lay upon Osiris' body and, in spite of the missing organ, took refuge in the marshes of the Delta and succeeded in conceiving Horus. Then she resuscitated her brother-husband.

The myth of Isis can be interpreted in several ways, but the aspect relevant to our discussion relates to divine healing. When you learned about the power of Isis, you believed that every sick person could impersonate Osiris and hope to be cured by the goddess. You can see that even after thousands of years the situation has not substantially changed. The almost universal belief underlying present-day healing practices that sickness

FIGURE 1-1. Grave Stele showing Isis and Nepthys. The bird flying above the dead, Ba, symbolized the spirit. A row of cobras overlooks the scene. From the Roman period 30 B.C.–ca. 400 A.D. From the Frederick Stearns Collection, Detroit Institute of Arts.

and death are unnatural and that they are the manifestations of mischief caused by magical influences, human or divine, can be traced back to ancient civilizations. The roles of the magician, the priest, and the physician evolved as an attempt to thwart the hostile powers. In ancient Egypt, the purpose of mummification was to preserve the body from decay and to protect the personal identity of the individual. These procedures were followed by a long series of ceremonies, generally known as the "opening of the mouth," which were magical in character, attempting to bring back to the inert corpse the faculties of which it had been temporarily deprived by death and embalming. Like the charismatics and spiritists of today, the Egyptians refused to accept death as the end of life.

The simplest method of treatment was the recitation of a spell in which the demon was ordered to leave the patient's body. Even today, when the medical condition is severe, particularly in chronic diseases like arthritis, incantations continue to be readily available.

The following charm, possibly used to relieve inflammation (redness), was offered to you upon arrival at the temple:

     Retreat, creature of Horus![4]
     Retreat, creature of Seth!
     Dispelled be the blood that cometh by Wnw[5]
     Dispelled by the red blood that cometh by wnw[6]
     You know not the dam; retreat before Thoth!

You were somewhat surprised by the requirement that this charm had to be recited over a rice pearl of red cornelian[7] to be placed in your anus. As G. Manjo (1975) commented in his book *The Healing Hand*, "Psychotherapy should help, no matter at which end it is applied!"

[4]Egyptian god of light and the son of Isis and Osiris.
[5]A city.
[6]By the hour.
[7]Cornelian, or carnelian, a cherry-red stone used in jewelry. It typified the blood of the goddess Isis, and its purpose was to stimulate the function of the blood.

If we change the names of the gods in the incantation, this charm could be used to great advantage by many modern professional "healers" to treat arthritis. However, the detail of the rice pearl of red cornelian clearly indicates that faith healers of our times do not have the sophistication that characterized their Egyptian counterparts.

Other outstanding features of Egyptian medicine can be brought up in a discussion about the roots of popular ideas on the causation of arthritis. One of these was the great interest and concern that the ancient Egyptians had about the anus. One of the seven medical papyri, and 81 of its 900 prescriptions, refer only to the anus. The Egyptians apparently regarded the anus to be the center and stronghold of decay. Near the pyramid of Gizeb, a tomb was discovered with an inscription about a physician who lived around 2,000 B.C. and who bore the curious title "Shepherd of the Anus." The Greek historian, Herodotus, related that "the Egyptians think it is from the food they eat that all sickness came to men." In your mind's eye you can see the roots of most of the popular folk remedies and quack cures relating to diet and arthritis in this aspect of Egyptian medicine, preserved with little modification for over 5,000 years.

A theory put together from many pieces of evidence was stated by Manjo summarizing the medical thought of the day in ancient Egypt: decay is typical of death, disease, and wounds; decay also occurs inside the intestine, so this internal decay must be a source of disease. The feces contained a very pernicious thing called ukhedu, or the rotten stuff. Ukhedu caused disease and pain; it could work its way into the blood vessels and travel around setting up disease. Ukhedu was thought to do what we now know bacteria can do. This was indeed a highly advanced idea, since physicians are still concerned with multiple problems related to bacteria harbored in the gastrointestinal tract. (The participation of the gastrointestinal tract in the development of some types of arthritis continues to be actively investigated at the present time.) Since, according to this theory of disease causation, Egyptians were condemned to walk around all day with an internal load of deadly material, they became the masters of internal cleansing. Parasites were very common in Egypt and became the symbol of disease. It was to expel the parasites from the body that various magical procedures and spells were utilized. After the episode of the rice pearl of red cornelian, you were ready for purgatives, emetics, and enemas. The enema is an Egyptian invention. One of the symbols of the god of medicine, Thoth, was the ibis. To him was ascribed the discovery of the enema, allegedly founded in the observation that the ibis injects seawater into the rectum with its long beak. Today enemas, purgatives, and colon cleansing are still offered as a cure to patients with arthritis.

Ricinus, the castor oil plant, was among the many drugs the Egyptians had at their disposal to induce diarrhea. You did not like the taste of castor oil and you were exhausted after 20 to 30 liquid bowel movements, but you were quite happy since you believed the treatment was quickly "removing the cause of your arthritis." You learned that emetics, purgatives, and enemas were employed in order to remove the *materia peccans*, according to the Egyptians' idea of the cause of disease. Your faithful companion on your pilgrimage was somewhat annoyed when you began practicing the advice that had been given to you to eliminate "unwholesome air" by stimulating eructation and flatus, which were supposed to serve that purpose. After the initial treatment you were advised to employ emetics and enemas for three consecutive days each month, for purely preventive reasons. You can easily see, from your own experience, that the obsession with internal cleansing by fasting, enemas, purges, and other means is not a practice recently developed by the champions of "naturalistic medicine," but that the brainwashing of mankind began thousands of years ago, at the peak of Egyptian culture. Although the Swnw did not cure your arthritis, you were certainly a happy customer because you were clean—as clean as one could be.

The 'Iatrós

More than 3,000 years ago, when you arrived in the land of Hellas looking for a cure, you were pleasantly surprised to find that the *'iatrós*, or Greek physician, was already talking about "arthritis" and "rheumatism."

You soon discovered that in Greek medicine, disease in general was also viewed as an imbalance. Any extreme of too much or too little was thought to cause disease. The celebrated four humors—blood, phlegm, and yellow and black bile—were thought by the Greeks to be harmoniously united. The theory of the four humors explained any pain or discomfort as a disharmony. The most likely humors to be imbalanced were phlegm and bile. Given this set of causes, the treatment followed logically: bleed, starve, and purge to get rid of the bad humors. Since in your visit to ancient Egypt your arthritis had been treated with enemas, purgatives, and emetics, these practices were not new to you. Here, in the time of the ancient Greeks, you soon discovered that the obsession with internal cleansing was already an established medical practice. This journey through history suggests that the use of fasting, enemas, or purging to "cure" any disease in modern times could be regarded as the vestiges of an archaic medicine that never developed, but that has survived entrenched in quack cures of today.

But the real test for you came when the 'iatrós prescribed the use of the roots of black hellebore, or Christmas rose, closely followed by those of white hellebore, or veratrum.[8] He told you that you could expect a cure, but warned you about some possible minor discomfort. Although the only desired effects to achieve a "cure" were diarrhea and vomiting (again cleansing), in you, Christmas rose and veratrum produced devastating effects. Indeed, armed with these weapons, the 'iatrós raised blisters, evoked sneezing, induced delirium, muscular cramps,

[8]Genus of liliaceus plants containing a family of alkaloids useful to treat high blood pressure.

asphyxia and, fortunately, did not cause your heart to stop. You experienced in your own flesh the reason why a treatment prescribed by a physician that causes side effects is called iatrogenic, that is, caused by the 'iatrós, or physician.

Even today, when a patient does not find relief through conventional medical care, he may in desperation resort to religion, faith healing, or magic. Similarly, for the patient in ancient Greece, when all else had failed and not even the 'iatrós could help, there was still one hope: the Temple of Asklepios, called the Asklepieion. Undoubtedly, part of the treatment of your arthritis while you were treated by the 'iatrós was a copper bracelet. Since your arthritis had neither responded to internal cleansing nor to the copper bracelet and you were quite distressed by stiffness and pain, you decided to visit the temple where Asklepios, the patron god of physicians, did some healing of his own.

The temple was located in a lovely sylvan spot, in the neighborhood of a spring. Even though you had but a rudimentary command of the Greek language, you found the ritual at the Asklepieion simple to understand. You were invited to relax on the holy grounds, take in the beauty of the surroundings, and wait for the night, while you listened to prayers and hymns. You were required to lie down in the sacred hall, and wait for the god to appear and give you advice in a dream. The priests received your gifts for the god and helped make you comfortable; but all the medical gestures would be up to the god.

The night you spent in the Asklepieion was unforgettable. You were told by one of the priests that the god sometimes appeared in person or in the disguise of a dog or a snake. Eventually, that night, the god appeared in the form of a snake, one of the sacred animals. Your memory of the events of that night was dampened by the prevailing heavy mist and the hallucinating gibberish of the snake god. Although your visit to the Asklepieion was a fascinating experience, your arthritis persisted unabated. The magic of the snake god did not alleviate your pain and in the morning, when the magic of the moment was gone, your entire body felt stiff as a board. The morning in Epidaurus was clear, warm, and dry and you felt compelled to read the testimonies from others previously cured that were carved in the stone. You learned that the god had danced over the paralyzed fingers of a man who rapidly recovered his mobility. If the god had jumped over your joints, perhaps you still could expect some late results. After you learned that a man badly infested rid himself of lice when Asklepios himself swept his body with a hard broom, you gave up. In our mind's eye, we can visualize the drama of the Greek version of divine and faith healing at the Temple of Asklepios, a precursor of the tent meetings organized by healing evangelists so frequently held in arenas, theaters, or on television programs commanding audiences of tens of millions of believers.

If you had visited Greece but a few centuries later, the treatment of your arthritis would have been different, since Greek medicine really began with Hippocrates, who was born on the island of Cos in 460 B.C. During the further development of civilization, the next step in the advancement of medical knowledge consisted of the elimination of supernatural and religious elements. Eventually, conclusions were drawn only from those observations which experience showed to stand the test of time. This step took place in Greece when the physician, the 'iatrós, became divorced from the priesthood. Hippocrates' recognition of disease as a natural phenomenon and his use of diagnosis and prognosis as we now understand them entitle him to be recognized as the father of medicine.

The Greek philosophers' approach to medical problems was ahead of their time. Socrates tells us in one of Plato's dialogues that the ideal approach to the patient had once been described to him by a Thracian physician: "You ought not to attempt to cure eyes without head, or head without body, so you should not treat body without soul." This philosophical admonition is in complete agreement with our present concept of medical treatment as being comprehensive and directed not only toward the disease but also toward the person. Although your consultation

with the 'iatrós in the time of Hippocrates did not result in a cure
for your arthritis, and did not provide the entertainment you
experienced centuries before at the Temple of Asklepios, the
concomitant treatment of body and soul was surely a step forward. This aspect of the 'iatrós' concept of medical treatment is
one of the tenets of orthodox medicine. The proponents of some
popular unorthodox "cures" have been able to exploit this approach, for although the body may not be healed by quack procedures, the person perceives that the soul is healed by the
touch of God, or by the touch of the healer, or simply by feeling
accepted. Thus, the placebo effect of quack cures on the individual is powerful and it is in this area, by deception, that such
practitioners shine.

Metaphysics in Ayurvedic Writings

About 1500 B.C. the original dark-skinned inhabitants of
India were overrun by lighter-skinned people who spoke Sanskrit and brought with them a huge body of literature, the *Vedas*,
the four sacred books believed to have arisen by divine
inspiration.

A system of medicine called *Ayurveda*, meaning knowledge
of life, was a product of Hindu culture. The fourth, or *Atharva*
Veda contained a collection of magic spells representing the lore
of the Atharvan priests directed against the demons of disease.
The principles of Ayurvedic medicine are described in two trea-
tises, the *Charaka Samhita*, mainly on medicine, and the *Sushruta
Samhita*, mainly on surgery. The spells of the Atharvan priests
contained formulas for almost any health problem, including
arthritis.

The Vedic religion, brought to India by the Aryan invaders,
is the oldest stratum of religious activity known to have existed
in India. It is the starting point of the religion variously called
Brahmanism or Hinduism.

It is very difficult to date the events in Indian history because the ancient Hindus believed that life is an illusion, a mere step to reincarnation and nirvana, and were not concerned with documenting their history. Thus, I will assume that in your fantastic journey through antiquity you are now arriving in India sometime between the 15th and the 5th century B.C., when Vedism was a living force. You immediately became acquainted with the *Rigveda*, or *Veda of Verses*. This is the earliest of Samhitas, a collection of hymns dating from no later than the second millennium B.C. Incorporated into the Vedic religion were the magical and the ascetic. Magic, in particular, was highly developed in India.

The ancient Hindus had the privilege of being able to choose from among an array of specialists. The *Krityahara* was the magic expert, and the *Vaidya* a general practitioner who also practiced surgery and developed the art of arrow removal. Just as in Egypt, you looked for a rheumatologist but found none.

When you began your inquiry into the quality of the Indian physicians, you were told that they were carefully chosen. Belonging to one of the higher castes was not enough to enable one to embrace a medical career. Sushruta indicated that the candidate should be "young, strong, and born of a good family, possessing a desire to learn, energy, contentment of character, self-control, a good retentive memory, intellect, courage, purity of mind and body, and should be found to have been further graced with the necessary qualifications of having thin lips, large, honest, intelligent eyes, a benign contour of the mouth and a contented frame of mind, being pleasant in his speech and dealings and usually painstaking in his efforts." Students oriented toward a medical career today may think it is very difficult to get into medical school and may be discouraged by the seemingly insurmountable requirements. How many of today's successful candidates would qualify for admission by Sushruta's criteria? Thus, your first contact with Indian physicians was satisfying, for they seemed knowledgeable and well qualified to practice medicine.

The Vaidya chanted verses of the Ayurveda in a monotonous rhythm while his apprentices repeated them. Initiation—into medicine—was imparted to students belonging to one of the three twice-born castes, those whose members were born first into ordinary life, then again, ritually, into one of the higher castes, such as the Brahmans,[9] the Kshatriya,[10] and the Vaishya.[11] The motivation to practice medicine was different for each: Brahmans to do good, Kshatriya for self-preservation, and Vaishyas for gain. Members of all three castes could gain religious merit, wealth, and pleasure, in that order, from the practice of medicine. You soon encountered problems while actually looking for a Vaidya. When you arrived in India, your arthritis was fairly advanced and you were quite debilitated by the disease and the long journey. You were shocked to find that Hindu physicians would not take on a patient with a complicated debilitating disorder or one considered fatal, although the sorcerers or magicians would. Obviously, treatment failure would damage the reputation of the ancient physicians, while sorcerers and magicians could work freely and with impunity. The latter feature of the art of healing by supernatural powers has persisted intact to modern times because faith and divine healers, spiritists, exorcists, and magicians thus far have had no legal responsibility, and their practice is not impeded by the regulatory machinery which is increasingly cramping medical practice. At long last, you succeeded in finding a Vaidya who was willing to risk his reputation and take your case. The Vaidya stressed, as had the 'iatrós before him, that the success of medical treatment depended not only on him but also on you, on the use of drugs, and on nursing care. This approach was a precursor of our contemporary concepts of teamwork and comprehensive medical care as well as that of patient responsibility, which are currently emphasized by orthodox medicine. It is clear that treatment

[9]Priests.
[10]Warriors and rulers.
[11]Free men.

cannot be successful unless you comply with your doctor's prescription.

Unfortunately, the treatment of inflammatory conditions in India was discouraging. Fever was thought to arise from the anger of the god Siva. The Vaidya resorted to fasting or purging and other cures similar to those used by the 'iatrós in Greece and by the Swnw in Egypt. You became aware that when everything else had failed, the Vaidya still could resort to the help of "Young damsels, beautiful and skilled in the sport of love, with faces glowing like the full moon of autumn and darting forth beams of love from their blue lotus-like eyes, with eyebrows moving in the ardor of desire...clad in their transparent garments, fumigated and scented...who were asked to take the patient into a firm embrace like a forest-creeper entwining itself around a sylvan tree, and to keep off as soon as the patient would feel himself heated." Perhaps the male chauvinism prevailing at the time prevented a similar treatment for you. I cannot find from the medical books whether the Vaidya utilized this method to alleviate the inflammation of the joints, but arthritic males could have enjoyed this treatment in lieu of a liniment or as a Vedic version of physical therapy.

Religion played an important role in Indian medicine. This is clearly revealed by Characa's words: "Medicines are of three kinds...first mantras[12] and religious acts; second, dieting and drugs; and third, the subjugation of the mind by withdrawing it from every kind of injurious or harmful act." When you followed Characa's advice, you experienced moderate relief of your symptoms, although the course of the arthritis was not changed by the treatment.

The Vaidya believed that "the mantras, full of occult energy and perfect truth..., never fail to eliminate the poison from the system." The mantras of the Vedic medicine and the points of acupuncture of the ancient Chinese were based on the existence of an occult or cosmic energy which is the alleged basis for metaphysical or spiritual healing. Although nothing in the orig-

[12]Magic formulas and incantations.

inal Ayurvedic or ancient Chinese writings gives credence to the claims of the existence of these metaphysical forces, this literature is marvelous reading and a tribute to the ingenuity, intelligence, and imagination of man who lived thousands of years ago.

In no other place did religion mingle so thoroughly with medicine as in India. The 'iatrós had split away from religion and from its psychological effect, leaving both to the temple of Asklepios. The Vaidya, instead, practiced the entire spectrum of primitive medicine, magic in particular. The magician used an extensive range of rituals and was familiar with the mysteries of divination. Your consultation with the Vaidya led you to participate in familiar rituals which you had seen before in Mesopotamia, Egypt, and early Greece. Your journey through ancient India could not help but suggest to you that the magical thinking fostered by ignorance has persisted throughout the centuries and still remains exploited in much of today's quackery.

CHAPTER 2

"CURES" THROUGH METAPHYSICAL FORCES

During your imaginary trip through ancient Mesopotamia, China, Greece, and India you were exposed to the roots of metaphysical healing. Life, sickness, and health were believed to be dependent upon supernatural forces, gods, and demons. Although a clear separation of religion and medicine was evident at the time of Hippocrates in Greece as well as in other ancient cultures, medieval Christianity maintained the concept of possession by the devil as cause and exorcism as cure of disease. During Roman times, there was a popular revival of interest in the occult but, except for Shamanism, metaphysical cures of disease persisted in relative isolation until the late eighteenth century.

There is no better example of the close association between charlatanism and conventional medicine than the impact of the theories of Franz Anton Mesmer who practiced medicine in

37

Vienna. In 1773, he ran a "magnetic clinic" in association with a Jesuit professor of astronomy and later, under the influence of a Swabian faith healer, became convinced that he could "cure" disease by manipulating a person's so-called magnetic fluid without magnets. When you learned about Mesmer, you were enthralled with the possibility that you might have a chance to meet him or some of his disciples. When his practice of "mesmeric" magnetism antagonized the Viennese faculty of medicine, Mesmer decided to leave for Paris, the mecca of eighteenth-century Europe. At that time, after a very long journey, you arrived in Paris eagerly expecting to find a cure for your arthritis. There you would have the opportunity to be mesmerized.

Mesmer attracted many followers in France, and despite a cold reception and opposition from the scientific community, his movement became extremely popular. He captivated his audiences and recruited fervent followers. You were certain that the medical community in France was conspiring against Mesmer and depriving you of a sure cure. After a long wait, you managed to make an appointment with one of Mesmer's aides. You were delighted, although your satisfaction was only slightly dampened when you were requested to pay for the consultation prior to the visit. But your excitement heightened because you were finally getting somewhere with the treatment of your arthritis. You rationalized that a cure was surely a bargain although the price was one hundred times that of a regular doctor's office visit. Later, you became aware that a few of Mesmer's followers were altruistic, just as were some of the practitioners of Ayurvedic medicine; but the motivation for most mesmerists was financial gain. Indeed, although Mesmer was probably not a quack, he himself profited handsomely from his dealings, and his followers were often satirized in cartoons with their pockets bulging with money (Fig. 2-1). The mesmerist was considered by the medical profession to be the king of the charlatans.

The winter in Paris was very cold and damp and you had severe pain and stiffness in your joints. By this time, you had been mesmerized off and on for more than six weeks. Coincidentally, you were fast running out of money. A royal commission consisting of widely known academicians including prominent men of the time such as Guillotin, Lavoisier, and Franklin, was appointed to investigate mesmerism. After weeks of examining the available evidence and interviewing a number of patients, the commission concluded that Mesmer's fluid did not exist, and that the convulsions and other effects of mesmerizing could be attributed to the overheated imaginations of the mesmerists and their followers. When you read the report of the commission, you felt inclined to believe that perhaps there was some element of truth in the reluctance of the doctors to accept Mesmer. Unfortunately for Mesmer, enough was already known about magnetism to disprove his claims about the mesmeric fluid. Nevertheless, mesmerism represented more than a passing fancy. Neither Mesmer nor the medical profession of his time realized that his success as a healer was due not to the nonexistent mesmeric fluid but to the power of suggestion, in some ways a precursor of today's psychotherapy.

The commission's report made the mesmerists very angry and they produced passionate responses defending their cause, which they claimed was the cause of humanity against the threat of self-interested academicians. By now, the mesmerist's rhetoric of 200 years ago should be familiar to you, since you are well acquainted with holistic practices and the vast array of unorthodox methods to treat arthritis. Old arguments are repeated over and over again. Today's quack healers also claim that their cause is the cause of humanity and that there is a conspiracy of the medical establishment against their "cures." Just as today's naturalistic and holistic practitioners do, Mesmer met the attacks of academicians with the same defense: "It is to the public that I appeal."

As suggested by Dornton (1968), mesmerism appealed to radicals because it served as a weapon against the academic establishment that seemed to impede their own advancement. Today's unorthodox healing movements do not have the same political implications that mesmerism had in its time; but they still appeal to the radicals because of the antiestablishment overtones of their rhetoric. Mesmerists claimed that they would restore a "natural" society in which the laws of nature would drown aristocratic privileges and despotic government in a sea of mesmeric fluid. First to go, of course, would be the doctors, and their academic allies who, to them, represented the last attempt of the establishment to preserve itself against the forces of the "true science of nature." In the rise and decline of mesmerism you can clearly see similarities to contemporary unorthodox healing movements. In like manner today, if naturalists, many faith, divine, or metaphysical healers, and charlatans were to have their way, medical doctors would be the first to go and the unorthodox claims of "true science of nature" would be recited as a litany.

Mesmerism had close ties with hypnotism and spiritism and, although Mesmer apparently did not practice hypnosis, some of his pupils did. Examples of "mesmeric somnambulism" were widely publicized. A mesmerized and apparently dead dog could be brought back to life, and a mesmerized "somnambulist" could see his own internal organs, diagnose his own illness, predict the day of his recovery, and even communicate with dead or distant persons. Contemporary spiritist literature overflows with similar anecdotes. The decline of the movement has not discouraged the occasional mesmerist from continuing to push his fluid for a profit on the boulevards of Paris.

For the cultured and sophisticated, there are attempts in the popular literature to build a rationale based on metaphysical forces responsible for healing. You read that to explain how these forces work, it is necessary to be conversant in the specifics of the health practices of Yoga and the readings of Ayurvedic, Tibetan, and Chinese medicine. Of course, you knew something about Yoga, which allows you to develop complete powers of relaxation. You had a deep respect for the teaching of Yoga and although your knowledge of Ayurvedic and Tibetan medicine was primitive, they were surrounded by an aura of mystery. You were told that the perusal of this literature might lead you to discover a subsystem of energy, called *Prana* in Sanskrit, which has been claimed to be at the basis of the human energy transfer in the healing act and responsible for regeneration and wound healing. From your trip throughout ancient civilizations you remembered that the subtle energy pervading all things was called *Ch'i* by the Chinese sages. In your more recent travels you could not help but recognize the similarities Ch'i and Prana had with the mesmeric fluid which enthralled the seventeenth-century world. Healthy people apparently have an excess of Prana. We further learn that Prana has its source in the sun. A proposed model envisions the "healer as an individual whose health gives him access to an over abundance of Prana and whose strong sense of commitment to help ill people gives him a certain control over the projection of this vital energy." The act of healing would entail the channeling of this energy flow, by the healer, for the well-being of the sick individual. The model is interesting, but in many aspects untenable. Even if man were the center of an electromagnetic field of some sort, able to interact by both body contact and at a distance, it appears implausible that the "strong sense of commitment to help the ill" would give the healer any control over this energy for the well-being of the individual to be healed. It is also not at all clear how this energy would have an influence on wound healing or any other vital process. Furthermore, there is no valid proof that it does, and there is no evidence that it even exists.

The use of mental power has been advocated as a unique metaphysical treatment for arthritis. Metaphysical healing is a pompous term that incorporates healing power, health, relaxation, the affirmation of being well, the rejection of negative and destructive thoughts, God, and religious feelings. Metaphysical healers claim that "arthritis, bursitis, and gout" can often be immediately cured, "by clearly visualizing the cure in a quiet place, relaxed, your eyes closed, with the positive affirmation that you are being cured." This method was purported to produce a kind of psychic effect that could also be healing and beneficial to others. Positive thoughts, a serene attitude, and relaxation certainly can be very helpful in relieving anxiety and minimizing the expression of symptoms. Doctors frequently stress this aspect of treatment because of its unique value in helping the patient cope with the problems brought about by chronic illness. Unfortunately, these measures do not succeed in "curing" any type of arthritis.

The Role of the Hands in "Healing"

The hands have been used from antiquity in an attempt to alleviate human suffering. The Egyptians gave deeper meaning to the gesture of touching the wound. Physical contact is reassuring. Shaking hands with a friend or taking the hand of a child conveys a feeling of empathy and facilitates communication. When a doctor touches the patient, both parties have the feeling that something is being done. Touching also means participating. Today, as yesterday, the hands establish a point of contact and are thought to be central in the act of healing. The comfort of physical touch has been considered to be reaching deep down to ancestral depths far older than mankind (Manjo, 1975).

The use of the hand by the Yang i — the Chinese physician — while taking the pulse, was a very important ritual which consumed considerable time. Body contact through the hand was an essential part of the treatment by which the Yang i undoubtedly provided much comfort to the patient.

The hands are used to apply firm finger pressure on the skin in the Shiatsu massage, which is one of the holistic practices taken from oriental medicine. The objective of Shiatsu is to stimulate the flow of Ch'i energy in the body by using the fingers to apply pressure to certain points on the skin. Practitioners of Shiatsu claim success in healing high blood pressure, neuralgia, migraine headache, and arthritis, among a variety of other illnesses.

Testimonials on the curative effect of the laying on of hands appear in the early documents of western church history. When "healing" occurs, there is touch involved—the laying on of hands—which is a comforting gesture, an act of concern and, to some extent, carries with it acceptance of the individual. We do not touch those whom we reject or toward whom we feel animosity. Recently, a similar gesture has been incorporated into the ritual of some of the traditional churches during which members turn to the people next to them, behind them, and in front of them to shake their hands. In this more formal setting, the hands are used as symbols as well as instruments of human interaction.

The use of the hands was developed to unforeseen levels by Mesmer, who professed that the entire universe was permeated by a superfine fluid that was the primary agent underlying heat, light, electricity, and magnetism. The best method of establishing "rapport" between patients and mesmerists was to rely on the use of the fingers (Fig. 2-1). In eighteenth-century seances, the patients transmitted the magnetic fluid from one to another by linking thumbs and index fingers in order to form a "mesmeric chain," something like an electric circuit. You certainly recall the beginning of your first session in Paris 200 years ago. To direct the fluid to your magnet, Mesmer's assistant laid his hands on your skin and ran his fingers all over your body. Then you felt a strange electrifying sensation in your spine and everything around you swirled and the world suddenly became dark. Here, your recollection ceased, but when you recovered your senses you were soaking wet with sweat, lying on the floor, and the world was still dancing around you. Again, you closed your eyes and noticed to your astonishment that all your pain had disappeared. In this manner, Mesmer was able to throw his patients into epileptic-like fits or somnambulistic trances, "curing" them of many diseases. Mesmer captivated you and your eighteenth-century contemporaries by suggesting that you were surrounded by wondrous invisible forces which could be manipulated according to the healer's desires to "cure" disease.

FIGURE 2-1. Mesmeric chain in eighteenth-century seance. The mesmerist was often depicted as a charlatan with his pockets bulging with money.

Unfortunately, all your aches and pains very shortly returned and it was evident that this treatment did not cure your arthritis.

The hand is even used by quacks in mail schemes. The believer is directed to place his hand on a printed tracing of the hand of the healer and write his prayer request in the palm of the picture. He is told his prayer will be answered, showing the power of the hand, upon returning the letter with a contribution. The laying on of hands continues to be used in the healing practices of the charismatics, pentecostals, and spiritists. The act of touching developed into various forms of body massage which became a popular form of promoting "whole health" by holistic practitioners.

The Pentecostal and Charismatic Movements

Religion and medicine have been intertwined since very early in the history of mankind. Although from the age of Hippocrates medicine became a distinct profession, in early times the services of physicians were not easily available to ordinary people. For centuries medicine was in the hands of clerics who charged high fees for their services until in the thirteenth century the Vatican forbade all priests from practicing medicine. In most cultures, religion and medicine eventually diverged and for many centuries the two pathways remained relatively independent. However, from the late nineteenth and the beginning of the twentieth centuries there was a resurgence of divine and faith healing coincidental with the appearance of Pentecostalism, one of the fastest-growing religious groups today.

Pentecost is the name of the Christian feast celebrated on the fiftieth day after Easter to commemorate the descent of the Holy Spirit upon the Apostles. Christian teaching tells us that seven weeks after Jesus was crucified, a group of his disciples met in Jerusalem on the Jewish festival of Pentecost. Suddenly, a sound came from heaven and filled the house where the men had gathered and a tongue of fire appeared over the head of each of them. They were filled with the Holy Spirit and could talk in foreign languages and had the power to prophesy and to heal. Pentecostalism is a name encompassing any of the various Christian religious movements which emphasize the activity of the Holy Spirit, stress holiness of living, and within the framework of organized worship, uninhibitedly express their religious feelings by speaking in tongues, giving spontaneous testimonials, uttering exclamations of praise, and practicing faith healing. In general, this activity has been called "charismatic." In theology *charism* is an extraordinary gift, such as the power to heal or to prophesy, and charismatic refers to those special talents or gifts bestowed by the Holy Spirit on individual Christians.

After your long pilgrimage throughout the ancient civilizations, you were living in Michigan at the turn of the nineteenth century. You were active in the church and, as many others did, you accepted the Pentecostal spirit. Since you were afflicted with a severe form of arthritis you were quite excited over the news that some of the special gifts had been received by members of your congregation, especially that of healing. In the church you learned that disease originates from disobeying the natural laws, from sin, and from the devil, and that God has the power to "cure." You were somewhat skeptical, since your visit to ancient civilizations taught you that similar beliefs are much older and not restricted to the two Testaments. You remembered that primitive thought saw in most illness the influence of the malevolent will of a demonic power. The antiquity of the idea of the demonic cause of disease has been established by the historians of ancient civilizations. The explanation of anything that surpassed contemporary experience was thought to be supernatural. Suffering could be caused by spirits of the dead, or by demoniacal animals which took up residence in the bodies of the sick. A more abstract concept of disease was that which considered sickness to be the punishment for evil acts. As primitive man's belief established the origin of sickness on a demonic hypothesis, his treatment was therefore causal—magic had to be met with magic. The influence of mysticism on medicine not only has survived the passage of time but also countless systems of religious belief. The connection between sin and disease has persisted in the human mind well into modern times. From your personal experience and from the study of medical art from the oldest civilizations, as well as from what we know about the practice of witchcraft by the aboriginal medicine men of today, it is clear that the prehistoric healers employed magical procedures that were not very dissimilar to the divine and faith healing practices of today.

Faith healing takes place in the body of an individual because of his mental attitude, and because of his faith. The presence of an outsider is not needed in order to win this favor from God. In contrast, divine healing is the direct work of God on the body of the afflicted. Thus, although healing occurs in response to faith, this is not a prerequisite since "divine healing" allegedly can be effective on unconscious persons, infants, and children. As a rule, a healer is a necessary agent of the "cure." Divine healing is not thought by religious bodies to be a metaphysical cure, such as that proposed by Christian Science or spiritism. Pentecostals believe that it is Christ in person who comes to the sick with his holy touch. As a consequence, it is neither the human healer nor his prayer, but Christ who "directly" does the healing. Divine healing is considered to be the same power that raised Lazarus from the sepulcher (Fig. 2-2).

The Value of Prayer

Some Pentecostals engage in a running clash with medicine. In church group discussions you were advised not to accept conventional medical treatment since, from the beginning of the movement, the tendency was to forbid the acceptance of medical advice as contrary to belief in divine healing. This

FIGURE 2-2. The raising of Lazarus, 1641, Rembrandt etching. The Toledo Museum of Art.

conflict with medicine is based on the biblical evidence that God performed healings without prescribing medicines. You excitedly looked forward to the prospect of being the recipient of divine healing, for after shopping for doctors and sorcerers through centuries of civilization you were quite disabled, and your joints were painful and swollen. Although you were steeped in prayers, you experienced no favorable change in your arthritis. Your excitement gave way to disappointment and finally to desperation, since you were prevented from having any medical treatment and God did not come to your rescue. Had you lived in Michigan and been affiliated with the same Pentecostal groups in the 1950s or 1960s, the advice of the church group would have been quite different. Officially, it was never suggested that medical treatment was wrong, but you were exhorted to first turn to God in prayer. The ultimate choice was left to you. You decided to give divine healing a chance; therefore you did not receive any treatment for your arthritis for a long time. By then you were crippled, unable to walk, and barely able to feed yourself. However, you were not unhappy, because this outcome was, without a doubt, the "unfathomable will of God."

Even though some brave souls have spoken out against the conviction that Pentecostals can invariably heal sickness, these voices are not heeded by the majority. Some Pentecostals continue openly to reject any medical care, while others have a softer, but equally dangerous attitude, putting their health and that of others at risk. There are more moderate views within some charismatic groups of the Catholic Church, but even in traditional religious circles the possibility that the hand of God could perform a "miracle" in our times is never denied. Although Protestants of the liberal tradition assert that miracles ceased after the Apostles in New Testament times, many Christians, even critics of the Pentecostal movement, do not agree with those who deny the possibility of divine intervention in the cure of human disease.

Almost every important Pentecostal church has one or more healers who exercise their power on particular occasions. The average Pentecostal member who has received the "healing ministry" once given to the Apostles through the Holy Spirit, is persuaded that it is available to each individual in the church. These persons firmly believe they have been blessed with the gift of the power to heal in order to alleviate the corporal ailments of their followers. They regularly visit the homes of the sick or the wards of the hospitals, read the names of the afflicted during religious services, or lead those who have already been cured to the altar as living testimony of the results of divine healing. As a rule, such healers shun publicity and are satisfied if they bring relief to others. They are altruistic, just like the Brahmans of ancient India. In addition to this multitude of local healers, some of the professional Pentecostal healers travel from city to city or from country to country to conduct large group healing sessions. Although they may be no less dangerous to the health of those seeking a "cure," there is a vivid contrast between the motivation behind the humble local healers and the flagrantly publicity-seeking professional healers who use methods never dreamed of by Christ or his early followers. Even though they usually work within some Pentecostal denomination, they may also be borrowed by Fundamentalist churches in order to "warm up" their revivals.

You were not surprised when you saw the healing practices used by Pentecostals. You readily recognized the imposition of the hands accompanied by supplicatory prayers, the handling of the handkerchief, exorcisms, and other techniques very much like those employed by the sorcerers of Mesopotamia, India, and Egypt.

There is no area of medicine left untouched by divine and faith healing. You heard innumerable anecdotes about the healing of diseases pronounced incurable by specialists. Some healers have been credited with restoring sight to the blind, causing the dumb to speak, and the crippled to walk. Healers claim fantastic success in the cure of cancer, thyroid disease, blindness, peritonitis, paralysis, ulcer, lameness, low back pain, muscle and bone disorders and, of course, arthritis. Your hopes soared in eager anticipation.

From extensive radio and press coverage, you heard about a forthcoming group healing session to be conducted by a famous professional healer. This propaganda, intending to key up the psychologic state of the audience, tremendously raised your level of expectation. You knew you had to apply well in advance since candidates are carefully screened by personal interview and many are rejected. You were certain you would be accepted because you were a member of the congregation in good standing and there was no question that you were in deep trouble. When you were accepted, you had no problem following the directives given to you in preparation to receive the healing. You simply were to attend daily religious services, to hear the Word of God, to see people being healed before your very eyes, and to hear the joyful testimonies of those who had been healed. It was also recommended that you fast and pray prior to coming to the sessions. The meeting was highlighted by rousing congregational singing and a vibrant exhortation by the healer, who told the audience of the blessings other people had already received, and of the even greater blessings awaiting those who were now stirred to hope. While you stood in the football field waiting to receive the healing, you could not help but think about the night you spent in the Asklepieion a few thousand years before. Although much less glamorous, this healing session was dramatic and its success clearly depended upon an excited, almost hysterical audience.

A professional healer does not ordinarily accept all the cases submitted to him. Since you belonged to the group that organized the healing session, you were familiar with the individuals who "took the line." You were somewhat disappointed when you had to sit in the back, far from the action, and certainly felt dismayed when the healer did not lay his hands on you. Certainly, no one could tell you that your faith was not strong enough for the blessing, so you were anxious to hear the reason for the refusal. Finally, you were told in passing that you required further personal attention. At that time you did not clearly understand what that meant, but you could clearly see that there was some element of truth in the healer's reply, since you had more joint pain and stiffness than ever before and simply moving around had become very difficult. The healer was right, but for the wrong reason; your arthritis truly did require further personal attention but you failed to benefit from the healing.

After the fact, how could you explain the healer's description of amazing miracles occurring in the midst of electrifying evangelistic sessions? Everyone saw the woman who was so crippled that she had to crawl on her hands and knees, and yet was instantly straightened. You also saw the man in the front row who came to meet the healer with great difficulty, and yet as soon as the healer touched him he threw his crutches away and began to run. At that time, you did not question whether there was real proof that these people were crippled, nor did you question what the long-term duration of the "cures" would be; but after your own experience you began to have serious doubts. When the thought of spiritual hustling crossed your mind, you had a hard time distinguishing the charlatans from the true believers.

Whenever we have the opportunity to look closely at the "miracles" claimed by Pentecostals, we often find them to be unsuccessful, prone to relapse, restricted to functional disorders (without a known organic cause or structural change), preceded by conspicuous buildups, and extravagantly publicized by the organizers. You should be aware that diseases which spring from psychological disturbances are not only treated with relative success (often temporary) by Pentecostal healers, but also by physicians, spiritual leaders, and gifted counselors. The recovery from hysterical paralysis by the power of suggestion can be astonishing, but cannot be considered a miraculous healing.

Not only new Pentecostal denominations, but also established religions are engaged in healing practices which have far-reaching consequences for the health of individuals. We are told by the historians of the Pentecostal movement that during the 1950s the charisms began to be received by members of the established churches who refused to withdraw and join Pentecostal denominations. This movement, called neo-Pentecostalism, or charismatic, was noted among certain parishes of the Episcopal, Lutheran, Presbyterian, and Catholic churches. The charismatic movement is neither a new religion nor a new church, but a movement of renewal affecting all Christian denominations. In addition to the established religious denominations, the post-World War II period witnessed the upsurge of a large group of revival ministries which established independent evangelistic associations. There were considerable differences in beliefs and behavior between and within groups, but the unifying feature was the belief that they had received the outpouring of the Holy Spirit.

Just as do most charismatics in the 1980s, you belong to a prayer group that has a considerable impact on your life. You really enjoy attending the informal group meetings which are usually held in people's homes. Members of the group know each other well, which fosters empathy and a strong sense of kinship. A group leader oversees the psychosocial and, to some extent, the physical welfare of the members of the group. Close interpersonal contacts are fostered and the idea that you are not alone in the world is reinforced. In charismatic thought, healing not only refers to physical healing, but also to the relief of inner unrest, wounding memories from the past, fear, depression, and unforgiveness. There is little question that this kind of deep interaction between the "healer," whoever he may be, and the patient, can have a powerful effect on psychosomatic symptoms and functional illness.

The "healings" you witnessed as the consequence of charismatic activity had much in common with your experience with the Yang i, the ancient Chinese physician, who took your pulse in a long ceremony during which body contact through the hands assured a powerful emotional impact. You thought that healing in the charismatic setting was also reminiscent of the ancient medical-religious practices of Akkadian or Ayurvedic medicine, in which religious feelings and supernatural powers were thought to provide relief.

Faith healing holds a prominent place in the charismatic movement, not in the dramatic, effusive style of the "tent-healers," but in a more subdued way. Many healers insist on the absolute need for prayer and faith in order to win divine favor. The charismatic groups began the practice of "soaking" sick persons in prayer. You could not but recall that you had been soaked in prayer way back at the Temple of Asklepios, and once again as a Pentecostal in the early 1900s. Now, as before, you could not observe any of the miraculous cures that had been reported. As a good charismatic, you are a fervent believer in divine healing, but in your prayer group orthodox medicine is not spurned. If the person is seriously ill and the physician effects a cure, the success is usually attributed to "the hand of God working through the doctor"—still a form of divine healing. If death occurs in spite of the prayers of the faithful, it is believed to be the will of God, which we are unable to understand.

The charismatic movement has had an enormous numerical success at a time when almost all other indices of religious practice in America have been declining. Assuming that there is a similar proportion of believers among arthritic patients as there is in the general population, there is no doubt that a large number of arthritics are involved in charismatic activities. This is a conservative estimate because there are large numbers of elderly persons with rheumatic diseases, and it has been noted that the elderly are strongly influenced by the charismatic movement.

Not only were you disappointed when your arthritis was not relieved, but you soon discovered that your health could be damaged in many ways by insisting upon following charismatic healing practices. Denial of the presence of disease is actively promoted by faith healers, who incite patients to stop taking their medications or to disregard their symptoms. Medical noncompliance is encouraged by healers who advise patients to disregard physicians' orders. Some voices have been raised calling for moderation. Francis McNutt, among others, has proposed that medicine and prayer are not in opposition, but together, the doctor, the nurse, and the person with the gift of healing form *God's healing team*. This naive supposition is negated by the claims made in reference to physical healing.

Anecdotes proclaiming the effect of prayer on patients who have recovered from life-threatening diseases are legion. Accepting these interpretations is only possible through gullibility and ignorance of the natural history of the rheumatic diseases. It is very consoling for people to believe that an observed favorable outcome is the result of prayer; but it should be noted that these favorable results may also occur in people outside the influence of the church and without the benefit of prayer. However, many times the outcome is less favorable, and the practice of faith and divine healing often results in interference with medical treatment. There are sad examples of patients with potentially remediable illness who delayed the beginning of medical treatment while engaging only in faith healing and prayer. When the individual makes a wrong decision that puts his life in danger, it is regrettable. It is even worse when adults make decisions that compromise the health of their children. An example of this aberration is the law in the state of Ohio that provides that no parent, guardian, or custodian of a child shall create a substantial risk to his health or safety by violating a duty of care, protection, or support, and indicates that "it is not a violation...when the parent, guardian, or custodian treats the physical or mental illness or defect of the child by spiritual means through prayer alone, in accordance with the tenets of a recognized religious body." It is striking that a proposed amendment to remove this exception so that a child treated through prayer by spiritual healing would be designated a neglected or abused child was successfully blocked by the spiritual lobby.

The objective efficacy of prayer was investigated by Joyce and Weldon in a controlled study. A group of patients with various chronic diseases was the object of five minutes of silent meditation per day by members of a church group, while their matched controls did not receive intercessory prayer. At the end of this long-term study, no significant difference was found between the two groups. Other attempts to document the efficacy of prayer in the treatment of disease have not been successful.

Prayer has been used since the era of primitive men and will continue to be used by millions of believers. I believe that meditation and a serene, philosophical attitude toward disease and adversity in general can only be helpful, but I am certain that it is not wise to use prayer as either the main or the only weapon to combat arthritis or any other disease. Unfortunately, it seems that as long as the participants are satisfied, this practice will continue to flourish, since the patient's emotional satisfaction may not necessarily be related to the cure of arthritis.

It appears that the faith healers are enjoying the best of two worlds. As did the sorcerer of King Ashurbanipal's time, they get the credit when the outcome is favorable, but have no legal responsibility when things go sour. The Greek historian, Diodorus, remarked that the physician in ancient Egypt was not to be blamed for unsuccessful results of treatment if it were carried out along recognized and prescribed lines, whereas a procedure going outside the bonds of tradition resulting in fatality carried with it the death penalty. It seems that in modern times the law has become more lenient toward quacks. After-the-fact, modern faith healers can resort to the acceptable clichés so often heard — "he was not prepared," "his faith was not strong enough," or "it was the Lord's will."

Healing through faith is not restricted to the charismatic movement. There is no question that spiritual healing has been practiced by the clergy for thousands of years. Sorcerers belonging to the clergy dominated Mesopotamian medicine for centuries. In ancient Egypt drugs and incantations were administered by both the sorcerers and the clergy, and the 'iatrós of ancient Greece did not object to the help of the gods offered at the Temple of Asklepios to treat his most difficult patients.

Thus, 3,000 to 5,000 years ago, religion worked along with medicine to soothe the spirit, relieve anxiety, and impart peace of mind. This is what religion does best, since it can have a positive impact on the health of the individual by easing anxiety and helping to control psychological factors. It is the extension of these claims to include physical healing which clashes head-on with medicine.

Shamanism, Spiritual Healing, and the Modern Medicine Man

Your eternal quest to find a cure for your arthritis found you in central Asia in the eighth century. You had heard marvelous stories about miraculous cures performed by the shamans of northeast Siberia. Thus far the advice of monks and physicians had afforded no relief, and you were anxious to test any new method. The journey would undoubtedly be perilous and costly, but you decided that undertaking it would be worthwhile. The risk of travelling through the lands of possibly hostile nomadic tribes did not stop you. You did not think twice about having to go over high mountains and through arid steppes to get to the land of the Yakuts. During your journey you learned all about the medicine man from your guide.

In Siberia a person most frequently became a shaman through inheritance of the shamanistic profession, although it could also be attained by spontaneous vocation. The shaman, you learned, was recognized as such only after a series of initiatory rituals and after he had been educated by qualified masters. During the trial the shaman-to-be becomes very sick and frequently wanders in the wilderness as though he were a madman. He becomes a shaman only if he can succeed in curing himself. The initiation involves the symbolic death and resurrection of the hallucinating candidate. In his agitated dreams he is tortured by demons, his body cut into pieces, he descends into the netherworld or ascends into heaven and is finally resurrected. This initiation allows him to interact with the supernatural world. The medicine man can now "see" the spirits, and he himself behaves as a spirit. We have to interpret trance as a phenomenon which developed as a normal religious experience, and it is likely that after this wild preparatory period was over, the shaman was a well-adjusted and balanced individual. Since his most important function is healing, the neophyte finally becomes a shaman when he is instructed by the masters on the art of recognizing and curing disease.

All this puzzled you. You were lucky to arrive in the land of the Yakuts in time to witness the consecration of a shaman, which was a public event in that part of Siberia. You and your guide followed the crowd to the outskirts of the village where there was a lone sacred birch out on the steppes. The shaman looked determined and almost appeared to be in a trance. His task was to climb to the highest part of the tree, just above the ninth notch, which indicated his ability to ascend into heaven. Each notch symbolized a specific heaven. It took little effort for the shaman to reach the top, his legs pressed firmly on the trunk, his arms reaching toward the heights in ecstasy and his eyes fixed on the infinite. Strangely enough, there was no visible reaction from the crowd of people, who remained silent showing deep respect and perhaps awe as they witnessed this encounter with the supernatural. The shaman was now ready, not only to ascend into heaven but also to descend into the netherworld to see and meet the spirits of the dead. Your guide told you that while he was in trance he was able to behave like a spirit, leaving his body to travel in ecstasy throughout the cosmic regions. A common belief regarding the causation of disease was that symptoms would appear when the soul was stolen by a demon or lost through the influence of supernatural powers. There in the land of the Yakuts, suffering from arthritis in its most severe form, you tried to recover your lost soul in order to be healed. You will probably remember your meeting with the shaman as long as you live.

You and your guide were rushed into a tent by an old man who seemed to see in the darkness. After standing for a few minutes, your eyes adjusted and you clearly saw the shaman wrapped in a long cloak, sitting on a leather stool in the middle of the hazy room. You extended your swollen and deformed hands so the medicine man could see why you were there; but he was not looking. His eyes were closed and his face bore a strange expression as though he were in a state of deep contemplation between sleeping and waking. He appeared as though his awareness was temporarily suspended, and he was being controlled by an exterior intelligence. He was obviously communicating with the dead. His trance seemed to be unending and your impression of the duration of your visit to the shaman's tent was vague. When you returned with your purse almost empty and your joints still hurting, you could not help but wonder whether you had really recovered your soul. At that time you could not be certain, but you were ready to wait. You waited and waited but your arthritis was not relieved and you were again disappointed. Your encounter with the shaman will always be remembered as a very expensive but exciting life experience.

Shamanism is representative of the mystical experience common to archaic religions. It is not only a religious phenomenon characteristic of the ancient Siberian and Ural-Altaic peoples, but it is also predominant in the religious life of the Eskimos, many North and South American Indian tribes, and people of the Malay Peninsula and Oceania. Healing practices of the medicine man in Native American Indian culture are related to mother earth. The priest-physicians used dance, music, and prayer to appease the anger of the evil spirits. Repetitious and rhythmic tunes created a mystic and almost hypnotic climate. In modern times you can see the close parallel between the ancestral shamanism of primitive societies and the common belief that bodily illness can be cured through spiritism with a medium acting as an intermediary between the living and the spirits of the dead.

Freelance healing has been with mankind from ancient

times. It has been continually sought after by the ignorant and the cultured alike. There have been testimonials praising the activity of healers for as long as written accounts have existed. The healer is not necessarily always motivated by the urge to heal the sick. Now, as in ancient times, financial gain is often the hidden motivation behind the activity of many healers. Although, for obvious reasons, no statistics are available on the subject, in all probability the healing "business" has developed into a multimillion-dollar enterprise which operates freely, unhampered by government regulations.

"Spiritual healing" is a blanket term used to cover the whole field of healing. Contemporary spiritists, like primitive people involved in shamanistic practices, believe that the spirits of the dead can work through mediums. Spiritists are legion and worldwide. Harry Edwards (1963), a well-known spiritual healer, claimed that "the largest healing movements are those of the Christian Science and Spiritualist religions." Spiritual healers claim to cure all diseases known to mankind, including arthritis, by touch or by the performance of simulated operations conducted over or near the body. Cures allegedly can be effected by absent healing—healing from a distance. The healer appears to act as a channel of communication between the dead and those still living in a way quite reminiscent of the primitive medicine man. The "statistics" reported by spiritual healers appear impressive to the gullible. They claim that over 80 percent of those patients treated report improvement of symptoms and of these, some 30 percent report complete recoveries. It is clear that the spiritual healer's "cure" is effective with those patients who improve by themselves because the disease follows its natural course and with the multitude of patients having psychosomatic symptoms who are prone to respond to a strong placebo effect. In a large proportion of human ailments, the individual will get well no matter what he does to treat the indisposition. There is no harm done to these individuals by the spiritual healers except for the financial loss. The positive results of spiritual healing have been attributed to the process of "spirit chemistry," which—healers claim—scientifically applied, breaks down adhesions but leaves the bone structures, membranes, and tissues unaffected. Of course, there is no such thing as "spirit chemistry," but we can recognize its historic links with mesmeric fluid, Prana and Ch'i. Your own experience in the land of the Yakuts showed you that spiritual healing with the same basic elements as those of modern spiritism was clearly practiced by the shaman many centuries ago.

To the spiritual healer, no disease is "incurable." The opposition to orthodox medicine can be seen in many aspects of the healing activity. As asserted by Harry Edwards, "It no longer matters whether the official policy of the medical profession is in favor of spiritual healing or not, for its truth is enthroned in the hearts and homes of countless people everywhere." These words are quite familiar to you since they seem to echo the defense of mesmerism against the medical establishment of more than 200 years ago.

Healing of the sick based on metaphysical principles is offered by Christian Science, and by the spiritualist movement, as well as by innumerable freelancers in the art of healing. Christian Scientists maintain that bodily illness does not exist at all, but is purely an illusion, and thereby insist that the symptoms of the diseases are only "in the head." This is a hard pill for you to swallow, for you have witnessed the beginning and progression of deformities in your hands and feet, the bulging of your knees, and the shrinking of your muscle mass. The Christian Science cure depends on the effects of prayer and is incompatible with medical treatment. Although it is easy to understand why children afflicted with infectious diseases have died after being treated with prayers alone, it may not be so obvious that the joints of children or adults suffering from arthritis progressively deteriorate when patients adhere to the Christian Science approach.

In the "healing" literature, it is frequently stated that spiritual healers are not opposed to medical therapies. Although this may very well be true of some healing practitioners, I have observed that many of my patients stop their treatments when they become involved in healing activities and do not return until they are desperate, when they again seek my help. I often learn about their experiences when they come back wiser but older, wasted, and more disabled. In this sense, most healing practices are contrary to the best interests of the patients because they lead to critical loss of time, allowing arthritis to progress from reversible to irreversible stages.

Part of the spiritualist literature appears to make some sense at first glance, other than the descriptions of the actual healings. We learn from Edwards about the case of a "young man who was suffering from acute arthritis." In spite of the "strong anti-faith attitude" of the patient, after a few moments, joint inflammation literally melted under the hands of the healer. Suggestion or hypnosis can rapidly alter the expression of pain, but the effect is not long-lasting. I have seen the effect of suggestion in my patients many times. It is not infrequently that I am able to move a joint with little pain when the patient and sometimes other physicians could not, due to severe pain. Although a better technique of physical examination, and relaxation induced by reassurance can sometimes be important factors, there is usually much more that remains unexplained. The healer—no matter who he is—can, by merely doing something to the patient, produce a strong placebo effect. This effect is associated with the release of endorphins,[1] which are potent substances produced in the body known to relieve pain.

Anyone attempting to critically analyze the "healing" of a young man with "an acute arthritis" described above should know the type of arthritis involved and the natural history of the condition. Acute gout, for example, is a self-limited condition that would be ideally suited to a faith healer's claim of close to 100 percent success, if the patient were able to endure excruciating pain for several days. After that period, the "cure" would be spontaneously forthcoming. However, anyone should be ex-

[1]Substances produced in the body which have a variety of actions resembling morphine.

tremely skeptical about the results of faith healing of an infection of a joint, which may lead to joint destruction and death if the correct antibiotic treatment is not given promptly. The point of the story of "the young man with acute arthritis" is that from the description given we do not know what the diagnosis was, nor are we even sure that he had arthritis. The "fantastic results" claimed by healers have several features in common. They are uncontrolled observations; no one knows what the real diagnosis is and the majority of the reports are in the form of short-term anecdotal accounts. If you realize that more than half of the conditions afflicting man are probably self-limited and a large number of other problems will respond to a strong placebo effect, healers can easily claim to "cure" about 70 to 80 percent of their clients.

I have very little doubt that "spiritual healing," as well as other forms of "faith healing," can give you a feeling of inner strength and comfort, soothing fears and tensions. Eliciting these feelings can have only a positive influence in the treatment of any condition, and has been accomplished by good physicians for centuries. However, there is a vast difference between giving moral support with an empathetic approach and telling lies and fostering false hope.

Harry Edwards (1963) claims that "all medical authorities agree that the origin of much disease is psychosomatic, and that the initial causation lies in mental unrest." This is only a half-truth. In these instances the healers are talking about the psychosomatic disorders thought to be based upon or modified by abnormal psychological reactions. Psychosomatic disorders are associated with abnormal life experiences, environmental stress, or social maladjustments, such as unusually protracted grief, obsessional fear of disease, or anxiety over family illness. Raymond Adams (1983) includes under psychosomatic diseases such common conditions as peptic ulcer, asthma, hypertension,[2] migraine, and, I hope to the surprise of no one, rheumatoid arthritis. These diseases have been set apart from others on

[2]High blood pressure.

the basis of three main features: the function of the affected organ can be influenced by the autonomic nervous system;[3] resentment, hostility, and suppressed emotion is common in these patients; and there is often an apparent relationship between onset and exacerbation of disease activity and the disturbing incidents in the patient's life. Thus, although the psychosomatic diseases are not caused by "mental unrest," psychological factors may greatly influence the expression of their symptoms. There is no question that mental unrest can influence the symptoms experienced by patients with arthritis. The quick improvement of inflammation frequently seen in a hospitalized patient is probably due to physical and mental rest. In some cases it is possible to witness the apparent triggering of the onset of arthritis by a catastrophic emotional experience. More frequently, exacerbations of the activity of the disease can be traced to an abnormal life experience or environmental stress. For these reasons, the patient's understanding of this relationship is one of the most important parts of the treatment. It has never been proven that any of these diseases is of psychological origin. Thus, it cannot be said that these diseases are caused by mental unrest, but rather that these disorders appear in individuals who are genetically predisposed to acquire the disease and when psychogenic factors, among others, are involved. It is important to note that in this group of patients neurosis[4] is found no more frequently than in the population at large.

Spiritists use a number of euphemisms, and death is never called death. It is likely that some people accept the myth of psychic healing because it is part of the total spiritualistic package that promises no death — they can deny death by claiming to be able to communicate with those to whom they refer as having "passed over." The superstitious person believes that supernatural forces are the cause of disease. To combat these forces,

[3]Part of the nervous system that controls involuntary actions.
[4]A psychological disorder in which anxiety is often the primary characteristic.

the aid of supernatural powers is deemed necessary. Greeting the spirits, and experiencing their presence, obtaining advice from them, and becoming convinced that they can even heal, fosters the denial of death. The ability of the spirit doctor to diagnose and treat disease and even perform surgery by removing organs without making an incision also attempts to demonstrate the survival of the person. It is amazing to discover the numbers of people who can believe this. Some patients cannot emotionally deal with the doctor's diagnosis. It is not uncommon that their initial reaction is to deny that they have the disease. Naturally, their first question is whether the disease can be cured. When they are told that there is no cure, they conclude—usually erroneously—that nothing can be done for them. If they think the doctor cannot help—again wrongly—they think they have nothing to lose, so they decide they may as well look elsewhere for a cure. For those who believe in miracles, there is little hope of benefiting from education. Perhaps, for them, it is difficult to deny miracles. When they are ill and desperate they tend to cling to these beliefs, isolated from reality.

There is no question that achieving peace of mind can be beneficial and provide some relief. However, it is quite different to believe that this practice will effect an "instantaneous cure through the healing power of the infinite," as asserted by H.D. Smith (1965). In the popular literature, the ability of spiritual healers to "cure" the incurable is either explicitly claimed or presented in testimonials. These bizarre claims compel the medical professional to warn patients that spiritual healing is a dangerous form of quackery.

CHAPTER 3

HOLISTIC TREATMENT OF ARTHRITIS

Ian Smuts coined the word holism[1] in 1926. In his book, *Holism and Evolution*, he developed the idea of wholeness as characteristic of the inner driving force behind the evolutionary process. Equally important in Smuts' holistic concept was that the whole has some undefined inner character that makes it more than the sum of its parts. When applied by the apostles of healing, the holistic concept encompassed a hodgepodge of approaches that originated in the East and exalted the virtues of old medical and nonmedical techniques. The promoters of whole health became involved in the "fitness craze," jogging, long-distance running, yoga, muscle relaxation, homeopathy, herbalism, chiropractic, ayurvedic medicine, various types of naturalistic diets, Shiatsu massage, foot reflexology, iridology, hypnosis, acupuncture,

[1]From the Greek, meaning "whole."

moxibustion[2] and many other techniques to prevent or cure disease. Shiatsu massage, macrobiotics, herbal medicine, moxibustion, and many of the principles basic to oriental medicine are very old and had their origins in Taoism. It is frequently mentioned that osteopathic medicine started as an unconventional approach to healing and health which later gained legal acceptance and approval from the orthodox medical community. This is by no means a triumph of the occult and mysterious, but simply that osteopathy evolved naturally through scientific lines and *converged* with medicine. It is surprising that the holistic health philosophy claims ownership of the spiritual element of health, recognizing the emotional factors involved in health and disease, because these are prominent features of medical practice. It does not make sense to talk about holistic health, because there is only one kind of health. Neither does it make sense to speak of holistic medicine, because there is only one kind of medicine.

Acupuncture and Hypnosis

Acupuncture had its origin in a serendipitous discovery made thousands of years ago in China. It is said that the Chinese sages noted that soldiers who survived the wounds inflicted by arrows often recovered from other maladies that had afflicted them for a long time. The early Chinese doctors began experimenting with needles made of stone, looking for a relationship between certain points in the skin and a large variety of human diseases. It became obvious to them that the results obtained with acupuncture were based on the equally ancient concept of the yin and the yang. As we can read in the Nei

[2]Oriental method of healing by small, discrete burns in the skin produced by the ignition of a cone of moxa, a flammable substance obtained from the leaves of a certain Chinese wormwood plant, *Artemisia*.

Ching, on the outside of the human body there is yang, and inside there is yin. Yin and yang are arranged so that yang is in the back and yin is in the front part of the body. The liver, heart, lungs, spleen, and kidneys are yin, and the gall bladder, stomach, lower intestine, bladder, and the burning spaces[3] are yang. The ancient Chinese philosophy taught you that if yang accumulates excessively, you will die from the disease.

Of acupuncture, the Yellow Emperor asked: "When the body is worn out and the blood is exhausted, is it possible to achieve good results?" Ch'i Po, his prime minister replied, "No, because there is no more energy left. This is the way of acupuncture: if man's vitality and energy do not propel his own will, his disease cannot be cured." The Chinese conceived a set of imaginary or spiritual vessels or meridians, containing not blood, but Ch'i. This principle described some type of energy which could be either drawn out or replenished simply by needling the right Ch'i vessel. This dual "inward" and "outward" purpose of needling is described in the ancient texts which claimed that the needles could let excessive Ch'i out as well as in when it was necessary to replace it from the outside. The basic purpose of acupuncture was to restore the balance between yin and yang, the omnipresent cosmic forces.

Modern-day acupuncture involves the insertion of fine stainless steel needles of various shapes and sizes into one or several hundred sites which are distributed on the trunk, head, and extremities. According to the theory, of the many possible acupuncture points, only one would do the right job. It was necessary to know the precise location of the diseases for the purpose of acupuncture. Proponents of acupuncture claim that this treatment is beneficial for arthritis, fibrositis, "rheumatism," muscle or skeletal pain, and many other unrelated diseases. Should you use acupuncture to relieve the pain of arthritis? Since you tried it during your visit to ancient China with disappointing results, you are not inclined to try it again to relieve your symptoms.

[3]Imaginary organs.

In 1971, the report of the journalist James Reston's experience in China brought acupuncture to the attention of the American public. Until recently, the medical profession in the Western World considered acupuncture a disreputable form of treatment. Acupuncture has been used in China—often with morphine injections—to induce anesthesia for some surgical procedures since the late 1950s and it is certain that it may relieve pain for a relatively brief period of time. Thus, acupuncture is legitimately used in some settings to relieve pain. Although acupuncture is a useful method of treating pain, it can be used by physicians or nonphysicians who do not have adequate training and it is frequently practiced without a definite indication. The mechanism by which it relieves pain is poorly understood; but it may be a combination of placebo effect, suggestion, or perhaps the production of endorphins. The insertion of needles would stimulate the nerves and would cause the brain to release endorphins. Endorphins, the morphine-like factors produced within the brain as a response to a variety of stimuli, have been offered as an explanation for the pain-relieving effect of stress, placebo, hypnosis, acupuncture, and other psychological methods. When animals are subjected to intermittent stress, they show an increase in the opiate-like activity of the whole brain as well as in their tolerance of pain. It is possible that the stress-induced relief of pain described in animal studies, under some conditions, may also be applicable to humans. As it is with the use of any other treatment that involves trust or hope, the placebo effect is of great significance in reducing pain.

For centuries the domain of magicians and entertainers, hypnosis was brought to the forefront of medical practice by Sigmund Freud. In the latter half of the twentieth century hypnosis has been increasingly used to treat a variety of conditions, one of which is arthritis.

Although hypnosis or acupuncture can relieve pain, there is no evidence to support their use as primary or even adjunctive treatment for most types of arthritis, because these methods may modify the perception of pain for a relatively brief period of time as compared with the lifetime duration of the chronic disease. Acupuncture and hypnosis have no influence on inflammation, although some disreputable publications report encouraging results from acupuncture in the treatment of systemic, inflammatory, autoimmune diseases including rheumatoid arthritis, and other diseases, even AIDS.

Acupuncture is a relatively safe method which has a limited legitimate use and a multitude of inappropriate indications. Acupuncture as well as hypnosis have been used increasingly to treat "end-of-the-line" patients, that is, those suffering from intractable conditions. There are, however, relatively few true end-of-the-line arthritic patients, since most can be improved or even live normal lives with adequate medical treatment. Although acupuncture has proved to be of value as a pain reliever, it is obviously not suited to treat pain in end-of-the-line patients who survive many years under these conditions. Its efficacy in low back pain, cervical spine problems, bursitis, tendonitis, painful shoulder, and a range of musculoskeletal problems is very doubtful. Many of these conditions can be treated successfully by other methods and some of them have a brief limited course. As has been noted, the use of any treatment in a condition that will improve following its natural course will make the treatment appear to be successful. However, in these cases, I will not argue with success. If it seemed to work, nobody will convince you that your money was not well spent. Acupuncture and hypnosis are not indicated in the treatment of any type of arthritis and, like most alternative methods, are expensive and time-consuming. When administered as either the primary or exclusive treatment, they prevent the patient from benefiting from conventional therapy.

Fascination with Food

Paradoxically, though the naturalists despise drugs, they are prone to drink herbal teas, eat concoctions of exotic vegeta-

bles, or adhere to deviant dietary practices. We call it food fad-
dism when people deviate from traditional food patterns. R. J.
Williams (1971) discusses this subject, very appropriately observing: "Many food fads are, of course, simple rubbish, a few
make a certain amount of nutritional sense and very few are far
from nonsense." When you are about to embrace a new dietary
scheme to treat arthritis, you should consider how this fad ad-
dresses your individual nutritional needs. A fad tends to identify certain foods as good for all people at all times without
allowing for the wide variation in individual requirements. Food
fads related to single kinds of food obviously do not promote
good health. You should not confuse the suggestion to improve
your diet with the primary message of the books claiming that
similar dietary changes will "cure" your arthritis. "Cure" means
to heal or to make well, and it implies a complete restoration of
health by the use of a specific treatment. Therefore, the "cure"
should be effective for a specific type of arthritis and for no other
disease—not even for another type of arthritis. To evaluate the
recommended "cure," you should keep in mind that many arthritides have a self-limited course, irrespective of the treatment. In other words, if you have a type of arthritis that will
spontaneously improve or disappear after some time, you may
feel tempted to attribute the disappearance of symptoms to a
diet or to other remedies, when in truth, the disease just followed its natural course. When you analyse the claims of a
"cure" of arthritis by diet, it would be helpful to realize that
there are wide differences in the dietary schemes proposed by
various authors. The daily ingestion of two teaspoons of honey
and vinegar, megavitamin[4] supplementation, drinking "immune milk," eating lacto-vegetarian diets, or diets high or low
in protein, abundant in cherries or alfalfa, high or low in fat, and
several other diets have been proposed as treatment for some or
all forms of arthritis. It is revealing that even though the recommended diets differ so widely, they all allegedly accomplish a

---

[4]A large dose of a vitamin, far in excess of daily requirements.

"cure." Common to these schemes are the anecdotal character of the observations and the absence of long-term follow up.

Undoubtedly you have already been exposed to the widespread belief that dietary aberrations or deficiencies are directly related to the cause of arthritis. The natural course of most arthritides has often led people to believe the periodic announcement of sensational "breakthroughs" promoted by the tabloids and some news media. Recently, it was estimated that arthritic persons spend about $2 billion each year on useless remedies, unapproved devices, unnecessary food supplements, and diet books that promise relief or "cure."

Reading the popular literature may allow you to become acquainted with the "wonderful" effects of goat's milk and raw potato juice. The daily ingestion of one-half pound of cherries has been credited with success in the treatment of "gout." You may also read about the evil effects of refined carbohydrates which make pain worse. Although this may be true for an occasional patient, it is rare, and there is no evidence that eating refined sugars in excess is the causative factor in any type of arthritis. There are, however, other sound reasons for which you should avoid excessive ingestion of refined sugars, since this practice often leads to obesity and may trigger the appearance of diabetes mellitus.[5]

In spite of the belief rooted in folklore that "miraculous cures" of arthritis can be brought about by specific diets, there is no evidence of a cause-to-effect relationship between any food and any type of arthritis. You can easily find anecdotal accounts of "cures" in many popular books, but their testimonials do not prove a relationship between diet and arthritis. Very frequently, as noted above, information that has not been adequately researched appears in the daily press. Quacks or even well-meaning but misinformed doctors who believe they have the answer to arthritis are frequently responsible for these news releases. These "breakthroughs" are at best half-truths that can

[5]Literally, honey-sweet diabetes, characterized by excessive amounts of sugar in the blood and urine.

divert you from seeking proper treatment. Physicians and scientists have shown to have an open mind on the question of diet and arthritis and it is encouraging that the role of low-fat diet and that of fish oils in the treatment of some types of arthritis continues to be investigated.

You have already been exposed to the ancient Egyptians' obsession with food and their belief that disease was related to what they ate. At that time the food available to the Egyptians was, as far as we know, "natural." Since then, the expansion of the world population and the problems related to feeding large populations in urban centers removed from farming and grazing areas have greatly stimulated the development of the food industry which adds, subtracts, and modifies natural foods, and even creates synthetic food.

A good number of vendors try to attract the buyer with the claim that the products they advertise are natural. Their slogans claim that unnatural things are bad and equate naturalness with wholesomeness. Some individuals who adopt nontraditional dietary habits follow these schemes in a pattern that takes on many aspects of a religious ritual. They appear to intertwine piety and abstinence from certain foods, attempting to justify the process they are putting themselves through as being meritorious in God's sight. This pattern of thought does not take into consideration that many natural foods are actually poisonous or that many natural things can be deadly. This issue has been ably discussed by H. B. Hiscoe (1983). The natural quality of lightning, an earthquake, a flood, or a volcanic eruption is evident, although they are natural disasters. You can easily think of many man-made products that make living in our times more pleasant or without which life would not even be possible. I agree with Hiscoe that "those who proclaim the evils of civilization are hypocrites who are unwilling to return to the way of life of the cave man, but blindly praise the virtues of the natural to support their own views."

One of the most common myths about nutrition is the belief that "health foods" improve health and prevent disease. Extolling the value of natural food is valid when we consider foods such as polished rice and white flour which are not natural because the germ of the grains containing most of the vitamins and other valuable nutrients has been removed in the refining process. The "unnatural" quality of white flour or polished rice can be dangerous only if they comprise the major part of the diet. This would not be a balanced diet, and most likely would be deficient in essential nutrients. However, the use of the word *natural*, as it applies to foods, can be carried to nonsensical extremes. There are practical problems in feeding the world population of today that justify the use of some unnatural foods containing adequate supplementation of the missing nutrients. The possible contamination of food with toxic substances is of great concern to everyone. Well-known examples are the PBB[6] contamination of meat and dairy products in the state of Michigan in 1973 and the contamination of cooking oil in Spain with toxic aniline derivatives. Although we all should be adequately informed, there is no doubt that this issue has been highly exaggerated. For example, numerous studies have shown no difference in pesticide levels between so-called organic and regular foods. Obviously, you realize that there are commercial interests behind natural or "health foods," just as there are behind "unnatural" foods.

Concoctions of sassafras for the treatment of "rheumatism" apparently originated with the Iroquois Indians who prepared tea from the root bark of sassafras. Some of the natural remedies used by the Navajo Indians with "great success" include a tonic made from crushed leaves and branchlets of the Gaillardia[7] added to lukewarm water and applied internally and externally, for the treatment of "gout." The Navajo Indians also "cured" rheumatic stiffness with a tonic boiled from the leaves and branchlets of the barberry bush.

Popular arthritis books claim that garlic and onions have

[6]Polybrominated biphenyls, originally introduced as fire retardants and later used in the manufacture of electronic parts and plastics.
[7]A carduaceous herb.

very powerful antiarthritic properties. Although no antirheumatic properties can be recognized in garlic or onion, these vegetables continue to be very valuable for their contribution to taste and their nutritional content when added to foods.

The root of a South African plant known as devil's claw is said to be "highly regarded by African natives for its healing powers, used in infusions in the treatment of rheumatic disease." R. Carston (1978), a supporter of the use of devil's claw root for the treatment of "arthritis," stresses that devil's claw root is "a completely natural medicine effective as an organic compound." Irrespective of the hypothetical "antirheumatic" properties of devil's claw root tea, the naturalists ignore the historical fact that many of the drugs most frequently used in clinical medicine were originally extracted from plants. Digitalis preparations still in use for the treatment of heart failure were originally extracted from purple foxglove, a perennial flowering plant. Colchicine, a time-honored drug used very successfully to treat acute gout was extracted from colchicum autumnale, a liliaceae plant. Infusions from this plant, known in antiquity as Hermodactyl, had been used for centuries. Due to its content of certain salicylates, the bark of the willow tree was also long known for its properties of relieving pain and fever. Today aspirin and other salicylates are widely used in the treatment of arthritis and other painful conditions. I doubt that even a hardline naturalist would nowadays drink extracts of foxglove, colchicum, or tea made from the bark of the willow tree to treat heart failure, acute gout, or even an attack of the flu.

"Magic" Alfalfa

On your pilgrimage seeking a cure for arthritis, you were in Michigan in 1980. You had already tried "everything" and you heard about the "magic healing power" and "high vitamin and mineral content" of alfalfa. The popular literature is full of testimonials reporting that alfalfa is "absolutely nontoxic" and in the form of tea or tablets is helpful in relieving symptoms of arthritis. Some of your friends told you that they benefited greatly by consuming up to 20 tablets of alfalfa per day over a period of time and strongly advised you not to overlook alfalfa *sprouts* for maximal effect. Alfalfa sprouts for your daily salads could be easily grown in a glass jar.

During the next few months you were very busy trying to improve your diet. You were quite happy with your doctor's treatment which succeeded in bringing your arthritis under control, but you really wanted to help make your health perfect, so you incorporated alfalfa sprouts generously into your salads and regularly took alfalfa pills. Since this had become a part of your new life-style, you did not even think much about it. By the fall of 1983 you were not feeling very well but your doctor did not find anything wrong. In the spring of 1984, you felt weak and sleepy. You kept dragging your feet for several months, your joints began to hurt again, and you had severe stiffness in the morning. You and your doctor thought your rheumatoid arthritis was coming out of remission. He changed your medicines, but you began losing weight and also—to your dismay— your hair was falling out. Your doctor was puzzled, but after new testing he broke the news that you had now developed lupus. You might not have been surprised if you had known the results of studies showed that chronic ingestion of alfalfa seeds and sprouts or alfalfa pills may produce serious and unexpected side effects.

In studies by Bardana (1982) and colleagues on dietary supplementation with alfalfa for its effect on lowering the blood lipids,[8] three out of five female monkeys fed alfalfa seeds became very ill 5 to 6 months after they began eating alfalfa supplements. Some of the monkeys became sleepy, lost their hair, developed facial rashes, and lost weight. Laboratory tests showed low white blood counts, anemia, and a positive test that is present in most patients with human systemic lupus

---

[8]Fats in the blood, mainly cholesterol and triglycerides.

erythematosus (SLE). Thus, monkeys fed alfalfa seeds and sprouts developed an illness with all the features of SLE, one of the rheumatic diseases afflicting man. Subsequently, it was discovered that a substance present in alfalfa can induce lupus in experimental animals, and that ingestion of alfalfa has similar effects in humans. The symptoms and laboratory abnormalities suggesting lupus improved after the intake of the food supplement was stopped. Roberts and Hayashi (1983) also described a flare-up of lupus in two patients after chronic daily intake of alfalfa tablets.

The point of this discussion is that alfalfa seeds and sprouts are natural products and the toxic substance they contain is also a natural substance. This substance is also a drug which, in the quantities found in alfalfa sprouts and seeds, has toxic effects on humans when ingested in relatively large quantities. This is an excellent example showing that natural products are not always beneficial for our health and that they are not wholesome just because they are natural. The opposite also seems to be true; that is, synthetic products are not bad for our health just because they are unnatural. Drugs, whether from natural sources or synthetically produced, can have either beneficial or adverse effects.

Certainly the recognition of the medicinal properties of plants has led to the isolation and purification of many of the useful drugs usually prescribed in clinical medicine, which are now prepared synthetically. In these cases, the plant is a natural remedy, but its medicinal activity depends on the drug or drugs it contains. However, the effects observed after eating its leaves, roots, or flowers, or drinking tea prepared from the plant are unpredictable. The use of leaves, roots, or flowers is cumbersome and the proper dosage is difficult to control. You should remember that the effect of the natural remedy is always due to the drug or drugs it contains. The purified drug, whether natural when isolated from the plant or synthetic if artificially produced, is easier to administer and far more effective and reproducible in its effects. The example of alfalfa also illustrates the principle that adverse effects may not necessarily be immediate but may appear after a long period of exposure to a dietary fad.

Holistic "Cures"—The Arthritic's Hope

The naturalistic approach to treating arthritis may be appealing, but you must recognize its actual dangers as well as its potential benefits. In general, the medical profession has treated this approach with disdain as plain quackery, primarily because its results have been presented to the public through testimonials, uncontrolled observations, and claims of "miraculous cures," in popular tabloids which are also very strong on quackery.

When you hear of the wonderful effects that treatment at a spa had on your neighbor's arthritis, you have to remember that not all arthritides are the same disease. Indeed, patients with some types of arthritis with little or no inflammation of the joints, flabby muscles, and obesity can benefit immensely from exercise, a rational diet, and the quiet, beautiful environment surrounding a spa. If you continue the treatment of your arthritis and you can afford a stay at a beautiful spa in the Alps, the results will most likely be excellent. The story is quite different for those patients with severe inflammation of the joints, such as rheumatoid arthritis, who neglect their treatment. I know that some of my patients have repeatedly substituted this pleasant approach for the conventional treatment without beneficial results. In general, the activity of the disease continues unabated and its progression is not halted. Of course, one can say—and it is a reasonable objection—that I only see the failures and not the "cures." However, I am certain—because I have seen the failures—that a good number of patients are not "cured" by this approach. I also know that a number of the patients whom I have not seen, who honestly claim to have been cured, could have spontaneously gone into a prolonged or permanent remission. This is a recognized feature of the natural history of the rheumatic diseases. It is also likely that a good number of self-limited rheumatic conditions—unrelated to rheumatoid arthritis—may have been confused with RA and may have been counted as "cures." Finally, we have the false claims of unscrupulous quacks who attempt to lure new victims into a particular scheme for profit.

For the many who engage in holistic practices and feel bitterly disappointed when a cure is not forthcoming, there is the potential damage related to dwindling hope, time lost, and additional disability. Under these circumstances, it is easy to overlook some of the common-sense features of these approaches which are also tenets of accepted medical practice. For example, correcting faulty nutritional patterns which lead to nutritional deficiencies or obesity, following prescribed exercise programs, and relieving stress are usually a part of conventional orthodox medical advice to maintain or improve health.

Other naturalistic schemes are extremely simplistic but continue to be popular among my patients, many of whom have read D. C. Jarvis' (1960) statement that "Vermont folk medicine does not recognize a difference among bursitis, gout, rheumatoid arthritis, osteoarthritis, and muscular rheumatism." If the reader does not know that these diseases are different, he may believe D. D. Alexander's (1956) suggestion that all of them can be relieved by taking one tablespoonful daily of cod-liver oil along with restricting the ingestion of refined sugar and controlling the total caloric intake. Undoubtedly, a daily dose of cod-liver oil can correct some nutritional deficiencies if they are present, and it does contain some EPA, which cannot hurt. Moreover, restriction of refined carbohydrates is probably helpful under most circumstances, and control of total caloric intake, if the patient is obese, is a sound measure that could be of benefit to many people. However, these measures do not cure bursitis, gout, or rheumatoid arthritis. Another tenet of Vermont folk medicine is that "people with arthritis do not make hydrochloric acid in the stomach." Many times I have been asked by my patients about the effects of the ingestion of hydrochloric acid or the addition of apple cider vinegar to a glass of water to be sipped before or during meals, as encouraged by Jarvis (1960). I have seen no evidence that adding apple cider to your diet makes any difference in the progression of arthritis, and it certainly cannot be credited with a "cure."

Drinking distilled water every morning has been recommended by quacks as very effective in reversing and controlling arthritis. Not only is distilled water ineffective in the treatment of arthritis, but I remind the reader that the distillation process makes natural water unnatural by removing nutritionally essential minerals.

The naturalists claim that factors related to prolonged abuse of our bodies predispose or lead to arthritis. P. O. Airola (1968) advocates: "The eradication of abnormal factors which lead to the development of disease...assisting the body's own healing forces...by rebuilding and strengthening the general health of the patient." There is general agreement that many of the health problems of man are self-inflicted. The prevalence of obesity and alcoholism in all strata of our society are concrete examples of how many of us subject our bodies to a great deal of abuse. There is ample evidence that aberrant nutritional patterns, overeating, or a sedentary and stressful existence are also widespread in our society. Although there is no evidence that these factors cause any type of arthritis, there is very little doubt that they can be aggravating factors because they are detrimental to your health. Common sense also indicates that correction of these abnormal patterns of behavior would be a positive contribution to your health. This is an area in which I agree with the "pitch" of the naturalists, although they misrepresent the actual facts, because, again, advice to correct these problems is not the monopoly of naturalists, but is one of the tenets of orthodox medical practice.

Those who advocate fasting, fresh air, brisk morning walks, exercise, relaxation, rest, and adequate sleep call themselves "hygienic practitioners." The practitioners of orthodox medicine could be considered to be only semi-"hygienic," for although we do not advocate fasting, there is wide agreement that fresh air, brisk morning walks, exercise, relaxation, rest, and adequate sleep are beneficial to everyone.

A popular book written by J. Ott (1958) claimed that "arthritis" improves if you spend long daylight hours outdoors without glasses. The alleged basis of this effect is purported to be the influence of the energy of the full spectrum of sunlight. Mankind has evolved in sunlight and is dependent upon its energy for much more than an indirect source of food through photosynthesis[9] and maintenance of earth temperature. For thousands of years natural light has been recognized for its health-giving powers. Our skin, eyes, blood vessels, and certain endocrine gland functions respond to exposure to the electromagnetic spectrum of the sun. The formation of vitamin D from precursors in the skin by solar ultraviolet radiation exposure has long been recognized. Although certain of our daily biological cycles are dependent upon sunlight, there is no evidence that it has any effect on the course of any type of arthritis. Sunlight can actually be harmful and damage or kill cells. Some patients with lupus erythematosus, a type of arthritis, are very sensitive to ultraviolet radiation and often develop a skin rash on exposed areas of their skin and exacerbation of the disease upon exposure to the sun. Excessively prolonged exposure to sunlight causes skin cancer, wrinkling, and premature aging of the skin, eye inflammation and, possibly, cataracts.

H. M. Shelton (1978), a proponent of fasting, presents an amusing view of the physician treating the patient with arthritis. "The physician...now comes forward with his array of therapeutic absurdities and makes forever impossible the recovery of the sick. He extracts teeth, removes tonsils, extricates the ovaries, cuts out the gallbladder, excises appendices, works over the nose, drains sinuses—even chisels them out, heats and elec-

[9]Formation of complex carbohydrates in plants from carbon dioxide and water, using sunlight as the source of energy.

trocutes the patient, fills him or her with anodynes and antibiotics, advises a different climate and, finally, provides an order for a wheelchair, but does nothing to remove the cause" (p. 280). I must remind you that the ultimate causes of most diseases afflicting man are not known, although for thousands of years sorcerers and magicians have claimed to be able to eradicate them. Some naturalists, in apparent defiance of science and the medical profession, proclaim the "law of healing" (Vetrano, 1978). "Every living thing...replenishes, renews, and heals its structures, or tends toward healing." "The human organism has the ability to adapt itself to every situation in a manner to preserve itself and to remove the offending agent, and heal itself under all circumstances."

The law of healing is equivalent to the reinvention of the wheel. There is nothing in the principle of this law that is not supported by scientific observation. As a matter of fact, this principle was developed by orthodox medicine. Hippocrates, the father of medicine, exalted the healing power of nature almost 2500 years ago. More than 100 years ago the great French physiologist, Claude Bernard, propounded the physiological principle of homeostasis, or the process by which the body maintains a constant internal environment through the use of various regulatory mechanisms. Later, the physiologist, Walter Cannon, extended the general concept of homeostasis as the mechanism of reaction responsible for bringing some aspect of bodily structure or function nearer a normal level. There is nothing magical about the "healing forces of the body." These forces are part of an extremely complex mechanism involving multiple cells of the immune system, the blood, and the connective tissue, specific organs, thousands of different molecules, hormones, and chemical mediators which constitute the natural defenses of the body. However, individuals can adapt to many or even most, but not to all situations and circumstances. If the damage is too great, the body defenses may be overwhelmed and complete healing does not occur and, if the insulting agent persists, chronic disease sets in. In chronic disease, the defenses of the body are no longer wise and they respond excessively. The inadequacy of the philosophy of homeostasis or of the "law of healing" to deal with chronic disease is obvious and has been noted by Bernard's critics. In many diseases the offending agent has still not been identified.

Patients with arthritis spend millions of dollars on herbal preparations, papaya leaves, chickweed, various roots, extracts of artichoke, paprika, kelp, cod liver oil, or tryptophan because these products are "natural." With the exception of the expense, you may think these "remedies" appear to be innocuous; but it bears repeating that the real harm they inflict on people lies in the effect they have by building false hope and the dangerous conviction that something substantial is being done to treat arthritis.

The literature of folklore is full of a mixture of common-sense advice and sound principles of healthful living, coupled with irrational, dangerous, unfounded, and dogmatic statements. The naturalistic approach ignores genetic predisposition, which is important in the development of the most common forms of arthritis. Its emphasis upon environmental factors is appropriate; but this in no way makes it a unique concept of medicine. Moreover, the scientific community has significantly contributed to our knowledge of disease susceptibility, and it is safe to assume that it will continue to do so in the future. Nothing could be more in agreement with the principles of orthodox medicine than the goal of "strengthening the general health of the patient by assisting the body's own healing forces." Although our knowledge of these factors is continually expanding, I believe there is an urgent need for research to identify the risk factors operating in the development of the rheumatic diseases.

One of the main research goals of the scientific community has been to define in great detail how the defense mechanism of the body works, and this effort has led to impressive advances in the fields of molecular biology, biochemistry, and immunology. These have led to the discovery of new drugs and methods to control various types of arthritis. A good example is the treatment of gout, which can be extremely successful. Thus, although I do not find anything wrong with trying to stimulate the "healing forces of the body," I do find fault in promising a "cure" which, at the present time, cannot be achieved.

Macrobiotic Diet

The word macrobiotic, "meaning the art of prolonging human life," was coined almost 200 years ago by a German physician, Christolph von Hufeland. This approach is thought to consist of "the application of factors essential for optimum health and longer life free from disease," based on preserving the life force underlying the universe. Von Hufeland's life force, reminiscent of *Prana*, was thought to be present in light, heat, air, and water. His macrobiotic diet was predominantly lacto-vegetarian, high in natural carbohydrates and low in animal proteins, although fish or eggs were acceptable if used sparingly. Foods that were encouraged included soured milk (such as yogurt, buttermilk, or kefir), other fermented foods (for example, sauerkraut or pickles, and sourdough bread), wheat germ oil and wheat germ, sesame and pumpkin seeds, unrefined honey, unpasteurized milk, unprocessed cheese and brewer's yeast, supplemented with kelp, cod-liver oil, and vitamin C. Other foods, such as sugar, white flour, coffee, tea, salt, canned and preserved foods, processed cereals, soft drinks and all refined or adulterated foods, and tobacco, were to be avoided.

It has been amply demonstrated that a lacto-vegetarian diet, or even a totally vegetarian diet, when well planned and well balanced, can sustain growth and maintain a healthy life. Some naturalists suggest that "the best therapeutic diet for 'arthritis' is a low protein diet with emphasis on raw, fresh vegetables and fruit, with the total exclusion of meat and fish." The

American diet is thought to be excessively high in fat and protein and not devoid of potential adverse effects (Williams and Caliendo, 1984). Although a relatively lower but sufficient ingestion of protein makes good sense, I consider "the total exclusion of meat and fish" to be a matter of personal preference rather than based on any evil effect that meat and fish may have on your health. Moreover, recent evidence suggests that regular ingestion of deep-sea fish containing eicosapentaenoic acid (EPA) can be advantageous for persons with some types of arthritis. I suggest that to avoid drinking an excess of alcohol and smoking cigarettes can be of substantial benefit to your health. The problems resulting from the excessive ingestion of sugar and refined carbohydrates have been widely recognized. These problems have been extensively studied by nutritionists for several decades. A revival of interest in nutrition has led to the recognition of the problems discussed above and to definite recommendations to bring about changes in the national diet. The use of these sound nutritional principles is advocated to prevent atherosclerosis, prevent or alleviate the complications of obesity, prevent or improve certain types of high blood pressure and, certainly, to promote better health. In addition, subjects adopting the macrobiotic approach are advised to get plenty of exercise, to avoid mental or emotional stress, to get sufficient sleep and relaxation, and to have an active sex life. I fully support these positive features of a life-style which is extremely helpful when adopted by patients with arthritis. There is some confusion among those who adopt macrobiotics and also some danger related to using these diets without a sound nutritional background.

The oriental version of macrobiotics is based on the yin-yang principle, and is also concerned with the art of longevity and rejuvenation. According to this approach, all foods fall into one or the other category. Disease is thought to be due to an imbalance in the yin-yang equilibrium, which can be restored by the appropriate choice of nutrients. The followers of the oriental macrobiotic approach believe "that every disease is produced by dietary excess." This dietary approach accepts no medicines, vitamins, or surgery, although in some cases certain time-honored oriental herbs can be used. The macrobiotic diet is tailored to each person's health problem by balancing liquid and salt, and the proportion of cereals and vegetables. Meat, fish, and fowl are classified as yang, whereas vegetables are classified as yin. The theory claims that a proper balance between these foods is necessary for health. The proportional balance of food for a normal healthy person is usually 5 of yin and 1 of yang. The proponents of this approach believe that natural brown rice is perfectly balanced between yin and yang. It has been suggested that the macrobiotic diet should begin with brown rice, each mouthful chewed 30 times and liquids to be limited to as little as possible, preferably to one and one-half cups of Mu tea or green tea after meals. Brown rice, seasoned as recommended, may be eaten as often as desired, as long as each mouthful is chewed 30 times for thorough mastication. Of course, a diet based on brown rice and Mu tea is not balanced and is nothing but a dangerous fad if followed for a long time. According to its advocates, as the health improves, this method allows the gradual addition of other grains and vegetables, some fish, fowl, salad, and a little fruit. Sugar or refined foods are never allowed.

The macrobiotic diet has been reputed to "cure" arthritis. Linda Clark (1971) quotes Dr. G. Ohsawa, a proponent of macrobiotics who asserts that "not only does macrobiotics heal present disease, but it also prevents [the development of] all kinds of illnesses in the future" (p. 128). The macrobiotic approach is described as "an oriental philosophy which is simply a practical discipline of life that everyone can observe with the greatest pleasure" (p. 129). This philosophical approach may be very attractive to many, but in practice it is necessary to have a strong background in nutrition to eat a balanced diet according to the principles of "zen macrobiotics."[10] There is a parallel between the German and the Japanese macrobiotic theory. A grain-centered diet, chewing food well, avoiding coffee, spices, and

[10]See Chapter 10, p. 233 (section on protein requirements).

alcohol, taking adequate rest, and avoiding medicines and tension are common features to both approaches. While the German method allowed small amounts of meat and dairy products, both diets recommend protein consumption considerably lower than that of the American diet. Although the macrobiotic approach does not cure any type of arthritis, its dietary recommendations would probably represent a considerable improvement for millions of Americans who unknowingly have aberrant diets. I caution you that very rigid vegan diets are not without risks. These persons usually have lower than RDA intake of vitamins B_2, B_{12}, and D and calcium. Children on vegan macrobiotic diets present with growth delay and may be dangerously malnourished. Again, the emphasis on the importance of mental rest and avoidance of psychological stress surely can be helpful in the treatment of any of the diseases known to mankind.

The Chinese Poor Man's Diet

It is worth discussing some less elaborate variations of the macrobiotic approach. Dr. C. H. Dong (1975) describes his return to the Chinese poor man's diet after he became quite disabled with joint pain and stiffness. He tells us that after eating foods common to the diet of most Americans for 7 years, he became obese and developed "arthritis." He described his amazement when stiffness improved and agility returned as a consequence of his weight reduction from 195 to 150 pounds. He accomplished his weight reduction by following a diet composed of seafood, vegetables, and rice, similar to the one he had as a child. The diet eliminated red meat, fruit, dairy products, herbs, spices, preservatives, and alcohol. It contained fewer calories and less fat than the diet he had previously followed. He further described an almost complete remission of his crippling disease, which convinced him that "rheumatic diseases are caused by chemical poisoning and allergy to foods."

We can analyze Dr. Dong's experience and attempt to explain the rationale behind his improvement. It is evident from the information provided that no precise diagnosis can be made as to the type of arthritis he suffered. Dr. Dong's description leads me to believe that the aberrant diet he followed for 7 years led to his obesity. This is the same dietary pattern responsible for high cholesterol levels and for the higher mortality from coronary artery[11] disease observed in people of the more developed nations. The dramatic improvement in general well-being, stiffness, and agility was to be expected and concurs with my experience in the treatment of those obese individuals afflicted with rheumatic diseases. Thus, you cannot interpret the improvement reported by Dr. Dong as evidence that rheumatic diseases are caused by chemical poisoning from food additives. Panush (1983) and colleagues performed an adequately controlled study using this diet in the treatment of rheumatoid arthritis. No significant improvement was observed in the group receiving Dong's diet as compared with a control group. However, we should have an open mind and recognize that negative results in a relatively short-term study do not totally eliminate the possibility of the beneficial effect of a lifelong dietary habit. Thus, this type of experiment cannot provide a definitive answer.

In the mid 1960s, when you asked your doctor if there were any connection between diet and arthritis, the answer was an emphatic no. The doctor told you that scientific experimentation had determined that diet is not a factor in arthritis. When you repeated the question to another doctor in the mid 1970s, the answer was the same. You were rather puzzled by the flow of information suggesting that nutrition is important in the development of cancer, hardening of the arteries, as well as in aging, immunity, and infection. Then, why not arthritis? When you asked this question in the 1980s, you heard a different story. The doctor told you that classic studies done 30 to 50 years ago

[11]Narrowing or obstruction of the arteries supplying blood to the heart by the process of atherosclerosis or by a blood clot.

seemed to indicate that diet was not a factor in arthritis, but these reports were old and inconclusive and, to your surprise, you learned that the relationship between food and arthritis is being reexamined.

As a result of your inquiry you learned that although allergy to food may occur and in rare instances can be responsible for joint inflammation, it is unlikely to be a common mechanism in the development of arthritis. You were very interested to learn that nutrition has a profound influence on the immune response. Animal experiments done in the last two decades have provided impressive evidence that high or low calorie diets or diets containing various proportions of saturated and unsaturated fat can have a profound influence on autoimmune disease and various processes vital to survival. The thought occurred to you that if nutrition is important for the immune process, it is possible that the composition of the diet may make a difference in the course of arthritis. The startling discovery that diets enriched in fatty acids uniquely present in fish oil[12] prolong survival in animal models of SLE has recently suggested that this substance might be useful in the treatment of autoimmune diseases in man. However, not all of the observed effects of fish oil have been beneficial in experimental animals. Nevertheless, several recent studies have shown that a diet supplemented with EPA[13] or the addition of dietary fish oil can produce some relief of morning stiffness and joint pain in patients with rheumatoid arthritis. Is this a cure for rheumatoid arthritis? Hardly! Short-term experiments have shown that EPA or fish oil can produce slight to moderate relief, though probably less than that which can be obtained by aspirin. You should realize that long-term experimentation now underway may show more substantial benefits, but the possibility of side effects of long-term and massive supplementation of these fatty acids should be considered.

The lack of present evidence establishing a "dietary cure"

[12]Eicosapentaenoic acid (EPA), docosahexaenoic acid (DHA).
[13]EPA and DHA are omega-3 fatty acids.

does not mean that nutrition is unimportant to the arthritic person. There is a great deal of experimental evidence suggesting that, in the future, diet may conceivably become an important part of the treatment of the rheumatic diseases.

The Naturalists' "Cure"

The naturalistic approach emphasizes the notion that a "cure" should be obtained without drugs. The naturalistic admonition that drugs are evil and should be avoided at all costs has both positive and negative aspects. The positive aspect exposes the very real problem of the excessive use of drugs.

The beneficial effect of any drug is coupled with the inescapable risk that it may also cause untoward effects. "Pill-poppers" frequently look for a drug to relieve their health problems and they often believe that all their afflictions can be solved with a "pill." In the second half of the twentieth century, in the eyes of the public, drugs have been thought to be a legitimate solution not only to perceived disease but also for the troublesome problems of everyday life. Not only do they take large numbers of prescription drugs, but they also consume an extremely large number of drugs available over the counter, as well as illicit "recreational" drugs. You should be aware that over-the-counter drugs taken alone or in combination with prescription drugs can also produce many adverse effects. Many spokesmen for orthodox medicine have attempted to moderate the excessive utilization of drugs. You may be surprised that one of the most powerful mechanisms that can control drug utilization is *your* responsible attitude. As creatures of civilization, we frequently demand instant satisfaction, thus neglecting behavioral changes that undoubtedly would require our personal effort. To exercise this control, you should understand and accept the complexity of treatment methods without necessarily demanding instant and total relief. For this to happen, you must be well-informed. Even more important, you must recognize and act upon previously identified factors responsible for human suffering, such as dietary aberrations, obesity, emotional tension, and a sedentary existence. Many drugs would not be necessary if smoking, alcoholism, and obesity were not problems common to our society. These factors, when present, undoubtedly add to the misery of patients with arthritis. Here, the naturalists do have a point. I agree that fewer drugs should be used, but this would be possible only if the existing priorities and the values of members of this society were to change.

As we have noted, many disease processes are self-limited and run their own course irrespective of the treatment. Drugs often can provide relief of symptoms, and the impact of their effect on improving human misery and raising the life-style cannot be ignored. However, when discomfort is mild and tolerable, drugs may not be strictly necessary, because they do not change the final outcome. It is very difficult for many people to understand that sometimes the best course of action is to prescribe no drugs, advise general supportive and conservative measures, and continue to observe. Large numbers of new drugs have become available for the treatment of many human afflictions. Many infectious diseases which were fatal 30 or 40 years ago can now be successfully treated with antibiotics, and the survival of individuals having many types of cancer has not only increased, but some of them can even be cured by anti-cancer drugs.[14] Pain and misery produced by some chronic incurable diseases can be relieved and the suffering can be diminished. The quality of life for people with many human afflictions can be improved, even if life itself cannot be prolonged. To ignore the many beneficial effects produced by drugs used in the practice of medicine is unreasonable and unrealistic. Although we should certainly curtail what is excessive and unnecessary, the naturalists fall into the ridiculous when they propose using no drugs at all. In a paradisiacal world where disease

[14]In reference to cancer, it is often said that a cure occurs when the patient survives 5 years or longer.

and aging are unknown, and all is happiness and enjoyment, drugs would have no place. Though the naturalists despise drugs, they are ready to drink herbal teas, to eat concoctions of exotic vegetables, or to adhere to dietary practices that deviate from the traditional. I venture to say that even a recalcitrant naturalist would accept antibiotic treatment for an infectious arthritis, or colchicine or other nonsteroidal antiinflammatory drugs for an acute attack of gout. There are hundreds of examples of medical situations which are best treated with a drug.

Drugs have been used with a different philosophy by the homeopathic movement. Homeopathy is a system of treatment developed by Samuel Hahnemann on the assumption that large doses of a certain drug given to a healthy person will produce certain symptoms which, when occurring spontaneously as manifestations of a disease, can be relieved by the same drug in small doses. Another idea behind homeopathic treatment is that dilution of a drug, and hence very small amounts, enhances the power of the drug. Neither of these assumptions has ever been demonstrated. Homeopathy has generally been regarded as a demonstration of the healing power of nature or of the value of placebos in treatment.

Recently, attempts have been made to determine the value of homeopathic treatment in rheumatoid arthritis by Gibson and colleagues (1981). These authors reported a significant improvement in subjective pain, number of painful joints, stiffness, and grip strength in the patients receiving homeopathic remedies, whereas there was no significant change in the patients who received placebo. In this study, matching of the series of patients given homeopathic remedies and those given placebo was a problem, since those given placebo had a higher value of ESR, longer duration of disease, more joint tenderness, lower hemoglobin values, and had probably more severe and active disease. Thus, changes detected between two unequal groups may simply reflect the natural course of the particular subset of patients.

In addition, the changes observed, although statistically

significant, were small and probably of no clinical importance. Another complication which makes the statistical analysis very difficult is that since, in homeopathic practice, the selection of the appropriate remedy depends on the patient's symptoms and signs and his reaction to his total environment, the remedies used were quite varied and could be changed during the trial. Although homeopathic treatment seems to be quite safe, it does not have any value in the treatment of musculoskeletal disorders and if used alone it may deprive the patient of appropriate and timely treatment.

The American Diet

What is overlooked in the controversy between physicians and the proponents of some of the dietary "cures" for arthritis, is that although such diets do not produce a cure, some of their recommendations make a lot of sense, and if followed, would probably have a positive impact on the health of the individual. These "pearls" are often lost because they are submerged under a sea of nonsense.

There is much evidence that dietary aberrations are common in our society. In the developed nations, excessive ingestion of alcohol and saturated fat are the most common nutritional excesses. There is much evidence that the contribution of fat to our diet is excessive since approximately 40 percent of the total calories in the American diet are derived from fat. When carbohydrate, protein, and fat are ingested in excess of energy demands, they are converted into fat. One gram of fat can release nine calories as compared with four calories potentially released by equivalent amounts of protein or carbohydrate. Essentially, obesity develops when more calories are consumed than are used. Obesity is a health problem that aggravates many common conditions including arthritis, particularly when weight-bearing joints are involved. Arthritic patients who are obese have an increased likelihood of having high blood pressure, diabetes mellitus, and elevated levels of blood cholesterol. For arthritic patients with lung problems, the additional weight of excessive fatty tissue carried on the chest will increase the effort needed to breathe.

Recent studies have revived general interest in the relationship between dietary fats and cardiovascular disease. Obesity is a serious risk factor in the development of coronary artery disease and stroke and some obese people have a tendency to develop high blood pressure. The matter of ingestion of saturated fat and cholesterol has been a highly controversial issue in the last few years. People are frequently confused when experts disagree on matters of public concern. However, as well summarized by Stamler (1978), the literature in general supports the conclusion that the excessive consumption of fat affects the level of cholesterol in the blood and increases the long-term risk of death from coronary heart disease in middle-aged American men. These studies point out the merits of a vegetarian diet and support the need for a change in the national diet toward a greater consumption of vegetables. I would agree that most people in the United States should consume fewer calories, less fat and meat, while eating more vegetables, cereals, and fruit, and reduce the intake of refined sugars, soft drinks, convenience or canned foods, salt, and alcohol.

Recent findings also suggest that it is not simply the *amount* of fat in the diet, but that the *type* of fat may also be important. A diet with a high amount of fish oil rich in omega-3 fatty acids can decrease the stickiness of platelets and might be helpful in preventing and treating atherosclerosis.[15] These considerations linking the ingestion of excessive fat and the quality of the fat intake to the increased likelihood of developing heart disease particularly apply to patients with rheumatic diseases, because they are frequently overweight and lead a sedentary existence. Another potentially harmful dietary excess is the overuse of salt, which is clearly an acquired habit. The average salt intake

[15]A type of hardening of the arteries.

in the American diet exceeds the "safe and adequate" intake recommended by the Food and Nutrition Board. There *is* convincing evidence linking high salt intake to the development of high blood pressure; therefore a reduction in the use of salt is probably in order, particularly for those arthritic patients being treated with corticosteroids. I believe that if you eat in this way you will probably feel better and it will be beneficial to your health, because with these changes you attempt to modify harmful dietary patterns.

Food Additives

Some popular literature has proposed a possible relationship between arthritis and chemical poisoning from additives and preservatives present in our food. I know of no evidence that suggests such an association. Although food additives or preservatives are not causative factors in any type of arthritis, their widespread use has been periodically suggested to be associated with several actual or potential health problems.

In our modern society, the food industry uses a billion pounds of chemical additives annually. These additives are used in various ways to improve the taste, modify the color, stability, or consistency, and to preserve, acidify, or sweeten food. The production and delivery of food for the enormous populations of our time pose complex logistic problems. Many food preservatives retard the chemical processes causing decay and the growth of microorganisms in food. Some preservatives are antioxidants, which prevent the oxidation of fats and other substances. The use of chemicals as food additives has probably not been thoroughly monitored to assess the potential causation of adverse effects. Even though many food additives are unnecessary and some may be harmful, an indiscriminately negative attitude toward these compounds does *not* appear to be justified. Artificial coloring of wine has been in use for more than

2,000 years, while butter and margarine have been colored for several centuries. In the late 1800s, synthetic colors were already being used in jelly, syrup, cheese, ice cream, pastries, noodles, and wine and liqueurs. Most of the beautiful colors that we see in the supermarket are not natural, but rather the result of the widespread use of food coloring. Of course, the fact that they have been around for centuries does not make them good; but it must be pointed out that over such a long period of time no ill effects have been detected. However, it did become evident to the United States Government that safeguarding the health of the population required the establishment of effective controls and regulations on food additives. At the present time, no new color additive intended for use in foods, drugs, or cosmetics can be marketed until extensive testing proves that it is not harmful for the uses and in the quantities proposed. In all probability, these new regulations implicitly recognize that by the use of a "grandfather" clause, those food additives previously certified had not been adequately evaluated in terms of their potential hazards to human health. Thus, the Food and Drug Administration has begun a program to provide for the periodic review of all food additives, including permanently listed colors, to make sure that they are safe by modern scientific standards. As a consequence of this surveillance program, one of the red dyes, Red No. 2, that was formerly very widely used to give color to soft drinks, ice cream, candies, baked goods, and maraschino cherries, was withdrawn from the market because of its cancer-producing potential.

Nitrites, tartrazine, sulfite preservatives, and monosodium glutamate are just a few examples of potential causative agents of health problems. Some segments of the food industry have heeded the warning of the medical profession about the potential deleterious effects of some food additives and many unprocessed foods having no additives are now available on the market.

You should also realize that the concern about food additives is being exploited by a multimillion-dollar "holistic" health industry. You may easily recognize the commercial interest involved in these "holistic" preparations which are supposed to solve the problems of the overweight, the underweight, and to satisfy literally everyone's nutritional needs. It is not true that you can no longer obtain adequate nutrition from regular foods and that everyone needs supplements of essential nutrients.

Does Treating the Part Improve the Whole?

Various holistic approaches are based on the belief that every part of the body is inseparable from the mind. The ancient art of touching with the hands developed into various techniques of body massage and in methods to promote whole body health. Some of them have flourished on the bandwagon of the fitness craze and health consciousness that blossomed around the 1960s.

Foot reflexology is based on the premise that various organs, nerves, and glands of the body are connected with certain "reflex areas" on the feet such as the soles, toes, or ankles. Practitioners of reflexology believe that energy flows through the body along meridians that terminate in the feet. This belief is reminiscent of the principles involved in acupuncture and Shiatsu massage. You may read in books on foot reflexology that "massaging reflex areas of the feet can be a solution to multiple health problems, from hemorrhoids to arthritis." You might be inclined to try it, since it will probably not harm you, and it is thought "to get rid of practically all types of poor health situations" and promises "prompt relief from practically all aches and pains." There are also claims that massaging these areas of the feet "stimulate your endocrine glands into their normal, healthy conditions." You will read about the striking cases of severe crippling "arthritis," describing people with curled feet, misshapen hands, and severe swelling of the knees and ankles who were restored to complete health by massage of their feet. Your hands are painful and swollen but they are not yet misshapen and your feet are not yet curled—so, why not? You will also be told by the foot reflexologists that it is possible to stimulate the pituitary or the pineal glands, or to influence the prostate, the uterus, the ovaries, and practically any part of your body, by pressing the "right buttons" in the reflex areas of your feet. Of course, there are no "right buttons" in your feet, but there certainly are "right buttons" to your purse! A variety of holistic methods are often offered to the credulous. Lectures or workshops promoting natural foods and nutrition, along with instruction in such healing methods as foot reflexology or the healing power of crystals and pyramids are frequently found at spiritualist retreats.

Several other methods have been claimed to improve the whole body by the treatment of one of its parts. Footbaths with herbal preparations containing garlic and onions have been claimed to "cure" some undefined chronic rheumatic conditions. Practitioners of chiropractic, iridology, tongue diagnosis, zone therapy, and many others claim to diagnose or treat the whole from the anatomical part. Most of these methods are not the innovations of twentieth-century man. On your trip through Mesopotamia you could see cuneiform inscriptions in the library of King Ashurbanipal describing prophecies based upon inspection of various parts of the patient's body. At that time you were surprised when you learned that sorcerers could make predictions by looking at the right or the left eye, the right ear, the outstretched right hand, the tongue, or the foot. Except for the art of foretelling events by looking at the right ear, which appears to be extinct, you can easily see in these practices which existed several thousands of years ago, the harbingers of iridology, palmistry, tongue diagnosis, and foot reflexology.

We know enough about the pathways in the nervous system to be certain that this complex reflex representation of multiple organs claimed to be found in the foot or in other zones of the body is simply untrue, and that manipulation of no single part of the body can restore the disorganized harmony of the whole.

It is possible that an area other than that which was treated might be affected by suggestion or, even more likely, by the placebo effect. In no way can the treatment of one single part of the body influence the entire body resulting in the "cure" of any disease.

CHAPTER 4

MONKS, BARBERS, APOTHECARIES, AND MOUNTEBANKS

In the thirteenth century, when the Vatican prohibited the clergy from practicing medicine, the way was opened for a multitude of mountebanks and quacks to offer their services as healers. Chaos continued for almost three centuries despite the edict promulgated by Henry VIII (1491–1547) of England which made it illegal for anyone to cure the sick without a license from the Bishop of London or the Dean of St. Paul's. In the early 1500s, barbers and surgeons formed their own professional association, allowing only their members to practice barbery, shavery, surgery, and the letting of blood, within the city limits of London. The red-and-white pole found in the front of modern barber shops represents the blood and bandage of the barber-surgeon of early times. A short time later, Henry VIII granted a charter to the College of Physicians that also restricted the practice of medicine to its own members within 7 miles of London.

101

The physicians also faced competition from the apothecaries who finally were chartered by James I in the early 1600s. At the same time, although the apothecaries were associated with the grocers, they looked down on them, considering them to be mere tradesmen who specialized in foreign drugs and spices.

The deluge of quacks took advantage of this turmoil in the establishment of the healing professions. Everyone wanted a piece of the pie. Arthritis was naturally one of the main ailments treated by quacks in the seventeenth century. The history of quackery clearly shows that not only are the poor and ignorant the easy prey of swindlers; the rich, the literate, and even royalty can be lured by their claims.

Quackery has remained unchecked for centuries. Even in relatively recent times in the U. S. it has been allowed to flourish. Both Adam Smith in the eighteenth century and Herbert Spencer in the nineteenth opposed governmental controls that sought to curtail quackery. Noninterference with business has been the prevailing doctrine in this country; but in 1906 the enactment of the first federal regulatory statute, the Pure Food and Drug Act, was thought to give a death blow to quackery. However, never before in history has medical quackery been such a booming business as it is today. The techniques of the quack had to be greatly modified to survive the greater scientific knowledge and improved educational level of the population, the upgrading of medical education, and the tightening of legal regulations. You may be lured into self-treatment by a motivated friend, another patient whose "arthritis was cured," a faith healer, a naturalist, or any number of other persons who make a living selling "health and cures." The word "health" used in this sense means health-giving or having curative properties.

Patients are constantly besought to buy physical well-being and to banish ailments by eating "health" foods. Dietary fanaticism, in particular, has been responsible for the failure of many people to seek and obtain adequate and timely treatment for their disease. If you become convinced that diet is all that is necessary in the treatment of arthritis, you may be inclined to experiment, with very little or no guidance. In my view, as I have pointed out, the time lost is critical, because affected joints will never be the same after a period of uncontrolled disease activity, and after several years the effects can be devastating. You should realize that destruction of the joints is a time-dependent event, and it is urgent that adequate treatment be instituted before the damage is extensive, for when it does occur, it cannot be reversed. I must warn you that the result of pursuing these pathways is frequently crippling and charts a lifelong course of misery and pain.

In the U. S. a change for the better was observed in the so-called "patent medicine" business at the beginning of the twentieth century. Influential in effecting this change was the "Great American Fraud" series by Samuel Hopkins Adams which was published in *Collier's Magazine* in 1905–06, the *Ladies Home Journal Crusade*, the passage of the National Food and Drug Act, the activity of the Better Business Bureau movement, and the responsible attitude of a large number—but not all—of the newspaper publishers who voluntarily curtailed fraudulent medical advertising. Early in this century, Dr. Arthur Cramp, director of the Bureau of Investigation of the American Medical Association (AMA), championed a campaign of education and enlightenment for the public which centered on "patent medicine" and "quackery."

Megadoses of Vitamins

Casimir Funk, a Polish chemist working at the Lister Institute in London, coined the word *vitamin* early in the twentieth century to designate a group of substances required in the diet for maintenance of good health. The discovery of vitamins was one of the great medical advances of this century, but quacks saw a bonanza in their discovery and soon developed a racket that mushroomed into the vitamin cure-all. Vitamins were soon incorporated into preparations claimed to be effective in a wide range of conditions, from growing hair and preventing grayness to the prevention or cure of arthritis. Vitamins are all-time favorite "remedies" used by patients with arthritis in their quest to obtain relief. It has become popular to use doses of vitamins 10 to 100 times or more in excess of the RDA[1] as a means of obtaining a cure or relief of symptoms.

Most of the naturalistic approaches to treatment regard nutritional deficiency as a common cause of "arthritis." Not only is there evidence that nutritional deficiency is often the result rather than the cause of many types of disabling arthritis, but it has been established that genetic makeup influences the development of most arthritides. From our knowledge that the various forms of arthritis are different diseases, it seems most unreasonable that they should all have the same cause.

If you take megadoses of vitamin supplements to treat your arthritis, you will expose yourself to the risk of experiencing serious side effects. Preparations containing enormous quantities of vitamins are available over the counter and in "health food" stores. Unfortunately, the dose ingested is often based on the common belief that if one is good, 10 is 10 times better. There is abundant evidence suggesting that excessive vitamin intake will not only be of no benefit, but in some cases can be dangerous. At best, megadoses of vitamins simply add to the expense and contribute nothing to alleviate the arthritis; at worst, alone or in combination with other drugs, they can cause unexpected side effects.

Very high doses of B vitamins taken three or four times a day, frequently enough to color the urine bright yellow at all times, have been advocated in some popular publications. The bright yellow color of the urine simply reflects the elimination of most of the enormous dose of the vitamin which the body cannot utilize. This obsessive preoccupation with maintaining high circulating levels of vitamins of the B group has no scientific basis, and this practice in no way relieves symptoms of arthritis.

[1]Recommended dietary allowance.

You can find support for these recommendations in the uncontrolled and inconclusive study by W. Kaufman (1981), who proposed the use of large doses of one of the B vitamins, niacinamide or B_6, for the treatment of patients with arthritis. There are reports of many patients with rheumatoid arthritis with low levels of pantothenic acid, folic acid, and riboflavin. Most of these patients had advanced destructive articular changes suggesting that the nutritional deficiency was the consequence rather than the cause of the arthritis. There are no grounds for the claim, based on an uncontrolled study, that daily supplementation of large doses of vitamin B_6 is effective in the relief of arthritic symptoms. I know of no rationale for the practice of administering large doses of vitamin B_{12} to patients with osteoarthritis, since they do not have anemia, are not deficient in vitamin B_{12}, and 99% of the administered dose is rapidly eliminated in the urine.

You have been exposed to the claims of popular writers who support the notion of the universal action of vitamin C in the treatment of the rheumatic diseases. You have probably read anecdotes about patients afflicted with "severe arthritis," which literally melted after they ingested large doses of vitamin C. There is no evidence in the medical literature to suggest that deficiency of vitamin C is a factor predisposing or leading to any form of arthritis. In spite of this, maximum amounts of vitamin C daily are recommended in some popular arthritis books with the remark that it is "nontoxic and completely harmless, even in massive doses." Pearson and Shaw (1982) not only openly recommend megadoses of vitamin C, but admonish patients to be sure that its levels in the urine oscillate between 500 milligrams per liter in the morning to about 2,000 milligrams per liter 3 hours after the morning dose, promoting the compulsive habit of measuring the vitamin in the urine. Phenomenal doses as high as 10,000 to 18,000 milligrams daily have even been recommended in some publications. This type of advice should be evaluated with the knowledge that doses over 250 milligrams per day are unwarranted and that the enormously excessive

dose ingested is eliminated in the urine. In some cases megadoses of vitamin C ingested over a long period of time can
produce side effects such as painful kidney stones. If you happen to have bleeding from your stomach, the test used to detect
blood in the stools may be erroneously negative when you take
massive amounts of vitamin C. Similarly, megadoses of vitamin
C make the control of diabetes difficult by altering the results of
the tests to detect the presence of sugar. An interesting complication of taking massive doses of this vitamin is that if for any
reason you stop taking it, shortly thereafter you may develop
weakness, malaise, and abnormal healing which is due to "conditioned" scurvy.

An issue has been made of the distinction between synthetic and natural vitamins. It is recommended in the popular
literature that "for day-in day-out use, natural vitamins are the
wiser." However, you should know that many synthetic and natural molecules are identical. Paradoxically, naturalists prefer vitamin C in tablet form to that which is present in fruits. All
commercially available vitamin C is produced by chemical synthesis, and is thus unnatural. The reason for this preference is
clear. In order to take the "modest" dose—by naturalists'
standards—of 1 gram vitamin C per day from natural sources,
you would have to consume about 5 pounds of Florida oranges,
22 pounds of bananas, or 27 pounds of lettuce. The amount of
vegetables necessary to provide doses of several grams of vitamin C per day from natural sources obviously cannot be ingested by even the most dedicated naturalists. An additional
reason that naturalists may prefer vitamin C of industrial origin
is the mistaken notion that "large amounts of citrus fruit or fruit
juices aggravate arthritis." Although an occasional patient may
have this complaint, and in these cases avoidance of citrus is
reasonable, there is no reason that you should be deprived of
orange or grapefruit juices or citrus fruits in general.

Doses of 10,000 I.U. of vitamin E have been advised in the
popular literature for their "antioxidant" properties as an effective treatment of "arthritis." Proponents of high doses of vita-

min E indicate that it causes no known toxic side effects, except for a temporary rise in blood pressure at the beginning of its administration. Not only is the efficacy of these elevated amounts of vitamins unproven, but it has been reported that the toxicity of vitamin E begins with prolonged daily doses of 400 I.U.

It should be clear that the multivitamin cure-all approach is expensive, heavily supported by commercial interest, and has no scientific basis. You should be aware of these practices, because policing the claims of nutritional promoters is presently very difficult, for salesmen are increasingly promoting food fads through oral communication rather than by incriminating pamphlets.

The Copper Bracelet

In relation to the continuing scientific interest in copper in the rheumatic diseases, you are probably well aware that mankind has been fascinated with copper for thousands of years. You were exposed to copper compounds when you visited Egypt at least 5,000 years ago. In general, the Egyptians called copper containing pigments *wadj*, which means "to be green." (The word *wadj* also stood for green eye paint and for women's makeup.) Women with arthritis—considering all types—greatly outnumber men. While you were seeking relief for your arthritic symptoms in ancient Egypt, you could not help but imitate the Egyptian women so you painted your eyelids a voluptuous green hue—after all, you were a woman.

You heard about the copper bracelet during your trip through Mesopotamia, and you certainly wore one as part of your treatment in ancient Greece. Although your arthritis kept getting worse, you were quite pleased with your exotic bracelet. Indeed, the greenish hue acquired by your skin in contact with the bracelet suggested that it was doing something to your body.

The popular use of copper as treatment in Greek medicine may betray Egyptian influence. The mines of Cyprus supplied the metal in such large amounts that the island, Kypros itself, gave its name to copper. A copper bracelet for the relief of arthritis has long been considered by the medical profession to be a harmless quack remedy. The many claims of relief from pain often have been attributed to coincidental improvement.

Recently, serious attempts have been made to test the possible beneficial effects of the copper bracelet in arthritis. In a series of interesting reports, Walker and colleagues (1981, 1982) studied the effect of metallic copper in the form of copper bracelets in relieving arthritic discomfort. Chemical experiments showed that copper may dissolve in sweat and that it may then be absorbed through the skin. Penetration of copper through the skin was demonstrated in cats, pigs, bulls, and humans, and it was shown that copper bracelets lose a measurable amount of copper per month. However, the issue of the clinical usefulness of the copper bracelet remains controversial. It was reported that people who wore copper bracelets for a period of one month experienced less suffering than nonwearers. The report added that previous users of such bracelets experienced significantly worse pain when not wearing the bracelets. In this study a placebo bracelet of anodized aluminum was used by the patients in the control group. Unfortunately, the blindness of the study was difficult to maintain. You are probably well aware, as are most arthritic persons, that one characteristic effect of a copper bracelet is to give a green coloration to the skin. This would obviously suggest to you that you were wearing a bracelet made of copper, negating the blindness of the study. In addition, the diagnosis of the respondents was not known, and as suggested by P. Simkin, the very low proportion of wrist involvement (one out of 250 patients) makes it highly unlikely that patients with rheumatoid arthritis were well represented in the group of patients reported, since the wrists are involved in the majority of patients with this disease. This subject clearly requires further investigation.

The scientific community has been interested in the anti-inflammatory properties of copper for a long time. In Germany, Fenz introduced copper in the treatment of rheumatoid arthritis in 1941 but, although promising results were reported, the treatment never became established. In 1927, gold began to be used in the treatment of RA and eventually became an established therapy, while copper ceased to be used. The resurgence of interest in the essential metals, particularly copper and zinc, in the field of the rheumatic diseases has been stimulated by the efficacy of the chelating agent penicillamine in the treatment of rheumatoid arthritis. Although the mechanism by which penicillamine suppresses the activity of RA continues to be investigated, some studies have suggested that penicillamine-copper complexes may be involved. Thus, although the chemical properties of copper are extremely interesting and there is a body of work suggesting that copper complexes have anti-inflammatory activity, there are no reasons to attribute curative properties to copper bracelets.

Hormonal "Cures"

Increasing knowledge of the glands of internal secretion stimulated the imaginations of quacks who rapidly concocted preparations for rejuvenation, beautification, and enhancement of sexual power.

The implications of the action of cortisone and the discovery of the relationship between the adrenal and the pituitary glands in the late 1940s and early 1950s were rapidly recognized not only by the medical profession, but also by the arthritic population and the public in general. Unfortunately, this momentous discovery also captivated the imaginations of charlatans who are always ready to capitalize upon the fears and afflictions of others by devising new "cures."

The apparent mystery surrounding the action of the endocrine[2] glands and the discovery of hormones stimulated the popular misconception that the cause of "arthritis" is related to an error in glandular metabolism, and that the ingestion of "mineral hormones in fresh fruits, vegetables, and dairy products" is beneficial for patients with "arthritis." It is true that endocrine disorders frequently produce musculoskeletal changes. Patients with acromegaly—a disorder of the pituitary gland—may have joint pain, stiffness, and effusions in their joints, and may develop carpal tunnel syndrome and osteoporosis. Muscle weakness and osteoporosis are common manifestations of excessive and prolonged use of corticosteroid drugs or of hyperfunction of the adrenal cortex resulting in excessive production of cortisol (the principal steroid hormone produced by the adrenal cortex having predominant action on intermediary metabolism). Patients with myxedema (hypofunction of the thyroid gland) often have stiffness and joint pain and swelling and those with hyperthyroidism may have painful swelling of the fingers, osteoporosis, and profound muscle weakness. If these conditions are diagnosed, the treatment is usually successful, but when they are not recognized, the patients may erroneously be thought to have rheumatoid arthritis or osteoarthritis. However, no other type of arthritis is generally recognized to be related to an "error in glandular metabolism." The need for fresh fruit and vegetables in a balanced diet is unquestionable, but this need is not based on the presence of "mineral hormones" that they do not contain. The impact of milk in human nutrition is mainly due to the high biological value of its proteins and to its rich content in calcium and other nutrients, but certainly not to "mineral hormones." It has been claimed by proponents of hormonal cures that a deficiency of cortisone, which is produced by the adrenal gland, is the basis of arthritic symptoms. This rationale is faulty on several counts. The adrenal gland is not deficient in its ability to produce cortisone in patients with any type of arthritis. Although in the 1950s cor-

[2]Any of certain glands that secrete certain substances or hormones directly into the blood.

tisone was initially hailed as a panacea to cure RA because of its potent anti-inflammatory effect, it was later discovered that its use in clinical medicine is often coupled with potentially serious adverse effects. It was also clearly shown that cortisone or related substances do not cure rheumatoid arthritis and do not halt the progression of the disease. The administration of a relatively low dose of prednisone, a synthetic corticosteroid related to cortisone, can be useful in certain patients with RA, but even in these instances it is an adjunct to other treatments, and not a cure.

C. Wade (1972) has also linked the hormone deficiency purported to be the cause of RA to the low levels of blood pantothenic acid reported in some patients. He tells you that when patients eat honey and brewer's yeast the levels of pantothenic acid in the blood increase. As a consequence of this treatment, "the two natural hormone foods, honey and brewer's yeast, stimulate the adrenal glands to issue a healthy supply of natural cortisone." The patients allegedly "improve and experience a rejuvenation of the joints and relief of their stiffness." Although honey and brewer's yeast are excellent foods that may be components of a balanced diet, they do not possess the power that the popular literature attributes to them. They certainly do not have the ability to stimulate the endocrine glands or to bring about rejuvenation of the joints. Neither is there evidence that the direct administration of cortisone produces any of these "wonderful" effects. Wade further surprises you with the statement that "yeast tonic helps the adrenals secrete hormones," namely, "cortisone which helps the body fight off arthritic infections by setting up a shield around bacteria and toxic substances, thus preventing them from spreading to surrounding tissues." Actually, cortisone does not help the body to fight any kind of infection. On the contrary, there is evidence that patients treated with cortisone derivatives may be *more* susceptible to infections. Cortisone is completely unable to "set up a shield around toxic substances and bacteria." The same can be said of the statement that "desoxicortisone can destroy its imprisoned bacteria." This cortisone derivative has neither the ability to imprison nor to destroy bacteria. These assertions constitute blatant abuse of the ignorance of the public about the action of cortisone.

Other mixtures of cortisone derivatives and sex hormones continue to be inappropriately used by large numbers of patients for the treatment of various types of arthritis. Liefcort is a combination of prednisone, estradiol[3] and testosterone.[4] The frequently recommended dose of Liefcort contains 15 milligrams of prednisone per day. It is the anti-inflammatory action of prednisone which makes these patients feel transiently better. This concoction has been used since the early 1960s, and has been purported to be effective in the treatment of rheumatoid arthritis and osteoarthritis. There is no evidence to justify the claim that sex hormones are beneficial in the treatment of RA or that they prevent steroid side effects. Moreover, there is no evidence that injections of sex hormones cure any type of arthritis. Numerous side effects can be noted in patients adhering to this treatment. To those adverse effects produced by the prolonged and unsupervised treatment with prednisone, most prominently osteoporosis, you can add those related to the use of testosterone, such as virilization, hoarseness, oily skin, acne, increased body hair, enlarged clitoris, stimulation of libido, menstrual irregularities, liver function abnormalities, and those potentially associated with the use of estrogens such as causing cancer of the cervix, uterus, vagina, breast, and liver, and possibly the increased tendency to form blood clots, as well as other serious side effects. If you take these hormonal preparations, you will be exposing yourself to these potential dangers from a treatment that is ineffective. Although patients often obtain some relief from pain and stiffness with prednisone, most types of arthritis follow their natural course and crippling is not prevented.

[3]Naturally occurring estrogen in humans.
[4]Sex hormone that stimulates masculine characteristics.

The Rise and Fall of DMSO[5]

DMSO is a commercially available solvent possessing many chemical properties that have both industrial and medicinal value. In 1963 Dr. S. W. Jacob reported that DMSO rapidly penetrates the skin, facilitates the transport of other drugs across biological membranes, has a local analgesic effect, decreases swelling, and promotes healing of injured tissue.

For over two decades, public consumption of the drug has continued to be encouraged by distributors selling DMSO labeled "not for medical use" to obvious medical users. Dr. Richard Crout summarized the FDA's position on DMSO when he testified before the select committee on aging of the House of Representatives in 1980. "DMSO is a solvent that crosses body membranes with ease and appears to have an analgesic effect when applied locally. There is much testimonial evidence to suggest that DMSO relieves pain after local application to injured or inflamed tissues. This is an effect similar to that which we associate with liniments. Properly controlled studies to prove this point are not available but are technically possible to perform. However, one of the main problems encountered by investigators trying to design blind studies using DMSO is that of masking its presence because it has a highly characteristic odor. Attempting to make placebos by using garlic to mimic the local and systemic effects of DMSO have been unsuccessful. There is no evidence that DMSO alters the course of any disease, or is, in any sense, a miracle drug. To suggest on the basis of the evidence available to date, controlled or uncontrolled, that DMSO is a major medical advance for any serious disease, is misleading."

The biological activity of DMSO continues to be actively investigated. Analysis of the literature does not support the notion that there is a conspiracy against the use of DMSO. The conjecture that DMSO acts in mysterious ways, defying ordi-

[5]Dimethylsulfoxide.

nary scientific principles, gives false hope to the thousands who suffer from rheumatic diseases. The mystique surrounding DMSO is maintained by those who sell you "solvent DMSO for non-medical uses," thereby encouraging you to treat yourself without proper medical supervision.

DMSO administered intravenously to patients with arthritis can produce serious illness with tremor and loss of consciousness, damage to the kidney and the red blood cells, abnormal liver enzymes, a drop in hemoglobin, agitation, bad breath, fever, low blood pressure, and rapid pulse rate.

Topical application of DMSO on the skin does not appear to produce serious side effects. The results of the experimental use of topical applications of DMSO to treat flexion contractures in patients with rheumatoid arthritis have been inconclusive. Despite the promising properties of DMSO, it has not proved to be a major breakthrough in the treatment of the rheumatic diseases, and it has no value at the present time in the treatment of any arthritis. However, millions of Americans have been able to purchase commercial grade DMSO for self-medication. Although its careful topical use is unlikely to produce major problems, and internal uses have been reported under experimental conditions, I would stress that DMSO is still in the investigational stage in the treatment of the rheumatic diseases, and I would certainly warn you against indiscriminate self-medication with the drug.

Amebas and Mycoplasmas

Some of my patients have explored the "cures" attributed to the use of clotrimazole,[6] metronidazole,[7] and other chemical substances related to nitroimidazole[8] in the treatment of RA.

[6]Antifungal agent for topical use.
[7]Antiprotozoan and antibacterial agent.
[8]Substance used to treat intestinal parasites.

The use of these chemicals is based on R. Wyburn-Mason's (1976) proposal that rheumatoid arthritis is caused by an ameba. This author claimed that an ameba causes "rheumatoid diseases" and that nitroimidazole is effective in their treatment. The claims of cure with this treatment also included osteoarthritis, although we know that this is a distinct disease with no known relationship to rheumatoid arthritis. The assertion that patients with lupus, those with complete ankylosis of the spine, and children with juvenile arthritis have been successfully treated with metronidazole also seems unfounded.

Diseases claimed by Wyburn-Mason to be produced by amebas include Paget's disease of the bone, ulcerative colitis, myasthenia gravis, arteritis, chronic pyelonephritis, some cases of diabetes, pericarditis, some cases of hepatitis, and uterine fibroids. Proponents of this theory claim that these amebas may also cause scleroderma, alopecia, psoriasis, vitiligo, dermatitis herpetiformis, asthma, and chronic bronchitis. In spite of the wide diversity of the diseases allegedly produced by the ameba, the treatment with nitroimidazoles is claimed to be "directed at the cause of rheumatoid disease and not simply at the symptoms." Not only is this untrue, but by following this treatment, patients with rheumatoid arthritis may be damaged in other ways. Exercise and heat are thought to be harmful by the proponents of this "cure," who suggest that the use of these time-honored modalities of physical therapy "guarantee the spread of the organism and make the condition worse."

The nitroimidazoles were not shown to have disease-modifying potential in a double-blind controlled study of RA performed by Wojtulewski et al (1980). In a 16-week double-blind comparison of metronidazole with placebo, Harkness and collaborators (1982) did not find any significant difference between the two groups. In conclusion, the amebic cause of any of the rheumatic diseases is unproven, and the claims of the curative effect of nitroimidazoles are anecdotal.

More recently, claims that a mycoplasma infection is the cause of rheumatoid arthritis have reached the public. Immediately patients began their inquiry on the use of tetracycline, an antibiotic that Thomas McPherson Brown, M.D. proposes as an effective treatment of rheumatoid arthritis.

Although Dr. Brown's contention is not recent, the public awareness of the possible role of mycoplasma as the cause of rheumatoid arthritis and that of tetracycline in its cure is new. This hypothesis has been examined in the past and a panel of experts appointed by the American College of Rheumatology[9] concluded that there is no evidence that mycoplasmas are implicated as the cause of RA. Moreover, the efficacy of tetracycline in the treatment of the disease was not proved in a controlled study performed by Skinner and colleagues (1971).

The public can recognize in the ameba and mycoplasma stories very similar arguments, and claims of the efficacy of nitroimidazole and tetracycline are certainly interchangeable.

Viper, Bee, and Ant Venoms

In ancient times there was a strong conviction that serpents had potent curative powers. The rod and serpent of Asklepios is today the symbol of the healing art. To the ancients, the serpent stood for two opposing ideas, as the symbol of evil on the one hand, and as man's protector and healer of disease on the other. Almost 2,000 years ago, Pliny told us that the snake is a rich storehouse of medical remedies. The Theriac of Andromachus, Nero's court physician, a fantastic mixture of ingredients with the reputation of being the supreme remedy in antiquity, owed its fame to one of its 64 components, the flesh of adders. The Theriac was believed to possess universal antidotal and curative powers to an almost miraculous degree. It is not surprising then that modern quacks have resorted to the use of vipers and their venom in the cure of arthritis.

[9]Formerly the American Rheumatism Association.

Cobra venom frequently has been extolled by the lay press as a cure for "arthritis." By 1980 the use of venom of cobras and kreits to treat rheumatoid arthritis, osteoarthritis, and multiple sclerosis was promoted by a pediatrician who was working with a snake handler in Miami. He claimed that some 1500 patients were treated with the venom and that many of them experienced long-lasting beneficial effects. The product was not of uniform purity and apparently was contaminated with moccasin venom. A workshop sponsored by the FDA concluded that there was no evidence indicating an antiarthritic effect. The existence of these ideas in ancient Greece is evident from the treatment of what is presumed to be a painful shoulder by the bite of a viper as depicted in an old relief (Fig. 4-1). Because of their ability to react with some specific serum complement proteins, some fractions isolated from cobra venom have received considerable attention from investigators. Analysis of the venom showed that the immunologically interesting cobra venom factor originally described by R. A. Nelson (1966) was not present in the product. Although interest in the immunological properties of some cobra venom factors continues, the use of these substances remains experimental. Several years ago the FDA banned two venom-based drugs, cobroxin and nyloxin, because they were found to be ineffective for the treatment of pain, arthritis, and other conditions. Thus, all available information suggests that cobra venom products have been offered as a cure for rheumatoid arthritis without a sound rationale.

In 1968, Gunther Holzman resorted to being stung by ants, hoping his arthritis would be relieved. After having a good response, he promoted the use of ant venom for the treatment of rheumatoid arthritis which was tried with allegedly dramatic response in some patients. Since then, a great deal of experimental work has attempted to identify and characterize venom fractions having anti-inflammatory activity. Altman and collaborators recently reported on a double-blind, controlled study which showed a reduced number of inflamed joints in 60% of the patients treated with a partially purified extract obtained

FIGURE 4-1. Viper biting patient, probably with a painful shoulder. Detail of a Greek bas-relief dedicated by Archinos to the oracular god Amphiaraos in Oropos (Attica), 380–370 B.C. From the National Archaeological Museum, Athens.

from ants. There were only few and mild adverse effects.

Although these results are encouraging, and justify further studies, this treatment remains experimental. Ant venom is still undergoing legitimate scientific study, but thus far there has been no outcome that would justify its use in anything other than a strictly experimental setting.

The venom of the honeybee has held a venerable position in the folklore of Europe and Asia, as well as in the medical community, for centuries. It is part of folklore that beekeepers never suffer from rheumatism or crippling arthritis, not because they eat the honey, but because they are frequently stung by bees. This became a very popular method of treating "arthritis" in Europe, where arthritic patients would travel long distances to visit the beekeepers.

The use of purified bee venoms in the treatment of human diseases is a more recent development. Serious scientific studies have been done to test the possible antiarthritic properties of honeybee venom and its derivatives. Shendirov and Koburova (1982), using an animal model of inflammation, reported on an interesting substance isolated from bee venom with pain-relieving and anti-inflammatory properties. However, reports of improvement of "arthritis" in patients treated with bee venom are based on uncontrolled testimonials or open trials. Although the use of honeybee venoms as a cure for "arthritis" has been given publicity from time to time in the lay press, this treatment has not received general acceptance because of the lack of support from clinical research studies.

Venom from bees, ants, and vipers have been studied by reputable scientists, and although some of these studies continue with great interest, thus far they have not provided the basis for use of venom in the treatment of any of the rheumatic diseases.

PART II

THE ALTERNATIVE
TO QUACKERY

CHAPTER 5

ARTHRITIS IS NOT ONE DISEASE

The diagnosis of arthritis may be confusing for the patient. When you see your doctor because you have recently developed joint pain and stiffness, you should expect a complete physical examination and not be surprised if further investigations are requested in the form of chest radiographs, laboratory tests, and other procedures called for by the diagnostic possibilities suggested by the clinical picture. The doctor is usually able to make a diagnosis, but some patients may require specialized studies, biopsies, or consultations with a rheumatologist.

Now you have been to your doctor and you have been told that you have arthritis. You are miserable and you want to know what can be done about it. Suddenly you realize that you and your family know next to nothing about arthritis, and you want to know what causes it and how it can be cured. In all probability, you are not aware that there are actually over 100 different kinds of arthritis, each so differing in cause, symptoms, prognosis, and treatment that frequently the only feature they have in common is pain and stiffness in the joints. Moreover, each of these types of arthritis has its own peculiar effect on your ability to function. They may look alike, but they are all different. We can't simply talk about arthritis as a single disease. You have to know the specific kind of arthritis involved, because each presents different medical problems. As long as you are probably going to live with it for a long time, you should learn as much as possible about the kind of arthritis you have.

The several types of arthritis that belong to a larger group of diseases affecting muscles, tendons, ligaments, joints, bones, and the connective tissue,[1] are collectively known as rheumatic diseases. Arthritis means inflammation of the joint.

The common term *rheumatism*[2] has been used since antiquity to denote the presence of any disorder of the extremities or back characterized by pain and stiffness. Just as the word *arthritis* refers to different diseases, rheumatism may be any of a number of completely different diseases in terms of cause, symptoms, prognosis and, most important, treatment. Rheumatology, which deals with arthritis and the diseases of the connective tissue, is one of the youngest subspecialties of internal medicine.

Although some of the rheumatic diseases may go away spontaneously, many are chronic in nature. Arthritis, as a group of diseases, is one of the oldest known to mankind and has been found in the oldest remains of our ancestors who lived 500,000 to 2,000,000 years ago. Osteoarthritis (OA) and rheumatoid arthritis (RA) in particular, account for the largest number of persons afflicted with rheumatic diseases. Both genetic and environmental factors seem to be important. The majority of the

[1]Supportive tissues in joints, bones, cartilage, tendons, ligaments, fascia, and blood vessels in general.

[2]From the Greek word *rheuma*, meaning flux or body humor, which the ancient Greeks believed flowed from the brain to the joints, producing pain.

chronic forms of arthritis are thought to be the consequence of multiple factors acting on a genetic predisposition. Many infectious agents have been considered as possible influences potentially able to trigger rheumatoid arthritis, but none has yet been shown to be involved. Although the cause of the spondyloarthropathies[3] and that of reactive arthritis are still unknown, considerable evidence suggests that microbial agents trigger these diseases in genetically susceptible persons. The clues supporting this probability derive from the strong connection of these diseases with the genetic marker HLA-B27 and the observation that some bacteria can trigger Reiter's syndrome.

Do you have a progressive kind of arthritis? Some of the rheumatic diseases are progressive. Progression of arthritis refers to the deterioration of joint structures usually due to persistent inflammation or degeneration of the articular cartilage. Your doctor can detect progression of your arthritis by observing impairment of the function of your joints, decreased mobility and muscle strength, appearance of deformities, or erosions seen in X rays of your joints. You can also become aware of the progression of arthritis when you realize that you can no longer do many things you easily could previously. You may experience difficulty in using your fingers or you may limp. Prolonged morning stiffness and pain and swelling in the joints over a period of several months are frequently indicators of disease progression. If you have any of these symptoms you should see your doctor. Examples of arthritis that can be progressive are adult-onset rheumatoid arthritis, some forms of juvenile rheumatoid arthritis, osteoarthritis, and any of the spondyloarthropathies. However, progression does not have to occur in all individuals afflicted with the same disease.

Do you have a systemic disease or a purely local condition? What is a systemic disease? The rheumatic diseases may involve not only the joints, muscles, and their fibrous envelopes, tendons and bones, but they may also involve the skin and internal

[3]Group of diseases producing inflammation of the axial joints of the spine and sacroiliac joints (Fig. 5-3).

organs such as the brain, heart, lungs, kidneys, gastrointestinal tract, or other organ systems. In this sense, some of the rheumatic diseases are systemic diseases. Rheumatoid arthritis, systemic lupus erythematosus, scleroderma, dermatomyositis, and many of the vasculitis[4] are systemic diseases. They are also known as collagen vascular diseases because collagen is the main protein in all connective tissue structures and these diseases tend to involve blood vessels which are located everywhere in the body. This is important to you, because the diseases in question may affect other vital organs, and medical care may be required by processes affecting almost any area of the body.

Do you have an acute or a chronic arthritis? Acute arthritis appears suddenly and usually without warning. The onset is abrupt and it can cause excruciating pain and swelling. The joints are usually red, hot, and tender and frequently filled with inflammatory synovia.[5] The duration of an acute arthritis is brief. While some may improve with adequate care in a few days or a few weeks, others are naturally self-limited. Examples of acute arthritis are infections of the joints caused by many different microorganisms and acute gout or pseudo-gout induced by the presence of crystals. However, gout as well as pseudo-gout can also cause a chronic form of arthritis. Chronic diseases are usually of slow progression and continue over a long period of time, not infrequently throughout the lifetime of the patient. If you have a chronic form of arthritis, it probably will remain with you as long as you live unless you have a spontaneous remission. This might be a hard pill to swallow, because people usually think of illness in terms of being curable. Therefore, your inability to understand or to accept the fact that you have a chronic disease might be at the root of many problems you will experience in the future. Present medical thinking does not eliminate the possibility of a cure for rheumatoid arthritis and other forms

[4]Group of diseases characterized by inflammation of the blood vessels.
[5]The fluid contained within the joint space, also known as synovial fluid.

of chronic arthritis. The fact is that a cure is not now available. When future research eventually explains the causes underlying the rheumatic diseases, prevention and cure will be reasonable goals.

Naturally, it is more comforting to believe anyone who tells you that you can be "cured"—now. Two of the main features of the rheumatic diseases are that the symptoms indicative of inflammation wax and wane throughout the lifetime of the patient and in some the disease may go into remission. A remission, for all practical purposes, may be equivalent to a "cure" if it is permanent, although more frequently the symptoms of the disease return. If you make the distinction between a remission and a cure, you may be motivated to live a more healthful life, to avoid obesity, and the abuse of alcohol, and to follow a program of regular exercise. You will also be able to recognize the very first symptoms that may announce the recurrence of arthritis. The word *chronic* should not throw you into despair, because the rheumatic diseases can be controlled in the great majority of patients. Control, as applied to arthritis, means the relief of your symptoms and the arrest of the progression of the disease, which will enable you to function in society. Rheumatoid arthritis, the prototype of the chronic rheumatic diseases, is a chronic, systemic inflammatory disorder with a worldwide distribution involving all racial and ethnic groups. Women are affected 2 to 3 times more often than men. Rheumatoid arthritis can strike at any time from infancy through old age, typically as a symmetric[6] disease, frequently involving the small joints of the hands and wrist, the MCP[7] and PIP[8] joints (Fig. 5-1), as well as other joints of the upper and lower extremities. The symptoms of pain and stiffness usually appear gradually and insidiously over weeks or several months. Occasionally, relatively brief episodes lasting a few weeks precede the development of

[6]Meaning that the joints of both sides of the body are involved with a certain degree of symmetry.
[7]Metacarpophalangeal.
[8]Proximal interphalangeal.

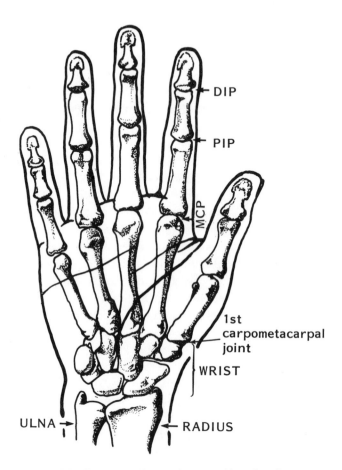

FIGURE 5-1. Small articulations of hand and wrist.

more persistent joint involvement. Extra-articular manifestations such as skin nodules, inflammation of blood vessels, involvement of the eye and of the peripheral nerves, pericarditis, and enlargement of lymph nodes and of the spleen are integral manifestations of the disease but do not occur in every patient. The lower spine[9] is usually spared but the cervical spine is frequently involved. Pain and stiffness can also be due to nerve entrapment when the inflammation occurs in a closed space occupied by a nerve. The most common of the nerve entrapments that occurs in RA is the carpal tunnel syndrome, although it can be produced by many different causes. It can be suspected when tingling and numbness localized to the first three fingers occurs along with some decrease in the grip strength. When carpal tunnel syndrome is present it can be relieved by the use of a canvas splint to immobilize the wrist and the use of NSAIDs to diminish the inflammation. If improvement is not forthcoming, a local steroid injection usually improves the symptoms; but surgical decompression provides permanent relief when conservative treatment has failed. There are a variety of musculoskeletal disorders producing hand deformities resembling those of RA. Admittedly, in a relatively few cases, RA may be present in atypical forms which defy diagnosis, even by the expert.

Marked destructive changes in the DIP[10] joints is usually not a feature of RA, but may suggest osteoarthritis or psoriatic arthritis. Osteoarthritis commonly involves the hands producing a bony deformity at the level of the PIP and DIP joints (Fig. 5-1). The first carpometacarpal joint at the base of the thumb is most frequently involved in osteoarthritis. Erosive OA is a less common variant which may resemble RA, producing erosions in the DIPs and PIPs. The severe destructive involvement of the DIPs of a patient in otherwise good health suggests that the diagnosis may not be RA.

Osteoarthritis, the most common form of joint disease af-

[9]Lumbosacral and thoracic.
[10]Distal interphalangeal.

flicting humans, is not related to rheumatoid arthritis. It is important to make the distinction between them because they have different prognoses and treatment. Osteoarthritis is not a systemic joint disease. Its lesions are localized to the joints, although many can be simultaneously involved. The pain and other disabling consequences of osteoarthritis can usually be successfully treated, enabling the arthritic to function with minimal discomfort. In osteoarthritis the articular cartilage and the adjacent bone are affected by a poorly understood process leading to breakdown of articular cartilage and reactive changes at the margins of the joints. OA may begin in a middle-aged individual, but it is much more common in the elderly. As the life expectancy in our society is progressively extended, the symptoms of osteoarthritis are more likely to appear. According to information released by the Arthritis Foundation, 37 out of every 100 adults in the United States have some manifestation of OA by radiologic examination; however, one can calculate that there are about 14 million Americans with symptoms and disability related to OA.

One can suspect osteoarthritis by the presence of slowly developing joint pain, stiffness, and bony enlargement of the joints with limitation of motion. Enlargement of the joint may result from prominence of bony structures, increased amounts of synovial fluid and, in later stages, from synovitis.[11] Morning stiffness is typically of short duration, lasting only a few minutes, but stiffness is usually marked after long periods of immobilization. Early in the course of osteoarthritis pain occurs after joint use and is relieved by rest. In a more advanced stage pain may occur with minimal motion or even at rest. Osteoarthritis of the hands may develop slowly over months or years but in some patients moderate inflammatory changes in the DIPs may appear rather rapidly with pain, redness, and swelling. Eventually the inflammatory changes become quiescent and a firm enlargement of the DIP appears. Osteoarthritis in the hand may also produce bony enlargement of the PIPs and involvement of

[11]Inflammation of the synovium, or tissue lining the joint space.

the first carpometacarpal joint producing a squared appearance of the hand and pain at the base of the thumb. Some patients may have primary generalized osteoarthritis which can be confused with rheumatoid arthritis. Laboratory examinations are normal in patients with OA; X rays may be normal in early stages but later, narrowing of the joint space, marginal osteophytes,[12] sclerosis,[13] and cysts in the neighboring bone are common findings. Not all patients suffering from OA deteriorate, but severe involvement of weight-bearing joints in particular may produce considerable disability.

For thousands of years the word *gout* was used much as the term *arthritis* is used now, probably indicating any of many rheumatic diseases. However, for over 300 years gout has been recognized as a specific joint disease. Patients with gout may have episodes of acute arthritis lasting from a few days to a few weeks. The stereotype of the obese male with a painful, swollen, and red big toe has been popular for centuries. About 90 percent of the patients are middle-aged and older men, but the disease can also affect women after menopause. Rarely, some forms of gout may affect younger individuals and children. Although the great toe is the most common site of initial inflammation, involvement of other joints is very common. The onset of the attack—which often occurs at night—is usually abrupt and, typically, pain and swelling peak within 24 hours. The affected joints are swollen and very tender. During the episodes of acute arthritis the patient seeks medical care because the pain is excruciating, but many patients may have numerous minor attacks of joint inflammation in between the classic attacks. A number of patients develop a chronic form of gout which is characterized by deposits of crystals in the tissues known as tophi.[14] Chronic gout with multiple joint involvement

[12]Reactive, bone growth usually located at the joint margins.
[13]Fibrous, dense appearance of the bone as seen in X rays.
[14]Subcutaneous nodules, usually appearing on the elbows, over the joints, or on the ear, containing a white chalky material consisting of accumulations of crystals of monosodium urate.

can mimic rheumatoid arthritis. Gout is the consequence of the deposition of crystals[15] in the tissues. These crystals can be found in the synovia or in tophi, and their detection is diagnostic of gout.

Another type of arthritis with a clinical picture that in many ways resembles gout is pseudo-gout, a distinct disease produced by the deposition of another type of crystal[16] in the tissues. The diagnosis can be made by finding the characteristic crystals by examination of the synovial fluid. Some patients with pseudo-gout may have a chronic arthritis that may resemble rheumatoid arthritis.

Although rheumatoid arthritis may also begin in the elderly, when multiple joints become symmetrically inflamed the problem may be the syndrome of remitting seronegative symmetrical synovitis with pitting edema (RS_3PE). This condition often begins abruptly, has predilection for elderly persons, and does not produce bony erosions. These patients often have inflammation of the flexor tendons and swelling of the hands and feet. It is important to recognize this condition because the prognosis is excellent. Morning stiffness and severe joint pain and stiffness frequently involving the neck, shoulder, and pelvic girdle, occurring in persons usually over 50 years of age, can be due to polymyalgia rheumatica (PMR). These patients, predominantly women, may have low-grade fever, malaise, and weight loss. Some individuals with PMR may have inflammation of the temporal artery and other blood vessels of the head called temporal arteritis. These patients may complain of headaches in the region of the temple and may experience sudden loss of vision due to involvement of the blood vessels of the eye. The apparent similarity of PMR with early rheumatoid arthritis may be striking, but the treatment is different and frequently successful. Its early recognition is important because treatment with corticosteroids can relieve the symptoms and prevent blindness.

Swelling of joints, bursae or tendon sheaths are important

[15]Monosodium urate.
[16]Calcium pyrophosphate dihydrate.

signs of musculoskeletal involvement (Fig. 5-2). The rheumatologist is usually able to detect minimal swelling that may go unnoticed by the patient or by examiners who have not been trained in the study of the rheumatic diseases. Frequently, patients are seen who claim to have "swelling" that even the rheumatologist does not see, in spite of the most careful examination. Not infrequently, affected individuals also have severe joint pains, though prolonged follow-up does not reveal the presence of joint disease, and even the most sensitive joint scans may not reveal evidence of joint involvement. One of the few conditions which can present in this manner is idiopathic edema.[17] Persons afflicted with this condition have some symptoms resembling those of RA. Most of these patients are young or middle-aged women with normal joints and normal routine blood tests. They may retain fluid in their legs after a period of standing, and may improve with treatment consisting of a moderate restriction of salt and the judicial use of diuretics.[18] Another relatively common condition which, in the eyes of the uninitiated, may resemble RA, is fibromyalgia.[19] In this condition that predominantly affects women, pain and stiffness may be very severe and the doctor can consistently recognize the non-articular location of tender points and the absence of joint inflammation. Symptoms are usually aggravated by fatigue, tension, excessive use of the affected part, immobility or cold, and are eased by heat, massage, gentle activity, or a holiday. Laboratory tests are normal. In many patients with fibromyalgia, a specific sleep disturbance can be identified that may be instrumental in producing or magnifying the pain. Patients with persistent symptoms but without objective involvement of the joints are sometimes incorrectly diagnosed and receive unnecessary treatment. The complications from excessive medication are widespread in this group of patients, whose

[17]Meaning swelling of unknown cause.
[18]Medicine which increases the volume of urine eliminated, i.e., water pills.
[19]Also called fibrositis.

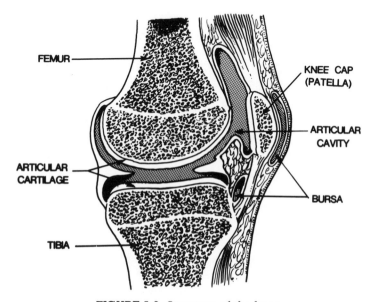

FIGURE 5-2. Structure of the knee.

disease is benign. When fibromyalgia is recognized, the treatment consisting of reassurance with a discussion of the nature of this condition, psychologic support, heat, treatment of trigger[20] points, the use of relaxation techniques, improvement of sleep, and mild and gradual resumption of physical activity to tolerance can be very successful. Drugs used to induce sleep such as barbiturates are not helpful, but very low doses of amitryptiline[21] or imipramine[22] taken in the early evening can be very helpful.

A skin rash, joint pain, and stiffness are the most common manifestations of systemic lupus erythematosus (SLE). The most frequent types of skin involvement are a typical reddish facial rash with a butterfly distribution and round or oval plaques, dry and scaly with darkening of the skin in the outside and central clearing, known as discoid lupus erythematosus. Hand deformities may be present in patients with SLE. Although the arthritis of lupus is frequently symmetric and can be deforming, it does not lead to bone and cartilage erosions. SLE is a chronic inflammatory disease with a strong tendency to affect young women. It may affect many organ systems, such as the joints, skin, heart and lungs, kidney, central nervous system, and the blood vessels of almost any part of the body.

SLE also occurs in children and the elderly. Several members of one family occasionally have been found to develop SLE, and some genetic factors have been found to be implicated. Hormonal factors are known to play a role as suggested by the predominance of SLE in women of childbearing age, the association of SLE with the Klinefelter[23] syndrome, and the possible effect of contraceptive pills inducing positive

---

[20]Sites of deep tenderness which can be identified by physical examination.
[21]Commonly used antidepressant.
[22]Commonly used antidepressant.
[23]Patients with abnormalities of the X chromosome, feminization, and testicular atrophy.

ANA[24] tests. One-third of the patients give a history of sun exposure before the onset of symptoms. Inflammation of the blood vessels—vasculitis—is common in patients with SLE. Some of the most severe manifestations of the disease include some types of renal involvement,[25] thrombocytopenia, central nervous system,[26] and pleuropericardial involvement.

Many patients are thought to have rheumatoid arthritis before the diagnosis of SLE is confirmed. The onset of arthritis or arthralgia during pregnancy or the postpartum period suggest that the diagnosis of SLE should be considered. In addition to positive ANA tests, patients with lupus have other abnormalities of the immune system.

Not only are there more than 100 different types of arthritis, but patients with the same disease may have completely different symptoms, prognosis, and treatment. For example, a patient with lupus and persistent arthritis, sensitivity to sunlight, and anemia, may have a benign disease with an excellent prognosis requiring only conservative treatment. Another patient with lupus may have severe diffuse glomerulonephritis or central nervous system involvement requiring aggressive therapy with high doses of corticosteroids or immunosuppressive therapy to achieve control of the disease.

A number of drugs, such as hydralazine, procainamide, oral contraceptives, and many others have been shown to be able to induce symptoms resembling SLE. In drug-induced lupus, joint pain and a nonerosive arthritis can occur, and pleuropulmonary involvement is common; but kidney involvement seldom occurs and skin involvement is much less frequent. The manifestations of the disease usually resolve within a few

---

[24]Antinuclear antibody (ANA) tests are positive in the majority of patients with lupus, but may be positive in other rheumatic diseases and can be induced by some drugs.
[25]Diffuse proliferative glomerulonephritis.
[26]Psychosis, seizures.

days or weeks upon discontinuation of the offending drug; but some patients may need a brief course of corticosteroid therapy.

Patients with pain and stiffness in the hands and swelling in the fingers may have a rheumatic disease called scleroderma. These patients develop thickening of the skin which may become darker or lighter in some cases. Often their fingers blanch or turn bluish upon exposure to cold.[27] Tingling or pain and the development of ulcerations in the tip of the fingers is the result of changes in and contraction of small blood vessels impairing circulation. Scleroderma is a systemic disease which may also affect the kidneys, causing severe hypertension, involvement of the lungs, and the gastrointestinal tract.

Arthritis involving the peripheral joints[28] is a recognized complication of intestinal disorders.[29] These conditions may also involve the sacroiliac joints and spinal articulations. Important differences from RA are exhibited in these and other reactive arthritides in that the test for rheumatoid factor is negative and the involvement of the joints tends to be self-limited, waxing and waning with the primary disorder, and less frequently leading to progressive joint destruction. Some cases with peripheral joint involvement may indeed resemble RA.

It has been recognized that ankylosing spondylitis[30] and related diseases are different from RA, and they now have been regrouped under the name spondyloarthropathies, which means that the articulations of the spine and the peripheral joints are both affected although the spine is more often and more severely affected (Fig. 5-3). Usually only a small number of joints is affected in these patients. One common characteristic

[27]This is known as Raynaud's phenomenon.

[28]Peripheral, such as those of the upper or lower extremities, as opposed to axial, such as those of the spine and sacroiliac joints (Fig. 5-3).

[29]Including ulcerative colitis, Crohn's disease, Whipple's disease, and jejunal bypass surgery for obesity.

[30]Inflammatory disease involving the axial articulations of the spine and sacroiliac joints, producing low back pain and stiffness of the spine.

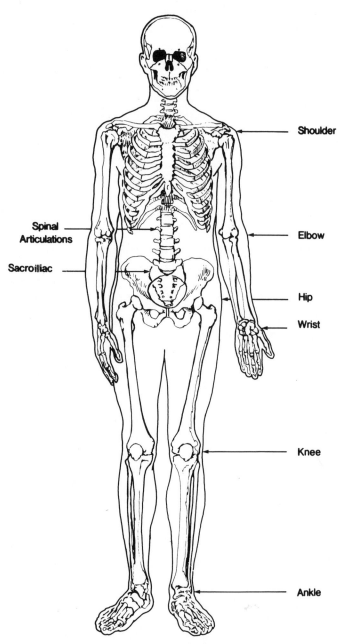

FIGURE 5-3. Peripheral and axial joints.

of these processes is inflammation at bony insertions of tendons and fascia.[31] These conditions have a tendency to develop bone formation and bony bridging of the joints. Young adult men are most frequently involved and a strong genetic predisposition is evident. In some patients with psoriasis, a symmetrical poly-arthritis indistinguishable from rheumatoid arthritis may be present. More frequently, in patients with psoriatic arthritis, involvement of the joints tends to be somewhat asymmetric with a progressive course resulting in considerable disability. Rarely, an arthritis of recent onset that looks very similar to rheumatoid arthritis may be caused by an underlying malignancy. In these cases a thorough clinical examination and often a chest radio-graph or other procedures are likely to suggest the diagnosis.

Do you have Lyme arthritis? The most common finding in this illness, which usually begins in summer, is a skin rash, a red lesion that may be flat or slightly raised forming at the site of the bite of a tick, which expands and may adopt the form of a ring. The skin rash is often associated with fatigue, malaise, headache, and a stiff neck. Weeks to months later, these initial symptoms may sometimes be followed by neurologic and car-diac abnormalities and a few weeks to two years later by ar-thritis. Pain may be of brief duration and affects one or two sites at a time. Later on, there may be intermittent attacks of pain and swelling in one or two joints, primarily in large joints. There may be more swelling than pain, particularly when the knee is involved. In some patients, large and small joints may be af-fected, and occasionally a chronic form of arthritis may develop, with erosions of cartilage and bone.

Even if you do not have Lyme arthritis, it is important for you to be aware of it. We have only known about it since 1977, when it was described in a group of children in Lyme, Connecti-cut, who were thought to have juvenile rheumatoid arthritis. Through a series of remarkable investigations, it was discovered by Steere and colleagues (1977) that Lyme disease is caused by a

[31]These processes are known as enthesopathies because they affect the entheses, or insertion of tendons and fascia on bone.

newly recognized microorganism, a spirochete, and is transmitted by a tick vector. The disease has now been recognized in three areas of the U.S.: in the Northeast from Massachusetts to Maryland, in the Midwest in Wisconsin, Michigan and Minnesota, and in the West in California and Oregon. Cases have been reported in Germany, Switzerland, France, and Australia. Most importantly, these investigations have demonstrated that the agent responsible for Lyme disease is sensitive to tetracycline and penicillin and that antibiotics can treat most forms of the disease successfully. It seems reasonable that research in the field of the rheumatic diseases will in the future discover the cause and cure of other types of arthritis which appear incurable at present. For this, medical research needs your continuous support.

This brief account is a sample of a few of the conditions that you may have if you have "arthritis." You should be aware that not all that appears to be arthritis is necessarily arthritis. It is also true that some arthritis may be difficult to diagnose in its early stages. Although deferring the diagnosis of some types of arthritis for a few weeks or even months may be inconsequential, failure to recognize systemic lupus erythematosus or temporal arteritis[32] may have cataclysmic consequences for the individual. In many cases, diagnostic errors may lead to excessive or inadequate treatment. Becoming aware of these possibilities should encourage you to raise specific questions related to your condition in the hope of obtaining a reasonable explanation from your doctor.

Although there are manuals available for self-diagnosis, I do not advise you to be your own diagnostician. This is true even if you are a physician, for in these cases self-diagnosis is difficult and most importantly, self-treatment is a disaster. However, once the condition has been properly diagnosed, you should be encouraged to get to know your specific problem well, for the more familiar you are with the disease process and its symptoms, the better able you will be to assume your respon-

[32]A type of vasculitis or inflammation of the arteries.

sibility in the most important and active phase of your own treatment. Your doctor, a rheumatologist, various consultants, physical and occupational therapists and rheumatology nurses, nutritionists, social workers, or other health professionals are invaluable sources who you should tap. You should be eager to ask questions and they may often recommend special reading. However, indiscriminate perusal of technical literature may create anxiety causing you to postpone making important decisions. In this atmosphere the treatment is fraught with difficulties and the best outcome may not be obtained.

Joint and Muscle Pain

Pain may or may not be due to inflammation. There are many factors involved in the expression of pain. Though the relief of pain is probably the immediate goal in the treatment of any of the rheumatic diseases, the main objective in the treatment of inflammatory types of arthritis is to lessen the intensity of inflammation, which is responsible for the damage to the joints and—in part—for the pain.

The most common characteristic of chronically painful states is that the part involved is usually sensitive, even to those stimuli which normally do not evoke pain. For example, the weight of the bed sheets may produce excruciating pain on contact with the skin covering a joint involved by an acute gouty attack. Once pain is elicited, it is felt beyond the involved part, outlasts the initiating insult, and can be magnified by fatigue or emotion.

How much pain is experienced by patients with arthritis? In general, arthritic pain is much more sustained and exasperating than that suffered by patients afflicted by any other disease known to mankind. However, we know that the pain experienced as a consequence of similar lesions in different persons varies in intensity, duration, and quality depending on the individual's perception of pain. The same stimulus may produce widely different responses depending on the background, past experience, sensitivity, associated anxiety, or even fear so frequently found in patients with arthritis. Not only stress and anxiety but also fatigue or emotion can modify the perception of pain. This variable response from person to person to similar insults cannot be overemphasized, because it may make a tremendous difference in the final outcome. It is common to see patients with very similar joint involvement, yet one is in a wheelchair, and the other is functional, enjoying a very fruitful life. The things that really matter are those that happen in your life; to what extent you can achieve your personal goals, how functionally independent you can remain in spite of the disease, and what the quality of your life will be.

Pain can be considered to be a warning signal. Though it is reasonable to expect relief of pain in affected joints, it is useful to realize that joint pain may respond to different treatments, because all joint pain may not have the same cause. Inflamed joints are usually stiff and hurt. Painful joints may be swollen due to thickened and inflamed synovium or to the accumulation of synovia. Pain due to inflammation is usually alleviated by rest, by treatment with anti-inflammatory medication, by removing excessive synovia, or by injecting corticosteroids within the joint cavity. The quantification of the activity of the disease, or how much inflammation occurs in the joints, is sometimes difficult. The duration of morning stiffness is one of the most useful clinical features by which we can quantify inflammation and assess the response to treatment. This can be measured from the time you get up to the time when you get as "loose" as you are going to get. An alert patient may become proficient in measuring the duration of morning stiffness. When the disease is quite active the stiffness in the joints may persist all day, although it is usually more pronounced in the morning. In active rheumatoid arthritis, morning stiffness frequently lasts one to several hours until the joints limber up. As a rule, morning stiffness of longer duration indicates persistent or uncontrolled activity of the disease. If the period of stiffness is considerably shortened to less than one hour, it usually means that the severity of the inflammation is decreasing.

If your disease has been in remission and you don't see your physician very frequently, the appearance of or increase in the duration of morning stiffness is a warning, suggesting that you should consult your doctor immediately to treat the flare-up of the disease. Stiffness lasting a few seconds or minutes, or experienced after prolonged immobility, does not have the same significance and is more characteristic of osteoarthritis, although it can occur in inactive RA. You may be one of those patients with arthritis neither seeking nor receiving medical care because you do not think you need any. You may have difficulties with your joints in the morning and thereafter you may be free of symptoms for the rest of the day. The presence of morning stiffness of more than one hour's duration probably indicates that you should see your doctor. Even if you can function for most of the day, low-grade inflammation continuously present over a long period of time may lead to destruction of your joints. Sometimes I see patients who give a brief history of joint disease lasting no longer than 2 or 3 months, yet X rays show erosions in the small joints of the hands. On further questioning it frequently appears that there had been a longer period during which they experienced morning stiffness that was regarded by the patients to be "normal."

Not all joint pain is due to inflammation. A destroyed joint may be the source of considerable discomfort and pain many years after the inflammation has completely subsided. In this case anti-inflammatory treatment may not be effective but aids for ambulation such as canes, walkers or crutches, a balance between rest and exercise, or a program of exercise directed toward strengthening the affected muscles, and pain-relieving drugs usually produce considerable relief. In some cases the replacement of the destroyed joint with a new prosthetic one may be indicated to relieve pain and restore function.

Antiarthritic medication can be inadvertently abused. If

your claims of severe pain are exaggerated, your doctor may unnecessarily step up the use of medication. Undoubtedly, there are situations in which pain is intolerable and there is no justification for parsimony in the dispensation of pain-relieving drugs. Severe pain caused by treatable or self-limited conditions as well as by terminal, incurable disease falls into this category. It is not a glorification of suffering which leads me to advise you to avoid the use of powerful pain medication. The physician may sometimes feel forced to escalate the doses of medication or to resort to other types of drugs, usually more dangerous, to treat inflammation, increasing the likelihood of side effects. In desperation, you may ask for stronger and stronger medication for pain, and the easy way out is to prescribe narcotics. In any case, you must realize that narcotics are not the answer for arthritic pain. Narcotics can indeed reduce and even transiently eliminate the pain, but narcotic addiction is a problem that would compound your difficulties. There is no question in my mind that the less narcotic medication you receive, the better off you will be in the long run. You should also be aware that narcotics may eliminate pain but not inflammation, and it is inflammation, not pain, that destroys joints.

What can you do if you are a highly reactive person with joints still almost normal and yet experience severe pain? Ask your doctor about techniques to relieve pain without drugs. Education is very important, for many believe that they will be better off if their pain can be completely alleviated. Although it is glorious not to have pain, you must understand that a level of useful activity must be maintained. If your doctor tells you to exercise despite some discomfort, it must be started at very low levels, and its intensity gradually increased with the help of other modalities of physical therapy, such as pool therapy or other forms of treatment in warm water. Gentle exercise in water or the use of a whirlpool not only relieves stiffness, but also allows you to move with very little pain and, probably even more important, to relax. This approach may require daily sessions in a rehabilitation facility before you can be given an independent home program.

Severe pain in the presence of minimal disease may also be related to anxiety reflecting family conflicts or the lack of understanding of the situation by others in the home environment. Education of your family on your diagnosis, prognosis, and treatment needs is a must for a successful outcome. Improved understanding of the situation by both you and your family can relieve your anxiety and immensely help you cope with pain. At other times this unduly magnified expression of pain may be related to the desire to obtain attention. Some individuals receive some type of reward from the environment when they complain of pain. In these situations the problem can only be approached successfully if the underlying causes are identified by the doctor and, most importantly, accepted by the patient.

For many patients with severe arthritis, pain becomes a way of life molding their personalities. The relief of pain will certainly help you develop a more positive outlook on life. Although it is understandable that you can be frustrated when pain and inflammation persist, emotional problems may greatly complicate your treatment. Arthritis is not the only cause of frustration and emotional turmoil, because these are both, to a certain degree, "normal" ingredients of everyday life. Treatment of rheumatoid arthritis with disease-modifying drugs will frequently produce relief by controlling the activity of the disease, but this will not happen quickly. NSAIDs can provide more rapid relief of symptoms, but do not influence the course of the disease. Unrelenting disease activity may in some cases persist for years and it may be necessary to deal with pain by a combination of modalities. Psychological aspects of arthritis must be dealt with on an individual basis.

A good deal of pain and discomfort can be produced by muscle contracture. The inflammation of the joint produces pain which tends to cause involuntary spasms in the skeletal muscles supplied by nerves from the same or adjacent segments of the spinal cord. When your joints are inflamed, pain is the basis for muscle contracture leading to joint deformities which usually assume a flexion position. The muscles contract, placing the joint in the most comfortable position in which pain is minimal. However, the increased muscle tension by itself causes more pain. If you use special joint protection techniques, ambulation or exercise may have a moderating effect on the pain. For this part of your therapy, the services of physical and occupational therapists who specialize in the rheumatic diseases are invaluable. You will often notice that during comprehensive rehabilitation, the same degree of physical stress that used to produce pain or discomfort can now be well tolerated.

The expression of pain is influenced by emotional states as well as by less well understood factors. Stoical individuals and persons who are excessively responsive to painful stimuli are at the opposite extremes of the spectrum. If you have chronic pain, it is very likely that you may also have weakness, as well as fatigue, troubled sleep, poor appetite, and emotional instability. It is a common observation that if pain can be eliminated, these symptoms regularly improve or subside. Of course pain subsides when inflammation is controlled by treatment or when the disease spontaneously goes into remission. There is no doubt that the expression of pain is greatly modified by psychological factors. Insomnia, fatigue, boredom, anxiety, isolation, fear, and depression usually exaggerate the response. Conversely, the intensity of pain tends to decrease when the patient gets adequate sleep, is able to rest, participates in diversions, and engages in positive human interactions. If the patient with arthritis can be helped to return to work through vocational rehabilitation training, or even if he can spend a few hours a day doing volunteer work, this may have a positive impact, not only on his mind but also on the disease itself.

Prognosis

You may inquire, "What would happen if I didn't do anything?" The development of a disease undisturbed by treatment is known as its natural course. It is very difficult to accurately describe the natural course of a chronic disease, since large numbers of untreated patients observed over a period of years in a systematic way are not available for analysis. Diagnosis is especially complex in the earlier stages of rheumatoid arthritis by virtue of its variable modes of presentation and evolution. Studies of populations have indicated that there are a number of patients with mild and nonprogressive disease which often goes into remission spontaneously. Some studies have suggested that rheumatoid arthritis exists most frequently as a benign nondeforming condition. Follow-up studies have shown that a substantial number of patients who are initially thought to have RA eventually prove to have other arthritic conditions. Patients with established deformities in a more advanced stage of rheumatoid arthritis probably follow a more predictable course.

Prognosis is even more difficult. The course of rheumatoid arthritis is highly variable and unpredictable. It has been estimated that approximately 10 to 20% of the patients will have either a complete remission early in their disease or will follow a mild intermittent course which will require little medical attention. The onset of rheumatoid arthritis is most often gradual and insidious. At the beginning, minor stiffness of short duration in the morning, with mild and transitory aches and pains in the joints may not be recognized by the patient to be anything abnormal. This discomfort can go on for months or even years with alternating symptom-free periods. Less often, the onset is more or less acute and sometimes even explosive. In these cases the patient is suddenly stricken with profound stiffness and severe articular inflammation in multiple joints with swelling and pain which may last all day. Some but not all of those patients with acute onset have been found to have a more benign prognosis than those with gradual onset of the symptoms. In contrast, approximately 10 percent of patients will develop relentless, crippling disease, leading to severe limitation of activity and ultimately to confinement in a wheelchair or bed. The majority of patients have intermediate degrees of joint involvement and fall between the benign and the severe groups. A course characterized by remissions or periods of decreased disease activity and reactivations is not uncommon. With appropriate treatment, the majority of the patients in this large group are able to remain quite functional in spite of the damage produced by the disease.

The presence of rheumatoid factors, antinuclear antibodies, bone erosions found in X rays of the joints, and subcutaneous nodules are predictors of relatively more severe disease. Several studies have suggested that the prognosis is better in men than in women. Men may have a more acute onset, especially if they are under the age of thirty, with subsequent greater improvement in the severity of the arthritis, than do women. In one of the few studies of early RA, Masi and his colleagues reported that more women than men had significantly greater numbers of swollen upper extremity joints, with an increased likelihood of developing bone erosions. In this interesting study, the variables which correlated with a better outcome included maleness, acute onset under the age of thirty, fewer swollen joints on examination, and a negative rheumatoid factor. It has also been found that a consistently low ESR[33] indicates a more favorable prognosis.

Other studies have shown that while symmetry of joint involvement in the early stages of RA has little value in predicting the course of the disease, when rheumatoid disease has produced established deformities, symmetric involvement of the joints is associated with a less favorable outcome. In spite of these prognostic indicators there are many exceptions, and even patients with severe and progressive disease may go into remission. Sometimes, during the treatment of a patient with rheumatoid arthritis, a complete remission occurs while the patient is being treated with a disease-modifying drug. The question arises whether this can be a spontaneous remission. The answer

[33]Commonly used blood test. Higher than normal values may indicate the presence of inflammation.

is yes. Controlled studies have shown that drugs like gold, penicillamine, hydroxychloroquine, sulfasalazine, azathioprine, and cyclophosphamide are effective and able to reduce disease activity and, in a few cases, induce remissions over and above those occurring in patients treated with placebo. For this reason these drugs are known as disease-modifying or disease activity retarding drugs. In an individual case there is no proof that the improvement is drug-induced, although it is very likely so.

When the rheumatic diseases are compared with cancer or cardiovascular diseases as matters of public concern, a frequent stereotype suggests that "arthritis does not kill but cripples and leads to a life of pain and misery." Although the latter is undoubtedly true, it has been documented by several studies that rheumatoid arthritis is accompanied by a greater mortality rate than expected.

The comparison of studies reported in the last several decades suggest that a more comprehensive treatment has probably improved the function and reduced the disability produced by the disease.

In ankylosing spondylitis the prognosis is generally good. Despite extensive bony fusion and deformity of the spine, 90% of the patients remain highly functional and can have a normal life.

Although the course of Reiter's syndrome is unpredictable, the majority of patients experience a single episode lasting less than one year, from which they fully recover. About one-third of patients have relapses, often separated by long symptom-free periods, and only 20% develop chronic arthritis and/or spondylitis.

Patients with spondyloarthropathies can reasonably expect to maintain as normal function as possible and to prevent deformities of the spine and the peripheral joints. Important aspects of the treatment are to suppress inflammation in the spinal articulations, and to relieve pain and stiffness. For patients with involvement of the spine, maintenance of normal posture and prevention of spinal flexion deformities are the primary goals.

The mattress should be firm, pillows should not be used, and position during sleep should avoid bending the spine. The posture should be maintained erect and adequate back support should be provided while sitting on chairs or on car seats. An exercise program should include range of motion exercises for the shoulders and hips. Swimming on a regular basis can be very beneficial. When arthritis of the peripheral joints is present, strengthening exercises of adjacent muscles as well as passive and active exercise of involved joints can prevent or minimize flexion contractures.

Many patients with various kinds of arthritis can experience a remission, and in the majority the activity of the arthritis can be controlled by treatment. Even chronic arthritis like rheumatoid arthritis can go into remission. However, these patients do not write books, and they are not judged particularly newsworthy by the press. There is nothing sensational about their condition. They know that their disease is in remission or that the arthritis is controlled by treatment.

To some extent, some types of arthritis like rheumatoid arthritis can be overdiagnosed. Many "miraculous cures" may occur in patients who have some other more benign and self-limited type of arthritis. Thus, dramatic improvement cannot always be attributed with certainty to a drug or to a diet or to anything we have prescribed for an individual patient. The value of any therapy can only be documented by the controlled observation of large numbers of patients over a period of time.

Controlling Arthritis

Many patients with arthritis can be successfully treated. The lack of a cure does not mean that "nothing can be done for arthritis." On the contrary, a comprehensive approach to the treatment of various forms of arthritis can allow the majority of patients to function normally with little or no pain or stiffness. I emphasize that these patients are among the many who cannot be cured by faith healing or any of the numerous quack treatments available. Of paramount importance is that you assume responsibility and become an active participant in your own treatment. Your first responsibility is to become educated. Knowledge of the nature of the disease process, its natural history and prognosis, and the rationale behind the treatment will allow you to ask intelligent questions and develop realistic expectations. For optimal control of the kind of arthritis you have, you need the help of a doctor qualified in the care of patients with rheumatic diseases. Family physicians, internists, and rheumatologists are usually qualified and have interest in the care of patients with arthritis. You should realize that adequate medical care of many arthritic patients requires the concerted attention of professionals with different skills, simultaneously or at various times during the course of the arthritic process. Thus, your doctor may call upon the services of physical and occupational therapists, nurses, psychologists, social workers, vocational counselors, nutritionists, or other health professionals, and the expertise of orthopedic surgeons or other medical or surgical consultants. Grasping the importance of rest and exercise, using the techniques of joint protection, and following the principles of adequate nutrition are essential for a successful outcome. Job modification or vocational rehabilitation are very important components. Education of patient and family is essential, but not sufficient in itself. Group therapy classes and arthritis self-help courses offered by the Arthritis Foundation are invaluable resources which can be tapped by a phone call to the local chapter. Emotional support from your doctor and your family will give you the strength necessary to become an active partner in your own treatment. Successful treatment of your arthritis must be powered by your strong motivation and sense of responsibility. Many treatment failures are, by and large, due to the patient's passive personality. Perseverance and tenacity are frequently indicators of a better outcome.

What can you do to control osteoarthritis? It is clear that the treatment from which you can benefit may differ from that of many other patients with osteoarthritis. You may just need an explanation of the nature of your problem and to be reassured that you do not have a generalized crippling form of arthritis. Joint protection from overuse is very important if weight-bearing joints are involved, particularly the knees and hips. The treatment of obesity, if this is present, is a must to prevent aggravation of OA. Principles of healthy eating should be discussed even with slender patients with early OA to prevent the development of obesity. Physical therapy can be invaluable to maintain range of motion and to relieve pain associated with muscle spasm. At home, the use of heat in various ways, long hot showers, hot water soaks, or warm tub baths may alleviate pain and discomfort. Isometric exercises are very useful to maintain muscle function and strength. Pain-relieving medications and NSAIDs are often beneficial, but you should not expect complete relief of pain or discomfort from the use of these drugs alone. An important point is that corticosteroids by intramuscular injections or by mouth are contraindicated in the treatment of OA. However, a limited and infrequent intra-articular injection of corticosteroids may be beneficial in the treatment of acute joint flare-ups.

Patients with severe neck pain due to osteoarthritis of the cervical spine, particularly when there are symptoms of nerve root irritation, can be helped by the use of a soft cervical collar, correction of abnormal posture, and cervical traction.

Osteoarthritis of the hands can benefit from hot soaks, paraffin baths, and avoidance of forceful, repetitive motions like weeding and gardening. Splints and intra-articular corticosteroid injections and the use of NSAIDs[34] can significantly reduce the pain and disability due to osteoarthritis of the first carpometacarpal joint.

Braces can be useful to allow protected motion of injured joints while healing takes place. Functional braces can be designed to assist or provide stability for unstable knees. Many

[34]Nonsteroidal anti-inflammatory drugs.

foot problems can be alleviated by metatarsal bars, shoe lifts, special orthoses, shoes with a large toe box, or custom-made shoes.

When the cartilage has deteriorated and the patient has considerable pain and disability which do not respond to comprehensive medical treatment, an orthopedic surgical procedure can be considered. For some patients with osteoarthritis of the knee, osteotomy can provide substantial relief. Osteotomy is a simple operation in which a wedge of bone is removed to realign the joints, shifting the weight-bearing surface to an area of the joint with healthy cartilage. If a single compartment of the knee is involved, the osteotomy of the tibia shifts the weight-bearing surface to the adjacent healthy compartment by correcting joint malalignment. Persistent pain and decreased function are the two main indications for a hip arthroplasty. Total hip replacement usually produces striking relief of pain and improvement of range of motion. Patients should not expect that the replacements will last forever. Durability of the prosthetic hip depends upon the patient's age and activity level and on the cause of the hip disease. In younger patients, the timing of the operation is important, and buying time can be a viable avenue when the destroyed hip allows some function. Besides these issues, you may raise the question of the material used. Acrylic-fixed total hip replacements have been very effective with very low complications in the elderly, but in younger age groups a relatively higher failure rate has led to successful experimentation with cementless prostheses. Total knee replacement in patients with advanced OA is not as successful as total hip replacement, but in selected patients can provide significant pain relief and improve function. The decision to undergo reconstructive surgery of a weight-bearing joint requires consideration of potential benefits against potential complications, the major of which are infection, pulmonary emboli, and prosthesis failure by loosening of the prosthesis or bone fracture.

A patient with rheumatoid arthritis can reasonably expect that treatment will relieve pain, reduce the inflammation, and preserve joint and muscle function with minimal side effects. The natural consequence of achieving these objectives is that the majority of patients are able to remain functional.

A comprehensive approach with a balance between physical and mental rest and exercise, sociopsychological support, physical and occupational therapy, adequate nutrition, the use of NSAIDs, disease-modifying agents, and even reconstructive surgery, when indicated, can produce gratifying responses in most patients. The existence of some patients with severe and progressive disease who fail to respond to the treatment does not justify a pessimistic attitude, because it is almost always possible to help the majority to function and enjoy an active and productive life.

Not all arthritis are chronic in nature. Many are self-limited or of relatively brief duration. Many patients with severe musculoskeletal pain or stiffness do not have involvement of the joints but rather of the soft tissues surrounding the joints, tendons, bursae, and muscles. Bursitis, tendonitis, and tenosynovitis are a few of the various causes of soft tissue pain. A combination of local corticosteroid injections, hot packs, ultrasound or diathermy, rest, protection of the involved area, and gentle range-of-motion exercises can usually relieve pain and restore function.

Sexual Concerns

There are many consequences of arthritis or of its treatment that interfere with sexuality, which is an integral part of living. Sex can be made progressively difficult or eventually impossible by pain and stiffness, involvement of the hips as well as other joints, fatigue, debilitation, the effect of drugs, or emotional complications. Although most of these problems can be solved or greatly improved when they are properly addressed, they are seldom discussed by the doctor or the patient because, despite the sexual revolution in the latter twentieth century, most people do not easily talk about sexual concerns. The doctor is usually the person with whom the patient discusses his or her sexual concerns.

For some patients the main problem is the deterioration of the sexual image as a consequence of perceived deformities. In other patients the sexual drive or the libido has been lost due to the severity of the disease and sometimes due to the effect of medications. What can you do about these problems? First, if your doctor has not asked about your sexual concerns, you should bring this up for discussion. Your doctor may advise you to take NSAIDs or pain medication to achieve maximal effects when this is most desirable. You may have to change the time choice for sexual activity, if this is possible, depending on your diagnosis and the diurnal pattern of pain and stiffness.

The use of warm-water baths or a whirlpool prior to sex may relieve pain and stiffness, allowing a broader range of sexual activities. The occupational therapist who is mainly concerned with your ability to function independently may help by teaching you alternate sexual positioning, depending upon the pattern of joints involved. If necessary, young women should also obtain counseling regarding the use of contraceptive methods.

Since your image in the eyes of your sexual partner as well as in the eyes of the world should be as normal as possible, you may use a number of coping strategies. You may try to conceal your disability and pain. Do not put an ad in the newspaper that you have pain—don't be a chronic complainer. However, communication is essential and a rough, demanding sexual partner must be helped to realize that sexual activity can be much more satisfying for both partners if passion is tempered with gentleness. The treatment of arthritis and the judicial use of NSAIDs may help you to conceal your disability. Although you may have to slow down in many situations, whenever possible, you may want to try to follow through with activities usually considered "normal," despite some increased discomfort or fatigue. However, this coping technique may backfire if you overdo it. To be able to appear normal you should pace yourself, allowing for periods of rest to restore your energy. The occupational therapist can also assist you in teaching techniques of joint protection and energy conservation which will go a long way to help you appear normal.

Conventional face-to-face intercourse may not be possible when there is destruction of the hip joint with severe pain and limitation of motion. A total hip replacement—when indicated—can eliminate pain and restore enough motion to allow normal sexual activities. There is still hope for sexual fulfillment in patients with severe disabilities resulting from arthritis, since there are many satisfying alternatives to the traditional forms of intercourse. If sexual concerns are not totally answered by the advice of your doctor, trained sex counselors are available and you can request a referral.

Drug Treatment

A relatively short-term goal of drug therapy in RA is to relieve pain and reduce inflammation of the joints. A longer-term objective is to arrest or retard the activity of the disease and in the best of cases to induce a remission. Drug therapy can be invaluable, but may not be the most important aspect of the treatment in some patients. Not all patients need to be treated with drugs. Nonsteroidal anti-inflammatory drugs (NSAIDs) are the first line of drug therapy. Aspirin (ASA)[35] is the most frequently used NSAID because it is effective and cheap. Problems posed by the use of ASA in OA and RA relate to the requirement of relatively large doses (from 10 to 20 tablets per day) in four divided doses, the frequency of gastrointestinal

---

[35]ASA and most NSAIDs inhibit the enzyme cyclooxygenase and thus the formation of prostaglandins, which are important mediators of inflammation.

intestinal irritation, its major side effect, and less frequently, the development of gastric ulcer. The risk of gastrointestinal irritation is greater when patients drink alcohol or take corticosteroids. ASA may also infrequently induce a dramatic hypersensitivity reaction in predisposed persons who may develop skin rashes, urticaria, swelling of the lips, the eyelids, or the airway, and severe asthma upon ingestion of small doses. In predisposed individuals, indomethacin, ibuprofen, and phenoprofen can also trigger an attack of asthma. ASA can commonly produce ringing of the ears which may progress to hearing loss that recovers when the dose of ASA is reduced. Renal toxicity can occur in the elderly and in those patients who are on a salt-restricted diet. NSAIDs should not be used in the last trimester of pregnancy since they may delay parturition and cause cardiac abnormalities in the fetus.[36] All NSAIDs share this side effect with ASA and should be avoided during the third trimester. ASA decreases the aggregation of platelets and antagonizes vitamin K, thus increasing the bleeding time. Its use also increases the effect of oral coumadin[37] and in these patients ASA should be used with caution or not at all. The diuretic furosemide[38] may not produce the desired effect in patients treated with high doses of ASA. When ASA is used together with other NSAIDs the blood levels of the latter can be reduced. Thus ASA or another NSAID are not usually used together.

Other alternative drugs are enteric-coated ASA and the nonacetylated salicylates, choline magnesium trisalicylate, [39] salsalate[40] and diflunisal.[41] These medications have at best simi-

---

[36]They may cause the premature closure of the ductus arteriosus, a communication between the aorta and the pulmonary artery which should be open during fetal life.

[37]Commonly used anticoagulant drug.

[38]Lasix.

[39]Trilisate.

[40]Disalcid, monogesic.

[41]Dolobid.

lar anti-inflammatory activity when compared with ASA but seem to produce less gastrointestinal irritation. When pain-relieving medication is necessary in addition to NSAIDs, acetaminophen[42] can be used since it does not have significant gastrointestinal toxicity. Ibuprofen,[43] fenoprofen,[44] and naproxen,[45] are very useful medications, somewhat weaker in anti-inflammatory potency compared to ASA, but with considerably fewer side effects. These drugs should be used with caution in patients with liver disease. It is wise that patients taking NSAIDs have white cell counts and be periodically checked for possible liver or renal side effects.

Naproxen is not only used in RA, but is also effective in the treatment of acute attacks of gout. In the choice of NSAID, one consideration is that the daily cost of therapy with most of the new NSAIDs is from 5 to 10 times higher than that of ASA. Other groups of NSAIDs are acetic acid derivatives, indomethacine,[46] sulindac,[47] and tolmetin.[48] Indomethacin is very useful for treating acute attacks of crystal-induced arthritis, and all these drugs can be useful to treat any of the forms of chronic arthritis. Indomethacin can produce severe headaches and gastrointestinal irritation rather frequently. It may also aggravate depression, epilepsy, and parkinsonism, and may increase the plasma levels of lithium in some patients. Sulindac is a useful NSAID that produces fewer gastrointestinal complaints than ASA. Tolmetin is used in the treatment of RA, JRA, and OA. Although the drug resembles indomethacin, it produces less gastrointestinal irritation and does not produce the central nervous system changes that may occur with that drug. Meclo-

[42]Tylenol.
[43]Motrin, Rufen, Advil.
[44]Nalfon.
[45]Naprosyn, Anaprox.
[46]Indocin.
[47]Clinoril.
[48]Tolectin.

fenamate[49] and piroxicam[50] are useful NSAIDs in OA and RA. Diarrhea is a special problem with meclofenamate which may lead to dehydration in the elderly. Piroxicam is a potent anti-inflammatory agent which needs to be taken only once a day. It is generally well tolerated. The possibility of central nervous system symptoms should limit its use in the elderly. Before making the decision to send an elderly arthritic patient who is confused and disoriented to a nursing home, a careful evaluation should be made. The label of Alzheimer's disease may be given to patients who are merely malnourished, who are depressed, or who are experiencing central nervous system side effects from NSAIDs. Two new useful NSAIDs, diclofemac sodium[51] and flurbiprofen[52] have an excellent safety profile. NSAIDs have not been shown to alter the course or rate of progression of joint damage in rheumatoid arthritis.

Corticosteroids are potent anti-inflammatory drugs which are extremely useful in the treatment of severe manifestations of SLE, including diffuse proliferative glomerulonephritis, pleuropericardial and CNS involvement, as well as severe blood manifestations, such as hemolytic anemia, thrombocytopenia, or bone marrow depression. These drugs are extremely useful in the treatment of severe vasculitis, such as polyarteritis, and other inflammatory diseases of the blood vessels. The use of corticosteroids may be lifesaving in some of these conditions. Intra-articular injection of corticosteroids is very helpful in the treatment of RA. These are usually given to patients who are responding well to the treatment but who have persistent activity in only a few joints. Oral corticosteroids are indicated to treat severe extra-articular manifestations of RA, such as vasculitis, pleuritis, pneumonitis, or pericarditis. Corticosteroids proved not to be the panacea for the treatment of RA, as suggested in the early studies of the 1950s. Although small doses of cor-

[49]Meclomen.
[50]Feldene.
[51]Volteran.
[52]Ansaid.

ticosteroids are sometimes used for a limited time while waiting for the initial effect of disease modifying drugs, or in those patients in whom first and second line drugs have failed, these drugs should not be used as the mainstay of treatment. Corticosteroids have not shown to have disease-modifying properties and do not retard the radiographic progression of RA.

A great danger is that their potent anti-inflammatory effect may provide enough relief of symptoms that patients may not realize the urgency of starting treatment with disease-modifying drugs, which offer the best chance of arresting or retarding the progression of the disease. Patients may become increasingly dependent upon corticosteroids for the control of symptoms, and may require increasingly higher doses to obtain the same effects. It is also not uncommon that patients are reluctant to discontinue these drugs, in spite of the physician's advice. An additional problem of the prolonged use of corticosteroids is the suppression of the adrenal gland, which eventually shrinks, so that after these drugs have been used for years it is no longer possible to discontinue them, because the adrenals cannot resume normal function. When it is still possible to discontinue these drugs, they cannot be stopped abruptly, but rather, have to be tapered gradually to avoid flare-ups of the disease. Most importantly, when corticosteroids are used for a long time, wound healing is poor, the body defenses are low, and these patients are prone to infections; the bones become osteoporotic, and, among other problems, diabetes may be induced. In juvenile RA, corticosteroids may also interfere with growth and development. There are no indications for oral corticosteroids in osteoarthritis. Local intra-articular injections of corticosteroids are very useful adjuvants of treatment. However, these injections should be given infrequently and judiciously since side effects may occur, among them the cartilage and bone breakdown that may occur with repeated injections.

In the treatment of RA, if aspirin or another NSAID fail to provide relief, your physician could try one or two other NSAIDs in relatively brief trials. If the disease is still not controlled, the use of slow acting or disease-modifying agents should be discussed with your doctor. If after a few months of conservative treatment with NSAIDs the activity of RA is persistent, particularly in women with positive rheumatoid factor and subcutaneous nodules, it is important to consider the early use of slow-acting drugs. To arrive at a mutual informed decision regarding the choice of drug, you should depend upon the advice of your doctor and what you know about these agents. All of them can—but do not necessarily have to—produce adverse effects, and with careful monitoring by you and your doctor these side effects can be minimized. Patients frequently think only of the potential side effects of medications and become very negativistic, ignoring the probable consequences of not using drugs. It is a common experience that many untreated patients with persistent disease activity develop progressive deformities and become crippled by its destructive effects. I have no doubt that for the patient with severe disease, the choice of a slow-acting drug is the most potentially beneficial and least hazardous decision.

The disease-modifying agents have several features in common. After a brief trial of one month or less you will know if a NSAID produces a beneficial effect, but the disease-modifying agents act slowly and a trial of 3 to 6 months is usually necessary before reaching a conclusion about their effectiveness. Many times it is difficult to be patient while you wait, but you should have a positive attitude and hope that eventually the activity of the disease will be reduced by treatment. Another feature common to these drugs is that when they are stopped, the beneficial effects are not immediately lost, but the symptoms return after a few months. Gold, hydroxychloroquine, and penicillamine are most frequently used, but recently Imuran and sulfasalazine have also been used successfully to treat some patients with active RA. These drugs may not be of benefit to all patients. In general, 60% improve or experience remission and the rest show no improvement, or are unable to take the drug because of side effects. Many patients do not respond to treatment or experience side effects with one drug, but have no problem with and benefit substantially from another. True remissions are few and far between and frequently the benefits of a single drug are lost or diminished after 3 years of administration. Often, another drug can bring about the control of the disease. It is important that you become aware of the potential side effects of any drug you may be prescribed, so their early recognition may allow you and your physician to act promptly and avoid major problems. The lines of communication with your doctor should always be open and you should recognize that any new symptom appearing while you are being treated with a drug can be a side effect.

Gold, either injectable or oral, is often the first choice. Oral gold, Auranofin[53] is effective, easy to use and usually well tolerated. Its major drawback is a tendency to cause diarrhea that can often subside spontaneously or can be controlled by transiently reducing the dose. The most frequently used preparations of injectable gold are aurothioglucose[54] and gold sodium thiomalate.[55] Gold seems to be most beneficial in patients with relatively early, active disease. If you elect to take oral gold, you should expect monthly office visits with laboratory tests for white blood cell counts and protein in the urine. If you choose injectable gold, you should initially make plans to go to your doctor's office for an injection on a weekly basis. After you have received 1 gram of gold at the rate of 50 milligrams per week, or, if you experienced a substantial improvement before reaching that level, the dose is given in alternate weeks and, subsequently, every third or fourth week. If your symptoms improve and no side effects appear, gold can be continued indefinitely. Common side effects are reversible upon discontinuation of gold. Serious blood side effects with depression of the bone marrow, and very low blood counts are very rare but may occur without warning, so continuous monitoring is imperative.

[53]Ridaura.
[54]Solganal.
[55]Myochrysine.

Many patients could benefit from hydroxychloroquine[56] but reject its use because of its potential side effects. This drug, as well as chloroquine,[57] can cause retinal lesions with loss of vision. This is a good example of inappropriate use of information obtained from the *Physician's Desk Reference*, or provided by the physician. Legally, he has to inform you that you can become blind with the use of these drugs. However, the use of hydroxychloroquine is safe if used at doses no greater than 6.5 milligrams per kilogram body weight and if a baseline and periodic ophthalmologic examinations are carried out every 6 months by the same ophthalmologist. Since exposure to sunlight increases the risk of retinal damage by antimalarials, dark sunglasses are recommended for patients spending much time in sunlight. Penicillamine[58] is also a very useful slow-acting drug. Its side effects are similar to those of injectable gold. Azathioprine,[59] cyclophosphamide,[60] and methotrexate are cytotoxic drugs that can be useful in selected patients with very severe and incapacitating disease. Cyclophosphamide treatment has been shown to induce long-lasting remissions and probably cures in patients afflicted with Wegener's granulomatosis, a severe form of vasculitis which was formerly a fatal disease.

Arthritis in the Child

If you are the parent of a child with arthritis, it is essential that you learn about your child's problems. Although, years ago, most children with inflammatory joint disease were lumped into one broad category of juvenile rheumatoid arthritis

[56]Plaquenil.
[57]Aralen.
[58]Cuprimine, Depen.
[59]Imuran.
[60]Cytoxan.

(JRA), this concept is at the present time undergoing revision. Three different types of onset have been identified, corresponding to equally different clinical pictures. In the beginning, one type of onset can hardly be recognized as arthritis. The child, more frequently a boy, develops fever of unknown origin, enlarged liver, spleen, and lymph nodes, and is usually thought to have some type of infection, leukemia, or lymphoma. Cultures and other diagnostic studies are usually negative. Diagnostic clues are the presence of joint pains or swelling; but these are often difficult to elicit since children do not frequently complain of joint pain. Another clue is the appearance of an evanescent skin rash on the trunk, face, and extremities. It is important to recognize the systemic onset of JRA, because many of these patients are subjected to exhaustive and sometimes unnecessary diagnostic studies, treatment with various antibiotics, and even exploratory abdominal surgery. About one out of five patients with systemic onset of the disease develops severe arthritis, and these children frequently may experience growth retardation.

All children who develop polyarticular disease do not behave in the same way. A subgroup, most frequently girls in their teens, develop clinical and laboratory features indistinguishable from adult rheumatoid arthritis. These children with positive rheumatoid factors as well as those with systemic onset of JRA present the greatest risk of developing destructive joint disease. Some children, also presenting with multiple joint involvement, have negative rheumatoid factors, fusion of spinal articulations, acute anterior uveitis, sacroiliitis, and a positive HLA-B27 test. At the beginning, the spinal involvement may be masked by the prominent involvement of the periperipheral joints. Almost half of all children afflicted with arthritis, primarily girls, begin gradually with involvement of only a few joints, usually a knee. These patients may develop chronic eye inflammation[61] and many have positive ANA tests. It is important to recognize that

---

[61]Chronic iridocyclitis.

a positive ANA in these children does not mean that they have lupus. It is also important to recognize that these children are at risk of inflammatory eye disease and should have slit-lamp examinations every 3 months by an ophthalmologist. Some children, usually boys, with only a few joints involved at the beginning may eventually develop low back pain and features suggestive of juvenile ankylosing spondylitis. Less frequently, some children may develop systemic lupus erythematosus, scleroderma, or other rheumatic diseases, inflammatory bowel disease with arthritis, viral hepatitis, or arthritis following rubella or rubella vaccination.

Joint inflammation can be satisfactorily controlled in most of the children with the drugs presently available. Salicylates are the mainstay therapy, but tolmetin and naproxen have been approved for use in children in the U.S. Gold, injectable or oral, hydroxychloroquine, and penicillamine can be beneficial in the group of patients with positive rheumatoid factors and chronic arthritis resembling adult-onset RA. Corticosteroids are not curative in any form of JRA and their known side effects, namely growth suppression, cataracts, osteoporosis, diabetes, adrenal suppression, and still others make their long-term use generally hazardous. Immunosuppressive therapy may predispose the children to fatal infection, pose the risk of malignant disease, and may interfere with their reproductive capacity. These drugs have been used to treat some patients with severe disease, but they are not indicated in the majority of patients.

The overall prognosis of juvenile arthritis in general is reasonably good with at least 75 percent recovering without significant joint damage, allowing normal function. It is clear that the prognosis and treatment have to be individualized depending upon the specific diagnosis. The main goal in the treatment of a child with any type of arthritis is to help him to live a normal life and to develop into a normal adult.

CHAPTER 6

NUTRITION AND DRUGS

Many types of arthritis are chronic in nature. If you have one of these types, it will probably stay with you for a long time — perhaps as long as you live. Because of the long duration of arthritis, occasionally you may be simultaneously treated with several drugs when you develop high blood pressure, pneumonia, indigestion, or the common cold. Although in many situations some patients may truly need the use of multiple drugs, some of these drugs are often unnecessary and at times even harmful. One of the routine tasks your doctor performs when he sees you as a new patient is to determine whether the medicines you have been taking for a long time are still necessary. Often, the reasons for their use may no longer exist. Patients are frequently ignorant of the most common possible side effects of each drug and almost always know nothing about the potential problems arising when certain drugs are used together. If you take medication over a long period of time, you must be aware of the possibility of drug toxicity and the mutual effects that food and medication can have upon each other.

Diet can modify the effect of drugs. Prescriptions for medication taken by mouth often include specific directions in relation to food intake, because what you eat can modify the absorption, blood levels, and efficacy of medicines. Certain medicines are more effective when taken with food, because food intake can prevent them from being destroyed in the stomach. Diet can also have an important influence on the toxicity of drugs taken by mouth. As we have mentioned, patients who take aspirin regularly have an increased tendency to develop gastric irritation or ulcer. You may better tolerate aspirin if you take it along with food, during your meal. Other NSAIDs are also better tolerated if they are taken with food, because their potential for gastric irritation is minimized. It is clear that the way you take your medicines in relation to food intake may make a decisive difference in whether or not they will work, and on your ability to tolerate them. Gastrointestinal side effects from medications can influence your nutritional status. The use of drugs can also interfere with nutrition by increasing or decreasing the appetite. For example, the continual use of corticosteroids may promote insatiable appetite, which may add to the problems of the obese arthritic. Although, for the undernourished arthritic, the practice of taking medication after a glass of milk may be desirable, this is not acceptable for all patients. For example, the 320 calories in a pint of whole milk may be particularly undesirable for the obese arthritic who is trying to lose weight. If milk is to be used with oral medications, skim milk is preferred, since it provides all the nutrients present in whole milk except fat and vitamin A, and provides only half as many calories.

Why can you lose the beneficial effect of some drugs? You may have observed that your arthritis substantially improved when you initially used a certain drug but, after a while, joint pain and stiffness reappeared. Obviously, the drug would not work if you forgot to take it, or if you took it improperly. But you took your medication faithfully, so this recurrence was very puzzling to you. For reasons unknown to us, this often occurs with all drugs used to treat arthritis, but sometimes this situation can be rationally explained. It is well known that the prolonged administration of drugs used to control seizures,[1] and some anti-inflammatory drugs,[2] as well as the excessive ingestion of alcohol, stimulate certain enzymes of the liver which are essential for drug detoxification. As a consequence, the drug in question is inactivated more efficiently, and larger doses are needed to produce the desired effect, explaining why certain drugs may lose their efficacy on repeated administration. Thus, you may not obtain the desired effect from certain medicines if you drink alcohol excessively or if you are also taking any of the above-mentioned drugs. Alcohol can have the opposite effect on other medications you may take. For example, the effect of blood pressure-lowering drugs, sedatives, and tranquilizers may be exaggerated by excessive alcohol intake. Unfortunately, we do not yet know all the reasons for the late failure of some drugs.

Many patients with arthritis, particularly the elderly living in isolation and young persons with destructive joint disease, are frequently prescribed antidepressants. Eating cheese, yeast extract, and pickled herring, or drinking some red wines has been shown to trigger episodes of dangerously high blood pressure and headache in these patients. Tyramine contained in these foods is believed to be responsible for the elevation in blood pressure. A wine and cheese party is obviously not to be enjoyed by those arthritics taking antidepressant drugs. Preparations containing L-tryptophan which are frequently used as "improvements" of the diet are of interest to the arthritic, since they can also trigger dangerous episodes of high blood pressure when taken with these antidepressant medications.

There are many examples of nutrition-induced changes in the way the body handles a drug. The use of tetracycline by

[1]Anticonvulsants, such as diphenylhydantoin (Dilantin).
[2]Phenylbutazone (Butazolidine).

patients who take calcium supplements or regularly ingest dairy products does present problems, since calcium forms an insoluble complex with this drug, impairing its absorption. Other medications, like antacids containing aluminum, and some preparations containing iron, also block the absorption of tetracycline, and should not be taken together. Oral forms of tetracycline should be taken 1 hour before or 2 hours after meals.

It is well known that diet influences the activity of the drug-detoxifying function of the liver. Debilitation resulting from starvation or from severely restricted diets enhances drug toxicity through depression of this mechanism. This is not uncommonly seen in the elderly or in younger individuals who have severe destructive arthritis. Undernourished patients with chronic destructive arthritis are more prone to develop adverse effects from drugs than those who are adequately nourished, particularly if they are simultaneously treated with many drugs. This situation is commonly found in elderly patients who need treatment for multiple organ failure in addition to treatment for arthritis.

A diet balanced in terms of protein, carbohydrates, and fats, which is adequate in calories, vitamins, and minerals, tends to minimize the potential toxic effect of many drugs. Patients with arthritis on marginally deficient diets, following food fads, fasting, or on severely restricted self-imposed diets are more susceptible to experience adverse effects from drugs.

Malabsorption of Minerals and Vitamins

The recent enthusiasm for high-fiber diets needs to be examined in relation to food-drug toxicities. Substances present in plant foods may bind to and prevent the absorption of metals through the intestine. When zinc or calcium supplements are prescribed, they should be taken at a separate time from fiber-containing meals, such as breakfasts consisting of bran-enriched cereals.

Some drugs can alter nutritional requirements by causing malabsorption which would make the nutrient unavailable to the body. Although you may not think of alcohol as a drug, it behaves in the body as such. Individuals who drink alcohol excessively can develop vitamin B and folate deficiency since it inhibits the absorption of these vitamins.

Patients with arthritis have frequently been prescribed antacids to alleviate discomfort produced by antiarthritic medication. Many continue to take unnecessarily these medications for years. The most widely used preparations in the last three decades have been those containing mixtures of aluminum and magnesium. Although new drugs[3] are now most frequently prescribed as antiulcer medications, arthritics still frequently use aluminum-containing antacids. Aluminum binds phosphate within the intestine, thereby preventing its absorption. Prolonged and repeated use of antacids may deplete phosphate in the body and may produce weakness, malaise, and lack of appetite. This complication is probably seen only in chronic alcoholics or when protein intake is severely restricted. This practice may also lead to osteomalacia. The indiscriminate consumption of self-prescribed antacid medication is not advisable.

A moderate anemia of the type seen in conjunction with chronic inflammation is common in rheumatoid arthritis. This anemia does not respond to iron supplementation because it is not due to iron deficiency, and it can only improve if the activity of rheumatoid arthritis subsides and the patient goes into remission. However, true iron-deficiency anemia may occur as a consequence of gastrointestinal bleeding induced by aspirin or NSAIDs or by excessive menstrual flow, or it can be the consequence of an inadequate diet. Aluminum-containing antacids taken with iron can make it insoluble and unavailable for absorption. It seems reasonable that when iron is prescribed, antacid medications should not be taken along with iron.

Treatment of rheumatoid arthritis with gold, penicillamine, or sulfasalazine can be complicated by adverse effects, such as

[3]Tagamet, Zantac, or Carafate.

ulcerations of the mouth and skin rash. Although in the patient's mind it is natural to blame a drug for any newly appearing symptom, sometimes these complications may not be related to drug toxicity, but to nutritional problems associated with vitamin (B_2, niacin, pyridoxine, folacin, biotin) or mineral (iron or zinc) deficiency as the underlying cause. Thus, for the wrong reason, it is possible that the arthritic may be denied the use of a drug which is potentially able to favorably modify the disease. When this is suspected, although it is wise to stop the drug immediately, the nutritional deficiencies must be corrected. Upon healing of the ulcer or the disappearance of the skin rash, your doctor may choose to cautiously restart the drug in question. The persistence of mouth ulcerations in some patients can have devastating nutritional consequences, leading to further weight loss, because eating becomes very painful.

Many patients with rheumatoid arthritis are treated with penicillamine, which effectively binds various metals, particularly copper and zinc. This drug can bind to many other substances present in food, and for this reason the drug should not be taken with meals. Penicillamine should be given on an empty stomach, at least one hour before any other drug, food, or milk. This method permits maximal absorption and reduces the likelihood of inactivation of the drug by binding with metals. While using penicillamine you may experience a substantial improvement of your rheumatoid arthritis. The stiffness and pain may disappear and you may function as normally as if you did not have arthritis. However, the honeymoon may suddenly be over. You may be surprised to learn from your doctor that the mineral supplements that you started to take last fall could probably be blamed. Because mineral supplements, zinc in particular, are very popular unrecognized "improvements" of the diet taken by many concerned patients, it should be emphasized that the administration of zinc may block the disease-modifying effect of penicillamine. Similarly, iron preparations and mineral supplements may diminish its therapeutic effect. Patients will be well advised to inform the physician about all food supplements, vitamins, and minerals taken to "improve" the diet.

The use of penicillamine may also result in pyridoxine inactivation. Patients being treated with penicillamine, particularly those with impaired nutrition, can benefit from a single daily supplement of 50 to 100 milligrams of vitamin B_6. There is also an increased requirement for vitamin B_6 in pregnant women and in those taking oral contraceptives. Emotional symptoms and depression occurring in arthritic women who are using oral contraceptives may improve with a daily supplement of 25 to 50 milligrams of vitamin B_6. Other nutrients affected by the use of oral contraceptives include folic acid, vitamins B_2, B_{12}, C, and zinc. Therefore, users of oral contraceptives who experience psychological disturbances can benefit from a multiple vitamin-mineral supplement.

Prednisone intake increases the urinary excretion of zinc and calcium and patients on long-term prednisone treatment are at risk of zinc deficiency and calcium depletion. Patients with RA or with psoriatic arthritis treated with methotrexate can have low folic acid levels because this drug interferes with folic acid metabolism.

Ingestion of mineral oil to treat constipation may prevent the absorption of fat-soluble vitamins (A, D, E, and K) which are stabilized by the mineral oil. If mineral oil is to be used, it should be taken 3 to 4 hours after a meal to prevent interference with the utilization of these vitamins.

Diet as a Source of Toxicants

Your efforts to "improve" your diet may be ill-advised and can actually harm you. Excessive dietary supplementation may result in a nutrient intake several times higher than could ever be achieved by eating a normal balanced diet. This irrational and excessive use of supplements is very commonly observed among arthritics who can experience unexpected adverse effects caused by excessive intake of vitamins A and D and possibly C and E. There is a growing concern among nutritionists that the consumption of certain vitamins has continued to increase and has become quite high in some individuals, exposing them to potential risks of toxicity and long-term side effects.

Arthritics frequently take megadoses[4] of vitamin C and some of them take amounts in excess of 5,000 milligrams daily.[5] Surveys of the general population have indicated that some people take from 1,000 to 40,000 milligrams or more of the vitamin daily. Since the massive intake of vitamin C has become very popular, you must realize that this practice does not result in a sustained high blood level of the vitamin. It is well known that after daily intake of the vitamin is increased beyond 200 milligrams, its elimination in the urine rises very sharply, and the pool of this vitamin in the body does not increase. Thus, there is no sound rationale for increasing your intake of vitamin C beyond 200–250 milligrams per day. Many studies have been done on the efficacy of megadoses of vitamin C to prevent the common cold. In general, no benefit was observed, and it is the consensus of most of the investigators who carried out the studies that the benefits, if any, are small. The multiple claims from the popular literature that massive intake of vitamin C assures great stamina, increased resistance to infection, superior mental prowess, enhanced fertility, and resistance to malignant disease have not been substantiated. Although the benefits of megadoses of vitamin C are doubtful, it has been found that high doses taken over a long period of time by predisposed individuals can have serious toxic effects. Absorption of massive amounts of vitamin C through the intestine is poor and the

---

[4]The term megavitamin therapy was initially used in the early 1950s to describe the treatment of schizophrenia using doses of nicotinic acid (one of the vitamins of the B complex) 200 to 2000 times the RDA.
[5]The RDA for vitamin C is 60 milligrams.

practice of taking large doses may produce nausea, diarrhea, and abdominal cramps. Unfortunately, your doctor, not knowing that you take megadoses of vitamin C, may interpret these symptoms as a gastrointestinal side effect of other antiarthritic medications. In patients being treated with anticoagulants for blood clots, large doses of vitamin C may interfere with the action of the anticoagulant drugs.

Gastrointestinal bleeding due to ulcers or to the effect of NSAIDs on the gastrointestinal (GI) tract is relatively common in patients with arthritis. To detect GI bleeding, a test for occult blood is often done on the stools. In the presence of large concentrations of vitamin C, current tests for occult blood will be falsely negative, even if blood is present in the stools. High levels of vitamin C may also interfere with the results of various other tests and may pose problems in the diagnosis and management of diabetes and liver disease.

There is also concern regarding the toxic effect that megadoses of vitamin C may have on the urinary tract by promoting stone formation. It has been found that adaptation may occur as a consequence of prolonged intake of high doses of vitamin C, so the body develops mechanisms for more effective and rapid disposal of the vitamin. Thus, scurvy can appear following cessation of prolonged high-dose vitamin C intake. In these patients, the above-mentioned adaptive changes underlie a conditioned deficiency of vitamin C with a relative lack of responsiveness to normal doses. Probably more common is the occurrence of fatigue and headache on withdrawal from high-dosage vitamin C supplementation. It seems obvious from the above discussion that if you are on a "generous" supplementation of vitamin C, you should make this known to your doctor. Although the adult RDA of this vitamin prevents vitamin C deficiency in normal persons, a moderate supplement of 200 to 250 milligrams is advisable for patients with arthritis. The increased pre- and postoperative requirements for vitamin C can also be met by this supplement. You may know that circulating levels of vitamin C in the blood are lower, and urinary elimination of the vitamin is higher, among regular users of aspirin. The low levels of ascorbic acid in aspirin users can also be corrected by the moderate supplement of 250 milligrams per day.

A common form of toxicity which may affect patients with arthritis is the result of chronic intake of high doses of vitamin A. High concentrations of vitamin A result in disruption of cellular membranes and degradation of the extracellular connective tissue. The average intake of some people is 20 times greater than or even higher than the RDA of 5,000 I.U. An intake as low as 20,000–40,000 I.U. per day over a number of years has resulted in toxic symptoms in adults. Skin rash, itching, cracking and bleeding lips, reddened gums, nosebleeds, hair loss, nausea, headaches, blurred vision, muscular soreness and weakness are common symptoms of chronic vitamin A intoxication. Lack of appetite may interfere with nutrition. High levels of blood calcium and excessive bone growths can occur. Deep bone and joint pain, frequently experienced by these patients may superficially resemble the symptoms of arthritis.

Vitamin D is a sunshine-dependent hormone which is produced in the skin upon exposure to ultraviolet light and further transformed into more active forms of the hormone in the liver and kidney. Vitamin D enhances calcium and phosphorus absorption from the intestine as well as resorption of calcium and phosphorus from bone. Excessive vitamin D intake, resulting in removal of calcium from the bones and elevated circulating blood calcium levels, can have devastating effects leading to calcification of soft tissue and bone demineralization. In most adults, a daily intake in excess of 50,000 I.U. is needed to produce toxicity, which is frequently manifested by muscle weakness, nausea, vomiting, constipation, polyuria,[6] excessive thirst, red eyes, itching, and renal stones. However, in certain susceptible individuals, toxicity may occur at levels of vitamin D intake only slightly above 1,000 I.U. per day.

Vitamin E is an all-time favorite of patients with arthritis. Self-medication with this vitamin is relatively common. Based

[6]Large volume of urine.

on its role as a preserver of the integrity of cell membranes, vitamin E probably contributes to the maintenance of normal muscular, vascular, nervous, and reproductive function. Its popularity is probably largely due to the unconfirmed claims that vitamin E is useful to treat many noninfectious diseases such as rheumatoid arthritis, or to promote well-being and sexual potency. Self-prescribed dosages up to 1,000 I.U. per day are not uncommon. Headaches, nausea, and double vision have been reported in patients taking as little as 300 I.U., although this dosage has frequently been given to people with no apparent ill effects. Higher dosages can produce severe muscle weakness and biochemical changes suggesting muscle injury. Interference of vitamin E with vitamin K explains the occasional occurrence of bruises in patients taking dosages of vitamin E above 1,000 I.U. Excessive vitamin E supplementation may also impair wound healing and produce skin rashes.

You should be aware that large doses of niacin can cause skin flushing, liver dysfunction, optic nerve disease, and can produce congenital malformations when taken during pregnancy. There are claims that megadoses of this vitamin (as much as 3 grams per day) improve joint mobility and alleviate "arthritis." There are no indications that this treatment is warranted for the rheumatic diseases.

Nutrition and Drugs during Pregnancy

Most of the problems discussed above involving diet and drugs may be applicable to the pregnant woman who may have special nutritional problems and is undoubtedly concerned that treatment of the arthritis may be harmful to her baby.

Though gestation may have a transitory beneficial effect on the activity of rheumatoid arthritis, some patients may require anti-inflammatory drugs which are potentially hazardous in the early stages of fetal growth. Even though the patient being treated with drugs has been warned about the potential dangers to the offspring, pregnancy sometimes takes place unexpectedly in spite of the use of contraceptive measures. The most vulnerable period is when the organs are being formed between the third and tenth week of gestation—the time when many women are still unaware that they are pregnant. Since some drugs can produce fetal malformations, particularly early in the gestational period, and many others may adversely affect the pregnancy, young arthritic women are often rightly reluctant to take any drug that might damage their offspring. The likelihood that the activity of arthritis may improve at this time may also justify the reluctance of the young mother to receive any drug. Another critical period is during late pregnancy, near term, when drugs given to the mother may adversely affect the child, who is less able than the adult to handle and excrete certain drugs.

For the majority of the drugs used in practice, there is no information available about their use during pregnancy or of their effect on the fetus. Although there are reports that salicylates, gold, and even azathioprine, a potent drug which suppresses the immune response, have been used during pregnancy with no ill effects on either the child or the treated mother, no one can guarantee that anti-inflammatory treatment given to the mother will not harm the baby. There is a report of a young woman treated with penicillamine during pregnancy who gave birth to a child with loose skin, increased mobility of the joints, fragility of cutaneous blood vessels, and impairment of wound healing. Women treated with methotrexate during early pregnancy may suffer spontaneous abortions, and in some cases there are congenital anomalies in term infants. When this treatment is given to arthritic women of childbearing age, proper contraceptive measures are a *must*. The use of any of the NSAIDs may be potentially dangerous in pregnant women, and if possible should be particularly avoided around the time of delivery. It is well known that the use of nearly all NSAIDs may prolong labor. The general rule for drug treatment during pregnancy and lactation is to control disease activity satisfactorily, but with the least hazardous drugs and the smallest possible dose.

CHAPTER 7

POOR NUTRITION
AND OBESITY

Undernutrition

Although starvation is seldom seen in this country, undernourishment still continues to be a major problem among the elderly, the poor, and the chronically ill. Patients with chronic destructive arthritis frequently fall into these categories. In addition to water and a source of calories usually represented by carbohydrates, the human body only requires the intake of a small number of organic substances and minerals, eight essential amino acids, one essential fatty acid, 13 vitamins, and a limited number of inorganic substances such as calcium, phosphorous, iodine, iron, magnesium, zinc, copper, potassium, sodium chloride, cobalt, chromium, manganese, molybdenum, and selenium, to maintain health. Marginal deficiencies of protein,

iron, folic acid, and vitamin C, although uncommon in the
United States, can be detected in the population of some regions. Your nutritional status can be assessed by taking a dietary history and performing a physical examination, various
body measurements, and a few laboratory tests. Not infrequently, unqualified practitioners exploit the patients' keen interest in nutrition with elaborate and expensive surveys of
various micronutrients. One example is hair analysis, which is
of questionable clinical value in evaluating individual patients.
Some patients with severe rheumatoid arthritis can have folic
acid deficiency, low zinc levels, marginal protein malnutrition,
and marginal deficiency of vitamin E. Marginal deficiencies can
also be found in alcoholics and in patients whose diets largely
consist of "snack foods" of low nutritional value.

Lack of appetite is a major contributing factor in malnutrition. Both the arthritis as well as depression may cause loss of
appetite and nutritional problems. Unrecognized depression
may be the main cause of weight loss, particularly in the elderly.
In these patients, the appetite is decreased, the choice of foods
is monotonous, and the preparation of meals becomes a difficult
chore. Nutrition can improve only when depression is recognized and treated. The elderly patient suffering from any form
of destructive arthritis may have special nutritional problems.

Depression, limited economic means, and restricted mobility place the elderly patient with disabling arthritis at risk
from malnutrition. Arthritic patients, just as other people, do
not like to eat alone or to cook for themselves. Depression, not
infrequent in these cases, may lead the patient to consume relatively easy-to-prepare, ready-made foods that can be kept in the
freezer for a long time. Although these foods usually contain
sufficient calories, they may lack the proper balance of proteins,
minerals, vitamins, and vegetables. Inadequate diets may lead
either to weight loss or to obesity depending upon the amount
of food consumed. The decreased caloric intake observed as the
individual ages can probably be accounted for by the decreased
basal metabolism and the decline in physical activity associated

with aging. The reduction in food intake associated with advancing age coupled with little or no variation in their diets make elderly people especially vulnerable to deficiencies in vitamins and trace elements. Some elderly arthritic patients may make meal after meal of toast with jelly and coffee or tea, which constitutes the basis for their undernutrition. This is an aspect of the treatment of arthritis in which the close cooperation of concerned family and friends can make a tremendous difference in the outcome.

Depletion of proteins impairs immune competence and wound healing. Debilitated patients with chronic disabling arthritis frequently have inadequate food and calcium intake, lose weight, and have diminished fat and protein stores, causing atrophy of the muscles and loss of bone mass. Poor nutrition frequently delays the healing of bone following a fracture. If protein depletion is allowed to progress, the immune system can be depressed in some patients. It has been recognized that malnourished individuals are more susceptible to infection than those receiving adequate nutrition. Malnutrition increases the risk of infection and has a potent adverse effect on the immune system which is an essential part of the body defenses.

A chronic destructive arthritis may result in increased nutritional requirements, decreased appetite, and decreased capacity for self-care. When the diet is inadequate, the carbohydrate stores are rapidly mobilized to produce blood sugar,[1] which is the fuel readily available to support energy needs. If caloric inadequacy persists, the body resorts to mobilizing fat and muscle stores to provide the needed energy, with devastating consequences to the muscles. These changes in the body are capable of altering not only the physical capabilities of the individual, but also his external appearance and his ability to function in society.

Severe malnutrition is relatively easy to recognize. Weight loss is confirmed by the patient's appearance. His clothing is loose and fits poorly and bony prominences are exaggerated,

---

[1]Glucose.

particularly in the face. Muscle wasting is pronounced and soft tissue swelling may be marked. The patient is very weak and may be lethargic. These patients are usually severely disabled and have a long history of joint involvement. However, the presence of chronic malnutrition in certain patients afflicted with arthritis may not be obvious. The weight loss may have occurred several months before, and subsequently became stabilized at a lower weight level. A patient may even appear to be obese and still have underlying muscle protein depletion, because in muscle-wasting, body protein can be replaced by fat.

When the factors leading to malnutrition are recognized, prescribing a balanced diet can produce dramatic improvement in the nutritional status.

Alcohol abuse can be a major aggravating factor in arthritis. Alcoholism occurs in all segments of society. Alcohol comprises at least 5% of the total caloric intake of the population of the U.S. Abuse of alcohol can be defined in many ways, but most of them tend to underestimate the magnitude of the problem. It has been estimated that about 15% of the men and 9% of the women in the U.S. are heavy drinkers. Ingestion of alcohol has been traditionally recognized as a provocative factor in gout. In spite of the fact that the consumption of alcohol has continued to increase and that alcohol could be a factor in the development or aggravation of certain types of chronic arthritis, the pattern of alcohol consumption in patients with arthritis is not known. The excessive intake of alcohol has also been reported to be a related factor in the arthritis associated with pancreatitis, and in the development of avascular necrosis of the femoral head. The term necrosis indicates death, and when applied to bone denotes dead bone. Avascular necrosis is thought to occur as a consequence of reduced vascular supply. Assuming that alcoholics will be found in the arthritic population in the same proportion as in the general population, one can calculate that in the U.S. there are at least 600,000 persons with RA and 2 to 3 million persons with other types of arthritis who abuse alcohol. One can argue that pain, isolation, and depression could more likely lead to the uncontrolled use of alcohol. This assumption was not supported by a 1985 study of hospitalized patients by Bradlow and Mowat in England who reported that men with osteoarthritis were more likely than those with RA to have been heavy drinkers at some time during their lives. It is a popular belief that patients with arthritis take alcohol for its pain-relieving effect. However, in this study a number of patients with RA felt that drinking alcohol made their joint pain *worse*, and that "alcohol and arthritis do not mix."

Inasmuch as heavy drinkers often consume nearly the same quantity of nonalcoholic calories as do nondrinkers, many arthritics who abuse alcohol are obese. Alcohol abuse in combination with poverty and social isolation can be the background for numerous nutritional deficiencies. The many effects of alcohol abuse have serious consequences on the function of the liver and the central nervous system. Protein depletion, low levels of blood sugar, malabsorption of carbohydrates, proteins, and other nutrients, anemia, and deficiency of several vitamins and minerals are well known consequences of the chronic abuse of alcohol. Research has shown that chronic alcoholics have an increased susceptibility to infection because the immune function is compromised.

Alcohol is known to affect the gastrointestinal (GI) tract, making these patients more susceptible to the adverse effects of NSAIDs, such as gastritis, peptic ulcers, and GI bleeding. There is little doubt that patients with arthritis who abuse alcohol are not serious in their efforts to fight their disease.

Weight loss is a common occurrence during the course of some types of arthritis, such as active rheumatoid arthritis. This is always a very important reason to consult your doctor, especially if you have not kept regular appointments. There are many reasons for poor dietary intake, including lack of appetite, nausea and vomiting, food aversions, changes in taste and smell, socioeconomic problems, lack of information about proper nutrition, and adherence to fad diets. Loss of appetite is common in the severely disabled arthritic patient leading to emaciation[2] and further deterioration of joint function due to loss of muscle mass and strength. Although weight loss may be caused by a concurrent medical condition unrelated to rheumatoid arthritis, it can also be due to the continuous activity of the disease. When, in addition to loss of appetite, a patient has abdominal distress and nausea or vomiting, the possibility that these symptoms may be drug induced is very high. Many patients with RA and other connective tissue diseases also have Sjögren's syndrome.[3] Dry mouth, one of its consequences, decreases mouth sensation and palatability of food during eating. A pureed diet, moist foods, and abundant liquids at mealtime may partially relieve the dry mouth. Arthritic involvement of multiple joints is a major cause of impairment of the ability of the individual to feed himself. Severely incapacitated patients with mutilating hand deformities, particularly when the shoulders and elbows are involved, frequently have nutritional problems. The decrease in the motion and the pain may produce awkwardness or enough inconvenience to restrict food intake. All patients are able to buy some food, but many are not able to purchase high-quality nutritious food. Instead, they must subsist on diets loaded with cheap calories, which may provide inadequate protein, and negligible amounts of fresh vegetables and fruits.

Before embarking on an extensive investigation to discover the cause of the weight loss, the arthritic patient should pay attention to the act of eating. Does chewing cause pain in the jaw just below the ears? Discomfort in this area can be due to inflammation of the small joints connecting the lower jaw with the temporal bone, which may be affected in rheumatic conditions (see Fig. 8-1). Has the arthritic lost some or all of his teeth? Does he wear dentures? The fact may be noted that the patient either has no teeth or that his dentures do not fit properly. On ques-

---

[2]Extreme loss of fat and muscle bulk which occurs whenever caloric requirements exceed the daily intake for a prolonged period.
[3]These patients usually have dry mouth and dry eyes.

tioning, it may become evident that he does not use his dentures to eat because they produce pain. Some patients may not be able to afford new dentures and may adopt a diet consisting of liquid or semiliquid foods which do not require the use of dentures. Usually, these diets are predominantly high in sugar and low in protein foods, with very few vitamins and no fiber. Dental cavities and gum problems can also make the afflicted individual omit foods that require chewing. If you have no teeth and your dentures have an improper or painful fit, you should consult a dentist and bring the problem to the attention of your doctor so that dietary adjustments can be made. Unfortunately, socioeconomic problems often put the arthritic at a real disadvantage, because proper dental care is not accessible to everyone.

The positive note is that many arthritics who eat poorly could readily afford a nutritious balanced diet if they set the right priorities. Money usually spent on tobacco and alcohol could be immediately diverted to buy high-quality food. Substantial savings can be made by purchasing the right foods, diminishing the content of sugar, refined carbohydrates, and fat, and by avoiding alcohol which only adds expense and provides empty calories of little nutritional value. The reduced earning power of the aged is compounded in the arthritic patient who has often lost his job many years before. Even though they may be well-educated and highly motivated, many patients may not be able to afford a balanced diet with abundant fresh vegetables and fruit. However, ignorance can contribute to making the diet more expensive. Indeed, ignorance rather than poverty may also be responsible for the individual having chosen the wrong priorities and consequently having adopted an inadequate diet. The following are risk factors which, when present in the elderly arthritic, strongly suggest that dietary abnormalities may exist: low income, living alone, crippling deformities of the upper limbs, inability to walk, physical inactivity, poor dental status, and low, high, or fluctuating body weight.

Recent nutritional assessments of patients with rheumatoid arthritis have suggested that the severity of the disease adversely affects the nutritional status. Painful deformities of the lower extremities make walking difficult or impossible. Access to the supermarket and food selection may become a real ordeal. Patients may be dependent upon the help of members of their families or friends for grocery shopping and meal preparation. However, orthopedic correction of some of the deformities, aids in ambulation, metatarsal bars, foam-rubber heel pads, therapeutic exercise, and other modalities of physical therapy can be successful in restoring function. Government and private insurance may cover some of the cost incurred in arranging assistance with meal preparation, if such resources are ordered by the physician. Disability resulting from arthritis and the limited independence brought about by destructive involvement of the joints of the lower limbs can also impede the process of bringing food to the table. The hand deformities may cause cooking to be a chore, making it difficult, painful, and sometimes even impossible to prepare nutritional meals.

Anti-inflammatory treatment and injections of steroids into the joints which reduce inflammation, warm paraffin baths for the hands, which may relieve stiffness and allow more mobility, the use of flexible canvas splints for the wrists, or the timely application of corrective surgical procedures may restore the function of the arthritic hand. In this way, improvement in function as a result of comprehensive treatment of arthritis may have a beneficial effect on the nutritional status of the individual. In the late stage of the disease when there is extensive destruction of the joints and little inflammation, the functional ability still can be considerably improved through retraining the arthritic patient in cooking techniques with the use of special tools and utensils devised by occupational therapists who specialize in activities of daily living.

Adequate nutrition can assure more energy, and can improve your body defenses. It can also help you to maintain an ideal weight, support the needs of your body in terms of bone and muscle mass and, in general, enable you to better function as a human being. The addition of a program of physical fitness to adequate nutrition will increase your endurance and respiratory capacity and the improved muscle mass and strength will make your joints more stable. The possibility of a more healthful life is more likely with adherence to sound nutritional principles and a lifelong program of physical fitness. These changes carry with them the potential to improve your economic status, which often can be translated into a better self-image, improved family relationships, and a happier life.

Nutritional rehabilitation of undernourished patients calls for multiple measures, including a balanced diet with adequate protein, fat, and carbohydrate intake, and calcium supplementation. It is wise for most debilitated and older patients to supplement their diets with a preparation that will provide an adequate daily requirement of vitamins and minerals. For patients whose intake of food has been markedly reduced over a long period of time, fats and dairy products should initially be restricted and gradually reintroduced. Rapid resumption of a normal diet may be complicated by cramping abdominal pain and distension. In addition, the treatment of the arthritis should be comprehensive, including a program of physical activity tailored to the needs and capabilities of the individual. In some cases there exists a basic socioeconomic problem preventing the patient from having access to existing potential solutions to his needs. Unfortunately, physicians or other members of the health team are seldom able to bring about a resolution of these problems. I would like to stress that the patient should exercise leadership and responsibility in his own treatment and that the cooperation of concerned family and friends is invaluable. Early retirement for a patient with RA usually means a low and progressively declining income. Control of arthritis pain and stiffness, prevention of deformities, adequate nutrition, and a fitness program may allow a patient to continue working, to be retrained in a new job, or to consider pursuing a new career. Vocational rehabilitation can be a possibility only for the fit and well-nourished individual. Neither patients nor physicians can wait until the much-needed modification of the social structure is brought about, but they must act with urgency to apply *existing* medical solutions to solve the patient's immediate medical problems.

Sedentary Life-Style and
Excessive Caloric Ingestion

History suggests that as a society becomes more prosperous, it becomes more sedentary, encouraging an excessive accumulation of body fat that results in obesity. Many studies have shown that patients with arthritis are usually physically inactive. Even if you are slim now, you should be concerned with the problem of dietary excess. You have enough problems dealing with the consequences of arthritis, let alone having to cope with obesity, which is often self-inflicted.

Obesity is the most common form of malnutrition in the U.S. In prosperous societies, obesity is primarily due to the abundance of food and overeating and to the sedentary life which is ingrained in the life-style of our time. Obesity in the arthritic is probably due to the same factors that are responsible for obesity in the general population.

Patients afflicted with any type of arthritis, at least when arthritis strikes, may not be different from other members of society in respect to dietary habits. The arthritic often adopts a more sedentary existence as a consequence of joint stiffness and pain. Although decreased physical activity is unlikely to be important as a cause of major weight gain in most obese subjects, a reduced level of physical activity can be a major contributing factor to obesity in the arthritic patient.

There is clear evidence that the proportional contribution of fat to our diet is excessive. Approximately 40% of the total calories in the American diet are derived from fat. When carbohydrates, protein, and fat are ingested in excess of energy demands, they are converted into fat. Essentially, obesity develops when more calories are consumed than are used.

One of the prevailing myths surrounding exercise is that it increases the appetite. On the contrary, a program of physical fitness may reduce the appetite, especially if the exercise is performed just before mealtime. Many overweight persons become discouraged when they learn how little weight loss they can expect from various types of exercise. Indeed, it is necessary to perform calisthenics for 22 hours to lose a single pound of fat. However, the energy cost of exercise should not be measured in terms of a single session. It has been calculated that the modest energy expenditure involved in playing golf 2 hours twice a week at an energy cost of 175 calories per hour could result in a loss of 10 pounds in one year. The slight weight loss to be expected from one session of exercise does not mean that it is unimportant to the obese patient, for exercise must be undertaken as a long-range program.

Obesity can reduce your life span and can aggravate common conditions. Experts regard obesity as mild-to-moderate when the weight is 10–30% above the desirable weight; severe, from 30–100%; and massive or morbid, when the weight is more than 100% above the desirable weight.

Life insurance studies have called attention to a considerable increase in the numbers of overweight people as the population advances in years. The significance of obesity as a health problem has been suggested by reports of an increased death rate in overweight persons from a variety of causes. It is well recognized that morbidly obese people die at younger ages than do non-obese people.

Why should you be concerned about the problem of obesity? Analysis of records during World War II suggested that the reduction in food supply was probably beneficial to the people's health. One can anticipate that weight reduction would be of similar benefit to obese patients with any type of arthritis.

Patients who are moderately obese have an increased likelihood of high blood pressure, diabetes mellitus, and elevated levels of blood cholesterol. Life expectancy of an obese person is decreased in the presence of these conditions. Information available on the relation of body weight to morbidity and mortality suggest that risk increases only when adiposity reaches more than 30% above ideal levels; and risk is clear in the morbidly obese. The consequences of overnutrition on the immune response in humans are presently being investigated.

That almost any organ of the body can be involved in patients with arthritis may be surprising to you. Arthritic patients may develop a variety of lung problems which, if not present from the onset of the disease, may very well develop later on. For example, rheumatoid arthritis may affect the lungs resulting in pleural effusions,[4] pulmonary nodules, or pulmonary fibrosis. Patients with systemic lupus erythematosus, ankylosing spondylitis, and other types of rheumatic diseases can develop severe lung involvement. Smokers may develop chronic obstructive lung disease unrelated to arthritis. A complicating lung disease in the obese arthritic should be strong motivation to attempt weight reduction, since the additional weight of excessive fat carried on the chest wall increases the effort needed to breathe. These patients often deny that overweight is a problem, but they huff and puff when they try to walk any distance or attempt to climb stairs, and may experience difficulty in breathing in the presence of respiratory infections.

The relationship between obesity and osteoarthritis is controversial. For example, Leach (1973) and colleagues suggested that obesity was related to the development of arthritic involvement in specific weight-bearing joints. Kellgren and colleagues (1963) observed an increase in osteoarthritis in the non-weight-bearing joints of obese individuals. However, Goldin and colleagues (1976) found very little evidence of osteoarthritis in patients with morbid obesity, suggesting that the obesity seen in patients with osteoarthritis may be secondary to the inactivity

---

[4]Fluid within the pleural spaces.

brought on by joint pain and limitation of motion. This and other studies have suggested that obesity per se may not be a factor in the development of osteoarthritis, but definitely aggravates its course.

Dietary Fats and the Arteries

The obese arthritic can undoubtedly benefit from restriction of fat in the diet. The importance of weight reduction to the weight-bearing joints should be obvious to you, but there are many other actual and potential benefits which you may obtain from a restriction of fat intake. Some obese people have a tendency to develop high blood pressure. Obesity is a serious risk factor in the development of heart disease and stroke.

The available information, well summarized by Stamler (1978), in general, supports the conclusion that the excessive consumption of fat affects the level of cholesterol in the blood and increases the long-term risk of death from coronary heart disease in middle-aged American men. These studies probably justify the recommendation to reduce the present level of fat content in the diet of the adult population of the United States. These studies point out the merit of a vegetarian diet and support the need for a change in the national diet. The pros and cons of this suggestion were thoroughly discussed by Blankenhorn (1985), indicating that the findings from recent studies add to the weight of evidence in favor of a change in the national diet toward the consumption of a greater proportion of vegetables. Recent findings also suggest that it is not simply the amount but also the type of fat in the diet that affects blood cholesterol and triglyceride levels. An increase in polyunsaturated fatty acids (PUFA) with a decrease in saturated fatty acids (SFA) in the diet has been shown to have beneficial effects on blood lipids. Also, a diet with a high amount of fish oil rich in omega-3 fatty acids can decrease the stickiness of platelets and might be helpful in preventing their clumping together to form blood clots.

The American Heart Association's statement on "Risk Factors in Coronary Disease" lists high blood pressure, cigarette smoking, hyperlipidemia, diabetes, obesity, male sex, heredity, advancing age, certain personality traits, and a sedentary lifestyle. Many of these risk factors can be changed and, some, like diabetes, hyperlipidemia, and obesity, can be modified through the manipulation of diet. Severe obesity is associated with an increase in heart disease and mortality, due in part to high blood pressure and to coronary artery disease. The heart of an obese person must do extra work to help supply the needs of the excessive fatty tissue. Correction of obesity often results in decreased blood pressure and an improved tolerance of sugar. Weight reduction is a blessing that allows arthritics to take less or even no medication to treat hypertension or diabetes. These considerations, linking the ingestion of excessive fat and the quality of the fat intake with the increased likelihood of developing cardiovascular disease, particularly apply to patients with rheumatic diseases who are frequently overweight and have a sedentary existence.

Effects of Sedentary Habits on Muscle

Even patients who maintain a constant body weight for many years may still be excessively fat, although not overweight. This may occur in the sedentary arthritic patient, who has drastically reduced his level of physical activity. In this patient the muscle is replaced by fat. The consequence of weak muscles is a more rapid deterioration of joint function, resulting in joint instability. Decreased muscle mass and strength has its greatest impact on the hips, knees, ankles, and joints of the feet which are weight-bearing joints. Unstable joints often hurt, are stiff, and are more likely to be damaged by normal activities such as walking or standing.

Obese persons tend to be physically inactive. Overweight is an important mechanical factor operative in the deterioration of joint function. The stress from the extra weight on the weight-bearing joints only becomes obvious to the person when it limits his physical activity, causing discomfort that he can no longer deny, such as feet that hurt and swell, or pain and stiffness in his knees when he stands, or when he gets up after sitting for a long time.

An obese patient is not usually a good candidate for reconstructive joint surgery. For example, the obese arthritic must frequently be denied this possibility because of the increase in the likelihood of postoperative complications. Also, mechanical stress brought about by excessive weight severely compromises the long-term results of the joint surgery. Even if the surgery is performed, the likelihood of long-term success diminishes when the patient is overweight.

It has been observed that overweight persons are frequently accident-prone. This finding may be highly applicable to the obese arthritic patient who is stiff and has a decreased range of motion of the joints. A heavy body would undoubtedly create problems when moving or changing direction. It is frequently difficult for an arthritic to get out of a car or out of a chair, but if he is obese his problems are compounded because of his excess weight. His knees and legs are stressed even more when he attempts to get up and he often has to depend upon others to lift him.

In many countries it is usual for body weight to increase long after growth in body length is completed. Because of the tendency for people to be less physically active in our society, many patients with arthritis experience a gradual weight gain before the appearance of the initial joint symptoms. In an even larger proportion of patients, there is an accelerated weight gain after the beginning of arthritis, probably due to the restriction in physical activity imposed by joint pain and the progressing skeletal deformities. However, the continuous weight gain with age, characteristic of the population of the United States, is *not* inevitable, since there are countries in which the increment in weight with age is smaller or nonexistent. It appears that two of the main factors involved in obesity are greater economic affluence, and physical inactivity secondary to a sedentary lifestyle. Although in affluent societies the poor seldom starve, they are often overweight because of the type of food within their means.

Body-weight changes in response to dietary recommendations show great variability among arthritics, partly because of differences in their compliance with prescribed programs of physical activity and partly because the truth about their dietary intake is not always easy to discover. With few exceptions, which undoubtedly would be recognized by your doctor, weight reduction is desirable in all obese individuals. Being overweight has negative psychological implications for the arthritic patient in that his self-image and social acceptance are both compromised. If not for strictly medical reasons, weight reduction should be accomplished to improve the general fitness, increase the employability, self-image, and social acceptability of the arthritic. A weight reduction program can be very helpful to patients with articular involvement of the hips, knees, ankles, feet, and to those with low back pain or those with varicose veins. I strongly advise that obese arthritic patients restrict caloric intake and reduce weight as prescribed by their doctors, nutritionists, or registered dietitians. Goals in the treatment of obesity are to achieve a weight within 15 percent of ideal body weight, to understand the nutritional principles necessary to develop a healthy dietary pattern, to prevent loss of muscle mass, and to maintain muscle tone by a fitness program during the weight-reduction period and, most importantly, to achieve long-term maintenance of weight loss.

Dangers of Drastic Weight Reduction

Obese arthritics are usually recommended a conservative treatment consisting of moderate restriction of caloric intake to no more than 40% of the usual dietary intake, with the restriction of total fat to about 20–30% or less of the caloric intake, and an increase of polyunsaturated fat with a corresponding decrease of saturated fat in the diet. The rapid weight loss often noted during the initial period of a calorie-restricted diet is mostly due to loss of water. Thereafter, patients should not become discouraged when the rate of weight loss is reduced. Behavioral modifications of eating habits and an exercise program are considered essential for long-term success. In this way, compliance is encouraged and weight loss is gradual. However, some obese individuals elect not to follow this conservative treatment but would rather embrace heroic reducing programs.

Because control of obesity is one of the chief measures available for the control of artherosclerotic heart disease, very low calorie diets have become big business. They were initiated in the mid 1960s for the purpose of producing rapid weight loss while preserving lean body mass. This approach attempted to provide a basal amount of calories, yet preserve body protein. It was expected that the resultant weight loss could be primarily derived from excess body fat and that lean body mass and body proteins could be spared. People following these diets can achieve substantial weight loss; but prolonged starvation may cause weakness, vitamin and mineral deficiencies, renal stones, and protein loss. Deficiency of vitamins and minerals can be prevented by supplementation during the period of fasting. In order to prevent loss of muscle mass, the addition of a small amount of high-quality protein was recommended during the fast.

The "Last Chance" diet and other very low calorie liquid protein diets became popular, and have been occasionally followed by obese arthritic patients. You should know that some deaths due to cardiac arrhythmias have been reported in patients subjected to very drastic weight loss. The Center for Disease Control reported that about 100,000 Americans used liquid protein diets during 1977. In that same year the FDA reported on 15 women who suddenly died as a consequence of cardiac arrhythmias while following these diets. This method was said to result in weight loss while preserving lean body mass by providing 1.5 grams of protein per kilogram of ideal body weight. Unfortunately, it has been shown that during rapid weight-loss regimens, loss of lean body mass can occur, and can involve critical organs such as the heart. These diets may lead to the depletion of body protein including cardiac protein, which may be responsible for alterations in the function of the heart. Current information suggests that obese persons who undertake unsupervised drastic weight-reduction programs are at increased risk from arrhythmic sudden death. At present, very low calorie formula diets containing high-quality protein and including vitamins and mineral supplements appear to be safer than the commercial liquid-protein diets. However, potentially serious hazards exist with all very low calorie diets, if they are used without medical supervision. It has also been reported that the long-term results of total starvation diets are poor. Within one year after the fast, about 80% of the patients have returned to their former weight or have even exceeded it.

The dangers of a fad diet are dependent upon the degree of nutritional imbalance and the length of time the diet is followed. For a brief period, many obese individuals may follow the majority of weight-reduction fad diets relatively safely and achieve weight reduction. The main problem with fad diets is that they do not promote the improved nutritional habits necessary for maintenance of weight reduction once the fad diet loses its appeal.

Behavioral modification, nutritional education with necessary dietary changes, support and encouragement from weight-reduction groups, and exercise programs have been used with moderate success in the treatment of obesity. In spite of the various avenues open to the individual, including patient understanding of the need for dietary treatment, poor compliance to dietary recommendations is almost the norm.

After weight-reduction goals have been agreed upon, supervised diet programs using special preparations can be very helpful; but for the obese individual overeating is not a transient problem. Weight loss can be considered successful only if the person can maintain his optimal weight over time, and this requires a substantial modification of life-style and a lifelong awareness of nutritional priorities.

Motivation—The Driving Force to Success

Although other factors may be involved, overeating is the cause of obesity in most individuals. Yet, even though there are those who do understand and want to change their habits, they may experience considerable difficulty in following through with their intentions. Consistency is not a universal human virtue, and to successfully lose weight, it is essential to change specific behaviors related to food consumption.

There is nothing magic about motivation, the ingredient necessary for the obese arthritic to succeed in his struggle to lose weight. There are many ways by which an overweight person who contemplates a program of weight loss may become motivated. Perhaps for years, even before he developed arthritis, he was told by his physician that he should weigh less. He probably was given the standard recommendation—"push yourself away from the table"—and not once, but many times was sent home by a physician with his list of "thou shalt not eat." He probably lost some weight, went back to his old eating habits, and regained that which he had lost—and a little bit more. He probably had this experience many times over a period of years.

Your doctor may strongly advise you to lose weight. Motivation can be heavily dependent upon your relationship with your physician. Although motivation is extremely important, it is not enough in itself. Patient education and encouragement as well as the relationship between the patient and the therapist are more important to success than are specific dietary constituents. Without a comprehensive program one cannot expect that a person who has been eating an inordinate amount of calories for many years will suddenly cut down to 1,000 calories per day. If he tries, he soon feels hostile and deprived, and noncompliance ensues. Compliance can be related to your perception of the image of your physician as a model for weight-loss behavior. You have to understand that the efforts of your doctor to help you with your weight problem do not mean he is rejecting you as a person. If your attitude toward the physician is negative, the attempt at weight-loss is doomed. So too is it jeopardized if you perceive a stereotyped attitude in your physician toward the problem of obesity. Assuming that your doctor will not accept you because of your overweight appearance can provide an excuse for not trying. A passive personality is frequently a prediction of failure—even among the highly educated.

The obese arthritic not only needs the support of the doctor but also that of his family. A good example is that of the obese young girl with juvenile rheumatoid arthritis and inflammation of the knees or hips threatening to rapidly destroy these joints unless she achieves substantial weight reduction. The grossly overweight mother sitting next to her in the waiting room suggests that the child has very little chance to succeed, for that was the way the family ate. Obesity in this case becomes a family problem, because to help the child, the whole family must modify its habits.

We are often proud of our intelligence and physical appearance. We like to look good. Many of us engage in interpersonal relationships which open to us the entire range of bittersweet human emotions, because other persons are important in our lives. We all have some ambition or a goal in life. For each of us the individual goal is probably different, but to reach that goal we are all dependent upon our capability to successfully perform certain tasks. Although that which you call happiness is heavily dependent upon these processes, you take them for granted when you are healthy. You also take for granted the many blessings which are dependent upon your health, because they seem so simple and commonplace. When you were healthy you could walk, move, eat, sleep, and function in life. When you woke up in the morning after a good night's sleep you felt refreshed, and you never thought much about pain and stiffness. You seemed to believe that this is something that may happen to others, but certainly not to you, so you were not concerned. The maintenance or preservation of your health appeared to be one of the lesser motivational factors in beginning a weight-loss program, probably because you did not believe you would ever become ill—at least not from eating. The situation may change drastically if you develop a stroke or a heart attack, or if you have to deal with a chronic disease like arthritis.

When the arthritic process has involved the knees, hips, and feet, walking becomes difficult and the discomfort is increased by obesity. When the arthritic wakes up in the morning he is usually stiff and sore all over. The obese arthritic patient is clumsy and moves slowly. He is dependent upon his environment and increasingly needs attention, loses jobs, looks unattractive, and his personal relationships are strained to the limit. One could surmise that a glance at his past and present way of life could reveal a great contrast in life-style. Many things that he previously took for granted may now take on greater meaning, especially if they no longer appear to be attainable. He wishes he could regain some of the ground he lost as his disease progressed. After he becomes ill he finds that his weight problem is aggravated by his sedentary existence and, as his physical problems worsen, for the first time he begins to take seriously the recommendation of his doctor that he must lose weight.

Diets are not among the things a patient most looks forward to in life. Actually, the decision to begin a diet is one of the minor choices by far that he must make. To the obese person, diet means deprivation which has the power to elicit a vast storehouse of embedded impulses from childhood conditioning. Because of these factors hiding in the back of his mind, food may make him feel better when he's hurt, angry, frustrated, lonely or bored, pep him up when he is tired, and give him something to do when he socializes. Food is charged with his childhood emotional baggage of which he may not be aware, and one of the most important things he must learn is how to distinguish between actual physical hunger and changes in appetite brought about by his changing emotional states. He must become aware of when he eats, where he eats, why he eats (not always out of physical necessity), and what the real feelings are with which he is trying to cope that mask as hunger. Education is essential if weight loss is to be achieved. The obese arthritic must realize that he used to eat not only because he was hungry but also because he was sad, angry, bored, lonely, or just because the food was there. If he admits to himself that he eats for reasons other than physical hunger, he may consciously organize his life around things other than food. There are frequently overlooked emotional aspects to obesity that probably account for a large proportion of noncompliance. To lose weight and keep it off, the person must learn to love himself, for in many cases overeating to the point of gross obesity is related to poor self-esteem. Feelings of guilt or inadequacy, perceived loss of identity related to interpersonal relationships, pressure derived from professional life, or change in social or economic status must be recognized and dealt with.

There are a number of support groups to help individuals who are attempting to lose weight. While attending these groups many people have experienced considerable weight loss. However, one of the characteristics common to some of these organizations is a constant preoccupation with food. If one follows the program, a large portion of one's day is spent planning meals, shopping for food needed for those meals, trading recipes, planning for the next day's meals, between-meal and before-bedtime snacks, and talking about food with other obese people. Unfortunately, once they cease to attend the groups, the majority of them tend to regain their lost weight.

Obese arthritic patients should ask themselves why they cannot keep their weight off. Some individuals are perpetually on a "diet." Many do not follow a program that will lead to weight loss, even though they will assure you that they do, and very few learn to eat a healthful balanced diet, not excessive in calories, when the weight reduction program is completed.

The task is difficult, because old habits die very slowly. Food is not only necessary to sustain life, but it is also a primary reinforcer to encourage a behavior. Food traditionally has been given to animals or humans as a reward for compliance. In his attempt to curb his eating habits, the obese person could be tremendously helped by finding another reinforcer to take the place of the food he is giving up, which would be just as strong or stronger than the satisfaction he has been receiving from food. He must be reeducated in the value of nutrition for his health; but this alone is seldom enough. Even though he may verbalize the will to be healthy, if he fails to discover what that reinforcer is for him, he will regress to the habit of eating to satisfy his emotional rather than his physical need. If he succeeds in discovering this reinforcer, which will probably differ for each person, he will lose weight and will have a good chance to maintain weight loss.

CHAPTER 8

NUTRITION AND YOUR BONES AND TEETH

You can minimize or retard bone decay. Osteoporosis is a reduction in the amount of bone without changes in the mineral content. Osteoporosis often affects patients with arthritis, primarily women after menopause. Healthy bones are essential for everyone, but are even more important for the arthritic patient. Bone is hard, but not inert, since it is continuously being broken down and rebuilt. The support that bone provides to cartilage[1] in the joints is critical to the integrity of weight-bearing joints, such as those of the hips, knees, ankles, and the spine. The osteoporotic bone is fragile and can easily break. If you have osteoporosis, the vertebral bodies of your spine can break without a noticeable injury. If you have arthritic pain,

[1]Firm, nonvascular connective tissue coating the bone ends in the joints.

bone fractures can be an additional source of pain which may make your life more difficult. The severe pain and swelling produced by a stress fracture of a bone adjacent to a joint may be mistaken for joint inflammation. A stress fracture can be suspected when pain and swelling suddenly appear in a patient who has destructive arthritis with no evidence of active inflammation in other joints. Healthy bones are also essential for the patient who faces the possibility of reconstructive surgery of the joints. All types of surgical solutions to destroyed joints rely on an adequate bone support.

Most patients with active inflammatory types of arthritis usually develop osteoporosis localized to the bone ends around the inflamed joints. Many patients with destructive arthritis and severe deformities develop diffuse osteoporosis of the entire skeleton. A sedentary life or immobilization as a consequence of chronic diseases promote bone loss. As a rule, patients with greater impairment of joint function and arthritis of longer duration experience a greater loss of bone mass. Treatment with corticosteroids, a relatively older age, a sedentary life, and the postmenopausal state in women are recognized factors potentiating or aggravating this generalized osteoporosis. Osteoporosis occurs earlier in young women if their ovaries have been removed, suggesting a role of sex hormones in this process. Multiple studies indicate that long-term treatment with corticosteroids accelerates osteoporosis. Even relatively low doses of corticosteroids block new bone formation and calcium absorption and increase calcium excretion. You should consciously work with your physician toward preventing steroid-induced osteoporosis. In predisposed patients, the careful administration of vitamin D, estrogens in postmenopausal women, increased calcium intake, and a program of physical activity can prevent or minimize the effects of osteoporosis. Many patients are reluctant to decrease or discontinue the use of cortisone derivatives because they become dependent on these drugs for relief of their symptoms. It is in your best interest to cooperate with your doctor when he attempts to wean you off corticosteroids. Self-treatment of arthritis, often with the generous use of steroids and without medical supervision, can be very dangerous.

There is some evidence that other dietary factors, such as excessive ingestion of protein, caffeine, and alcohol also promote bone loss. When osteoporosis is seen in young men, it is almost always associated with the abuse of alcohol. An additional factor which enhances calcium loss and bone resorption is the frequent use of aluminum-containing antacids.

An important but frequently neglected factor in the prevention of osteoporosis is dietary calcium. Calcium is the most abundant mineral in the body, 99% of which is in bone and teeth. In addition to its major function in building and maintaining bone and teeth, calcium is also required in the process of muscle contraction, blood clotting, neuromuscular transmission, and in the regulation of heartbeat.

Dietary surveys indicate that many diets do not meet the recommended dietary allowance for calcium. Long-term dietary deficiency is probably one of the factors responsible for the high incidence of osteoporosis in the general population. The healthy aged should have at least the equivalent calcium requirement to that of younger adults, if not more, because of decreased absorption. The frequent occurrence of osteoporosis in many elderly persons indicates the need for an even greater dietary intake of calcium within that population.

Milk and dairy products are the best source of dietary calcium. Eight ounces of whole or nonfat milk supply about 300 milligrams of calcium. Sardines, kale, turnip greens, and broccoli are recognized sources of dietary calcium. Although many vegetables contain a considerable amount of calcium, it may not be available for absorption. It is difficult to meet the RDA for calcium with a diet without milk or milk products. Calcium is absorbed through the intestines by a mechanism which is dependent upon vitamin D. The calcium from some vegetables such as rhubarb, spinach, chard, and beet greens is not readily available for absorption.[2] Substances,[3] principally found in the outer husk of cereal grains, especially oatmeal, combine with calcium, preventing its absorption. There is some evidence that fiber itself may decrease calcium absorption from the small intestine. These are good reasons for not taking calcium supplements at breakfast time but rather at night, far-spaced from consumption of fiber-containing foods.

Although the RDA for calcium is 800 milligrams, it is recognized that a somewhat higher intake may be necessary to maintain adequate calcification of the bones in elderly individuals, particularly in postmenopausal women. For the preservation of bone integrity and calcification, it is essential to establish an adequate nutritional status. Adequate calcium intake is especially important for women approaching the fifth decade, as well as during the subsequent years of life. This goal can be accomplished with a calcium intake between 1.0 and 1.5 grams per day. Since most dairy products have a high fat content, the amount of whole milk and cheese needed to meet the increased calcium requirements of these patients would be undesirable if obesity were present. For those who must be concerned about their weight, skim milk, nonfat dry milk, or low-fat yogurt may be more appropriate.

The ingestion of lactose, the principal carbohydrate of milk, can produce abdominal cramps, bloating or distension of the abdomen, and diarrhea, when lactase, the enzyme necessary to digest lactose, is deficient. Milk intolerance due to lactase deficiency is observed in 5–15% of the adult white population, and in 80–90% of black Americans and Orientals. The vast majority of lactose-intolerant patients are aware that they are milk intolerant and avoid milk. A daily oral calcium supplement of 1000 milligrams is a reasonable alternative when ingestion of milk and dairy products is insufficient or undesirable. There is evidence to suggest that osteoporosis can be prevented to some extent, or retarded by augmenting calcium intake. To what ex-

[2]Calcium oxalate is insoluble and is not absorbed.
[3]Phytic acid forms calcium phytate.

tent osteoporosis can be prevented by such long-term calcium supplementation is uncertain, but some benefit is highly probable and there is no known associated risk. However, the unsupervised and indiscriminate supplementation of calcium is not advisable, because an excess of calcium can generate problems in some persons, for example those who have or are predisposed to developing renal stones. However, there is no adequate evidence that high calcium intake per se is a primary causal factor in a number of conditions associated with excessively high levels of calcium in the blood and urine or in deposits of calcium in the kidneys and soft tissues. If the blood and urine calcium levels are normal, calcium supplementation appears to be safe.

In contrast to the small portion of dietary calcium absorbed from the intestine, the absorption of phosphorus is remarkably efficient. Adequate amounts of phosphorus can be obtained from cheese, egg yolk, milk, meat, fish, poultry, whole grain cereals, legumes, and nuts. If your dietary intake of protein and calcium is adequate, you should not be concerned about the phosphorus in your diet. However—of interest to patients with arthritis—there is an increased need for phosphorus during prolonged treatment with aluminum-containing antacids taken to obtain relief from gastrointestinal side effects of NSAIDs. Persistent low levels of phosphate in the blood may cause loss of appetite, osteoporosis, bone pain, and muscle weakness. Low phosphate levels due to deficient intestinal absorption does not usually occur unless excessive amounts of nonabsorbable antacids are consumed; the antacids bind the phosphorus and prevent its absorption through the intestine.

Normal metabolism of calcium is dependent upon the presence of adequate amounts of vitamin D. Calcium deficiency in adults may produce osteomalacia, resulting in a reduction in the mineral content of the bone. It seems that some elderly people with osteoporosis may also have osteomalacia, presumably representing vitamin D deficiency. Although osteomalacia can occur in patients with rheumatoid arthritis, particularly in areas of the world with reduced exposure to sunlight, it does not appear to be a common complication in the U. S. With adequate exposure to the sun, vitamin D supplements are unnecessary. When the sun is seldom seen, as in cloudy climates, particularly combined with smog, vitamin D becomes a required supplement in the diet.

The presentation of osteomalacia in adults may not be as dramatic as it is in children and it may be overlooked in a patient with chronic arthritis. Low back and hip pain and muscle weakness may produce a waddling gait. Osteomalacia in the elderly may be responsible for vague bone achiness and muscle weakness. When present in patients with rheumatoid arthritis, these symptoms may be confused with those due to an increase in the activity of the disease. Even if the climate provides adequate sunlight, the patient with severe arthritis may not have access to it due to difficulty in ambulation, or because of being bedridden or confined to a nursing home.

Treatment of generalized osteoporosis has often been disappointing. There is currently no acceptable mode of therapy that safely stimulates bone formation. However, it is possible to retard the rate of bone loss in the elderly and in postmenopausal women by suppressing bone resorption. Prevention is a more useful approach. Women who smoke have an earlier menopause than those who do not, presumably because of an effect of smoking on the circulating estrogen levels. It has been suggested that cigarette smoking promotes bone loss after menopause. This is an additional reason for you to quit smoking. A woman of menopausal age should raise the question of estrogen replacement with her physician, since long-term estrogen replacement is the most effective measure for significant protection against bone loss and fractures in postmenopausal women. The closer the beginning of estrogen replacement to the cessation of ovarian function, the more effective is the protective effect. Several studies have shown that the rate of bone loss can be retarded if women are treated with estrogens, especially if this treatment is begun within 3 years of menopause.

You should be aware that estrogen treatment is contraindicated in patients with estrogen-dependent breast cancer and in women with benign fibrocystic breast disease. Potential dangers of this treatment include an increased risk of uterus and breast cancer, a tendency to form blood clots, and high blood pressure. The danger of cardiovascular complications is decreased substantially in those women without additional risk factors such as smoking or obesity. The results of recent studies suggest that the risk of cancer of the uterus remains elevated for many years after cessation of long-term use of estrogens. The implication of these findings is that all women who have used estrogen for a year or more, and who have not had hysterectomies, should be under long-term gynecologic surveillance. A postmenopausal woman not taking estrogen has one chance in 1,000 per year of getting cancer of the lining of the uterus. A woman taking estrogen has 5 to 10 chances in 1,000 per year. It has been suggested that cyclic administration of low doses of estrogens, as usually given for the prevention of osteoporosis, carries less risk than continuous administration. Also, it is interesting to note that there is evidence to suggest that the use of oral contraceptives containing a combination of estrogens and progesterone may actually reduce the risk of cancer of the lining of the uterus. These potential risks to which postmenopausal women treated with estrogens are exposed should be weighed against the risks of *no* estrogen therapy; including severe osteoporosis and vertebral and hip fractures. Hip fractures have catastrophic consequences to the individual by curtailing her independence and life expectancy. It has been estimated that osteoporosis-related fractures cost nearly $6 billion per year in the U. S.

The concern about calcium intake should be accompanied by an equal preoccupation with increasing the level of physical activity, within the limitations imposed by arthritis, because a program of exercise stimulates bone formation. Women with destructive arthritis, who lead an extremely sedentary existence, are at risk of generalized osteoporosis. Attempts to minimize bone loss should be started years before menopause when the joint involvement does not limit physical activity. Preventive measures include regular exercise which moves bones against gravity. Walking is the best exercise available to most patients with arthritis that qualifies under this category.

Tooth Decay and Sugar Intake

The reason for talking to you about your teeth may not be immediately evident. You are probably so anxious to obtain help for your ailing joints that you may feel that talking about your teeth is superfluous. Although teeth and gums are not directly involved in any type of arthritis, there are important considerations linking them to nutrition and general health.

Malnutrition has a significant influence upon your teeth and, reciprocally, dental problems may affect your nutrition. There is evidence that the continual consumption of sugar-containing foods leads to tooth decay in susceptible persons. If you habitually chew gum or eat candy, foods high in natural sugars such as raisins, figs or dates, and other foods containing sugar between meals, more dental decay will occur than when you eat the same foods during regular meals. Evidence suggests that it is not the amount of sugar you consume, but the *frequency* of its ingestion that increases tooth decay. This is a significant factor in the formation of cavities, because teeth are exposed to acid derived from sugar for a greater length of time. Candies, sweet drinks, and sweetened fruit juices are especially a problem, because they contain sucrose, the common sugar that most frequently favors the development of dental cavities. More complex carbohydrates, such as starches,[4] cause fewer cavities and can be used advantageously in the diet in preference to sugar.

It is well known that bacteria must be present to cause the

[4]Such as those occurring in potatoes and other tubers or roots (tapioca) and cereal grains (wheat, rice, oats, corn).

destruction of tooth substance characteristic of tooth decay. The initial lesion is the dental plaque. Bacteria in the plaque break down sugars to form acids. Dental cavities will result from the transformation of sugars into acids which dissolve the minerals in tooth enamel. Tooth decay may progress to involve the dentine until it ultimately reaches the dental pulp and destroys the tooth. Bacteria in the mouth will not form as readily if you brush your teeth regularly after each meal.

One of the most important steps in the prevention of caries is the modification of the oral environment by restricting the use of foods high in natural sugar and candies. The elimination of undesirable snacks or eating items of low tooth-decay-producing potential, such as fresh fruit and vegetables can be helpful. Tooth decay does not develop when the food does not contain the necessary refined sugars to sustain the activities of the bacteria causing tooth decay. Changing the composition of the diet along with adequate dental hygiene can go a long way toward eliminating this problem. For instance, cereal grains as a source of carbohydrates do not encourage the activity of microorganisms that produce dental caries and can be substituted in the diet for sugar. To preserve dental health, it is best to have three main meals in which as many of the foods as possible are consumed in their natural state without being excessively refined. It is also advisable to include foods in the diet which require vigorous chewing rather than to rely upon soft foods, liquid, or semiliquid food mixtures which do not stimulate the various tissues and organs involved in the processing of foods in the mouth. If for some reason, sticky, adherent, high sugar-containing foods are included in the diet, dental cleansing should be very thorough. Genetic factors and faulty oral hygiene both play a major role in predisposing the individual to dental decay. The formation of caries and the extent of tooth destruction are also influenced by the frequency of eating, the habit of snacking, and the fluoride content of the available drinking water. Snacking is a widespread habit that should be avoided if possible.

The preservation of your teeth is also dependent upon your desire or your ability to obtain professional dental care. The dental plaque adheres to the tooth surface and can be detached only by mechanical cleansing such as tooth brushing or dental flossing.

Good nutrition is fundamental to the development of sound teeth. In children, proper nutrition with adequate complements of vitamin D, calcium, phosphorus, and fluoride must be present to insure proper development. Fluoridated toothpaste can be helpful in the adult. Dental education and dental cleansing leading to the prevention of tooth decay is very important for all patients with arthritis.

Mouth Pain and Nutrition

Any condition producing pain in your mouth may affect your nutrition. Pain or stiffness due to arthritis of the temporo-mandibular (TM) joint is relatively common in adult and juvenile rheumatoid arthritis. These joints unite the temporal bones and the lower moving part of the jaw (Fig. 8-1). We use this joint hundreds of times each day as we speak or eat. Abnormalities in closing the mouth, thinning of the jawbone, difficulty in opening the mouth and even in eating may occur as consequences of TM joint involvement. An overbite occurring as a consequence of erosions in the TM joint may be an annoying problem and chewing can be painful.

Pain in the face, jaw, or ear, initially thought to be due to dental problems, may not be due to arthritis but rather to abnormal function of the TM joint. In these cases, pain may be intermittent and localized to one side of the face. Tension, trauma, previous dislocation of the TM joints, dental manipulation involving the forceful opening of the mouth, prolonged courses of

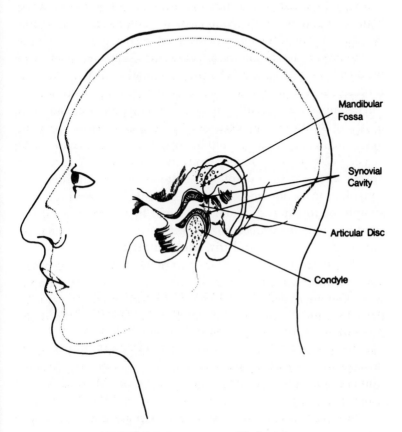

FIGURE 8-1. Temporomandibular joint.

cervical traction, compulsive gum chewing, habitual and pur-
poseless grinding of the teeth, dental malocclusion, loss of
teeth, and the use of ill-fitting dentures can all be found in the
history of patients with TM joint pain. The pain may be aggravated by spasm of the muscles involved in chewing, causing the
face to be very tender on the affected side. Reflex muscle spasm
produced by a trigger mechanism originating in the TM joint
produces severe pain. If it is properly recognized, this condition
can usually be successfully treated. Although malocclusion and
ill-fitting dentures may occasionally be the cause of TM joint
pain, and in some cases should be corrected, patients may waste
considerable time and money in involved dental procedures that
do not alleviate the symptoms. Self-medication and delay in
consultation is not uncommon in patients who attribute the
symptoms to ear and dental problems. In severe cases, if the
condition remains unrecognized or untreated, nutrition may be
impaired.

Reassurance—an important part of the treatment—is based
upon communicating the precise diagnosis to the patient and,
when known, explaining the causes of the abnormal function of
the joint and the mechanism of the production of the pain.
Appropriate treatment to relieve anxiety and tension is essential. Anger and frustration must be recognized and worked
through in order to help the patient understand that these unre-
solved feelings are major contributors to muscle spasm and
consequent pain.

In some forms of juvenile rheumatoid arthritis, severe involvement of the TM joint, with pain and restriction of motion
very early in life, may impair the normal development of the jaw.
Eventually, in most children, the pain and disability produced
by inflammation of the TM joint is controlled by treatment, or
the symptoms may even disappear if the disease goes into remission. However, some patients may be left with a small, dis-
figuring jaw, and may have impaired ability to open their
mouths, increased overbite, crowded teeth, and altered jaw
function. These problems can be successfully treated by orth-

odontic procedures and jaw surgery which make possible the correction of the dental and chewing abnormalities and may improve facial appearance.

The development of mouth ulcers in a patient with arthritis requires urgent attention if significant weight loss and deterioration of health are to be avoided. Although mouth ulcers can be a feature of some types of arthritis such as Behçet's disease, lupus erythematosus, the arthritis of inflammatory bowel disease, and Reiter's syndrome, they can also be the side effects of some common medicines used to treat arthritis like gold, sulfasalazine, or penicillamine.

Jawbone Loss, Receding Gums, and Tooth Loss

After the third or fourth decade of life, bone resorption predominates. As a person ages, his "normal" bone loss in the jawbone leads to decreased tooth support, loosening of the roots, and ultimately to the loss of teeth. Abnormalities of the gums, bone, and other supporting structures of the teeth are very common among the elderly, and major causes of the loss of teeth in adults.

The exercise needed by your jawbone to prevent osteoporosis is the chewing of solid and fibrous foods. It is likely that the habit of ingesting a liquid or semisolid diet which does not require chewing *is to your jawbone as a sedentary life is to your spine*. It is well known that lack of exercise is one of the main factors in spinal osteoporosis.

Inadequate ability to chew food increases with age and is very common in the older arthritic population. Frequently, a nutritional disorder arises as a consequence of the loss of teeth. Some time after the loss of teeth, the gums and mucous membranes of the mouth and lips shrink to some extent, so the wearing and fitting of dentures becomes difficult. Patients who have lost their teeth and who do not wear their dentures, either because of negligence or because they are unable to afford them, frequently have problems with chewing and consequently with digestion. As a result, they may prefer to eat liquid or soft foods.

The salivary glands are of considerable importance in the maintenance of healthy teeth. Debilitating conditions may alter the quality and quantity of saliva. In the condition known as Sjögren's[5] syndrome, which frequently coexists with rheumatoid arthritis and other connective tissue diseases, there is dryness of the mouth due to the involvement of the salivary glands. Because the saliva normally prevents the growth of bacteria, decreased production of saliva, or changes in its chemical composition may permit greater bacterial activity, encouraging the formation of dental cavities. Patients with Sjögren's syndrome frequently have early dental decay, and many of them eventually lose all their teeth.

Healthy teeth contribute to social acceptability and improve the self-concept of the arthritic patient who is constantly threatened by physical problems inflicted upon him by the disease. In the absence of teeth, the skin around the mouth sinks, and the facial features are usually altered, causing them to look different, older, and unattractive, thereby damaging their self-esteem.

Oral hygiene is very important for everyone, and particularly for those afflicted with a chronic disease such as any type of arthritis. For those individuals having restricted motion of their upper extremities with severe destructive lesions of the small joints of the hands, wrists, elbows, and shoulders, cleaning the teeth properly becomes a very difficult task. Consultation with the occupational therapist, who can modify toothbrush angle and handgrip, provide long handles, or substitute an electric toothbrush, may be of assistance to the patient. In extreme cases, the person who is caring for a debilitated patient must take the responsibility for the patient's personal

[5]Chronic autoimmune disease characterized by diminished lacrimal and salivary gland secretion leading to dry eyes and dry mouth.

hygiene. Regular dental checkups are a necessary component of the care of the arthritic patient and, if you are not under the care of a dentist, your physician should make the referral when it is appropriate. This will enable you to preserve your own teeth as long as possible. Should you lose your teeth, they should be replaced as soon as possible and dentures should fit well without eliciting discomfort during eating.

CHAPTER 9

THE RELATIONSHIP BETWEEN FOOD AND ARTHRITIS

Multiple studies have clearly suggested that nutrition plays an important role in the development of cancer, atherosclerosis, and the aging process as well as in immunity and infection. Similar information relating nutrition and arthritis has been sparse and contradictory.

Since the mid-twentieth century, any possible suggestion of a relationship between diet and arthritis was usually dismissed by the statement that thorough scientific investigation failed to reveal any such association. Although these statements appeared to be true when the classic studies were carried out, they cannot now be considered conclusive. In the light of new information obtained through research in nutrition since the 1960s, the issue of the relationship between nutrition and the rheumatic diseases is being reevaluated.

Not infrequently, arthritics expand their inquiry about nutrition and arthritis and accept the advice offered in popular books promising a "dietary cure." I believe that a report to the public on the role of nutrition in the treatment of the rheumatic diseases is long overdue.

Food Allergies

Many theoretical possibilities suggest that nutrition may be an important factor in the development of some of the rheumatic diseases and that dietary manipulation may have a role in their treatment.

The topic of food allergy is controversial. It has long been known that generally safe food substances can produce illness in susceptible individuals. Many food substances can cause allergic reactions in sensitive individuals. Although some symptoms can be attributed to food intolerance, the cause-to-effect relationship between certain foods and an adverse effect is frequently difficult to prove. Recent evidence supports the view that some components of ingested foodstuffs are capable of producing an allergic response in the skin and the lungs. These reactions are usually immediate and most frequently consist of asthma, hives, or both.

Other sites of allergic reactions to food are less convincingly established. However, a small number of observations linking food intake and rheumatic diseases have been reported. Allergy to sodium nitrate was thought to be responsible for attacks of palindromic rheumatism, and ingestion of black walnuts has been related to exacerbations of Behçet's syndrome. In spite of these provocative isolated reports, there is little objective information to support the popular belief that the majority of rheumatic diseases are caused by food allergy. Most rheumatologists have found an occasional patient who is unable to tolerate certain foods. When this is the case, the elimination of that food from the diet is reasonable. This intolerance for food is not usually related to the arthritis; therefore, omitting the food involved does not have an influence on its course, although the patient will feel better because symptoms produced by the offending food will be eliminated. Recently, the unusual occurrence of the exacerbation of pain and stiffness triggered by milk ingestion was described by Parke and Hughes (1981) in one patient with rheumatoid arthritis. It was reported that remission occurred following elimination of dairy products from the diet. Although in this case the omission of the offending agent was successful, this is rarely applicable to patients with rheumatoid arthritis. Carefully controlled observations by Panush (1984) have suggested that food can exacerbate symptoms in some patients with rheumatoid arthritis. These observations support the suggestion that individualized dietary manipulation may be beneficial for selected patients. The proportion of patients whose condition can be improved by this type of dietary manipulation is unknown.

Nutrition and the Immune Response

You should be aware of the evidence suggesting that immunological abnormalities are important in the development of much of the tissue damage found in the lesions of rheumatoid arthritis. An obvious link between nutrition and arthritis is the well-known effect nutrition has on immune responsiveness. Depression of the body defenses by nutritional deficiency could make patients more susceptible to infection. Although we do not know what agent or agents trigger the immunological abnormalities found in RA, the infectious cause reviewed by Phillips and Christian (1985), although not proven, continues to be discussed and investigated.

It has been demonstrated that dietary fatty acids can influence the immune system by governing the composition of the cell membrane of lymphocytes. Cellular behavior depends upon recognition of signals by receptors located on the cell membrane. It is possible that nutrition, by altering the structure of the cell membrane, may modify recognition phenomena which take place on the cell surface, with far-reaching effects on cell–cell interactions. A nutritionally "sick" cell could possibly explain cellular malfunction and a host of secondary immunological manifestations, including autoimmunity. Fatty acid intake could also influence the immune system by regulating the quantity and quality of important mediators of inflammation.[1]

Impressive experimental evidence, largely obtained in animals, has been collected, supporting the view that diet has an important effect on the course of autoimmune disease. These experiments are pertinent to the problem of arthritis and the rheumatic diseases in humans because of their profound immunological changes, including autoimmunity. Animal models of autoimmunity have been widely used to investigate the effect of different diets on the course of autoimmune disease. Extensive studies performed by Good (1984) and colleagues have shown that nutrition can have a profound influence on various processes vital to human survival. Nutritional changes associated with malnutrition, protein deficiency, reduced caloric intake, deficiency of zinc, and low-fat diets have all been shown to affect immunological responsiveness. Among the processes known to be affected by nutrition are aging, the propensity to develop tumors, and resistance to infection. Animal experimentation has amply demonstrated that dietary manipulation of fats or caloric intake can produce profound changes in the immune system. The mechanism by which diet may profoundly influence the immune system in animals remains to be determined, but these observations suggest the urgent need to investigate the relationship between nutrition and the rheumatic diseases. Although experimentation in humans is in its infancy, it is clearly conceivable that what you eat may modify your immune reaction.

[1]Prostaglandins and leukotrienes.

Fish Oil

Not only a high- or low-fat diet but also the composition of the fat ingested seems to bring up different responses in the immune system. Various proportions of essential fatty acids (EFA), different ratios of saturated and unsaturated fatty acids, and also fatty acids of nonmammalian origin have been used experimentally. Diets limited in EFA have been reported to improve arthritis and experimental inflammatory joint disease in animals.

EPA and DHA are the omega-3 fatty acids present in fish oil and marine mammals. EPA is present in large quantity in fish oil and found in high concentration in the diet of Eskimos. Omega-3 fatty acids have been recently brought to the attention of the public because the Eskimos have a low incidence of coronary heart disease. In the early 1970s it was proposed that the low incidence of coronary atherosclerosis and myocardial infarction in Greenland Eskimos might be related to their unique dietary habits. The fat of Greenland Eskimos had lower concentrations of linoleic acid and arachidonic[2] acid (AA) and higher concentrations of EPA. Major effects of these fatty acids include a reduction of circulating triglycerides and lipoproteins, reduction of the ability of platelets to promote blood clots, and retarded development of atherosclerosis. Omega-3 fatty acids also inhibit the formation of substances active in inflammation.[3] Ingestion of fish oil fatty acids also leads to the formation of derivatives with diminished biological activity which are less active in inflammation. Indeed, preliminary studies have reported that marine fatty acids have influence in reducing inflammation.

Dietary supplementation with EPA has a profound influence on the course of autoimmune disease in various animal

[2]EFA precursor of prostaglandins (PG) and leukotrienes (LT). The PG and LT formed from EPA are much less active in inflammation than those formed from AA.
[3]Prostaglandins and leukotrienes.

models. Improvement and marked prolongation of life was accomplished by Prickett and his colleagues (1983) in a mouse model of systemic lupus erythematosus by feeding a diet rich in EPA. Kelley and his colleagues (1985) showed that when a fatty acid component uniquely present in fish oil (Menhaden oil) was used as the exclusive source of fat, the onset of renal disease was delayed and the animals had prolonged survival in an experimental model of lupus in mice. These studies have opened the possibility that EPA may have some value in the treatment of some of the rheumatic diseases. Recently, Kremer and colleagues (1985) reported that a diet supplemented with EPA and low in saturated fat improved morning stiffness and decreased the number of tender joints in patients with rheumatoid arthritis. A controlled study performed by the same group of investigators reported that EPA supplementation to patients with RA improved fatigue and reduced the number of tender joints. It was recently reported by Sperling and colleagues that the addition of dietary fish oil to baseline treatment during 6 weeks produced significant decrease in the number of painful joints in patients with RA. It should be noted that although these differences are statistically significant, *all* patients still had considerable disease activity, and the improvement was generally mild.

It is important that you realize that the long-term effects of dietary manipulation leading to drastic changes in the quantity or quality of prostaglandins are not known. The complexity of the results from animal investigations and the chronic nature of the disease suggests that short-term experimentation in humans afflicted with rheumatoid arthritis is probably not adequate to determine whether dietary manipulation can make a significant contribution to its treatment. It is certain that the relative composition of the diet in terms of the proportion of unsaturated and saturated fatty acid and the absolute content of linoleic acid (LA), the precursor of arachidonic acid, as well as the presence of EPA in the diet, potentially can have an effect on autoimmunity in humans and on the chronic phase of rheumatoid inflammation. This line of investigation is being actively pursued. These effects of EPA have made headlines in major newspaper columns and many patients are already medicating themselves with large quantities of EPA. What the results of current research mean for the patient with various kinds of arthritis is difficult to determine. There are potential dangers in the abuse of EPA, and the long-term effects of large doses in particular are not known. For example, a recent study has shown that daily dietary supplementation with 5.4 grams of omega-3 fatty acids results in a rapid deterioration of carbohydrate metabolism in patients with type II (non-insulin-dependent) diabetes mellitus. It is also to be noted that some of the commercial preparations containing EPA also contain selenium, hawthorne berry, vitamin E, and other substances, the effects of which can be toxic if consumed in excess, or may produce unforeseen effects during long-term administration. In my opinion, it is reasonable at this time to eat more fish *in place of* other sources of protein and fat of animal origin, rather than engaging in massive *supplementation* with EPA. Quantities of EPA equivalent to those contained in a fish dinner can not be harmful and probably can be helpful. The unsupervised intake of large amounts of omega-3 fatty acids by arthritic persons having type II diabetes is not wise.

Morris Ziff (1983) has discussed the problems inherent in experimental studies of diet in rheumatoid arthritis. In spite of the difficulties encountered in proving a beneficial effect of diet, it is clearly possible that it may eventually prove to have a role in its treatment. Although it is still unreasonable to expect a cure, one can expect that dietary changes in the future could afford some of the relief of pain and stiffness now provided by NSAIDs. This would give patients and physicians another important option that would reduce the need for medication. It appears reasonable to investigate the possible role of diets with a reduced fat content and those that differ in fat composition in the treatment of human rheumatic diseases. The results from animal experimentation are extremely interesting and suggest new avenues for future intervention in humans, but they have

only modest applicability to man and to the treatment of the
rheumatic diseases at the present time.

Effects of Fasting and Low-Fat Diet

Intermittent fasting in one form or another has been advocated for years in the popular literature as one dietary approach
to "cure" RA, as well as a valuable way to treat arthritis in
general. Although fasting does not cure any type of arthritis,
the bodily changes occurring as a consequence of food deprivation are of considerable theoretical interest. Fasting has been
found to modify the function of cells[4] involved in the immune
reactions, to enhance the ability of white blood cells to kill bacteria, to increase the level of immunoglobulins, and to enhance
the general defenses of the individual. In fasting, the fat stores
of the body are mobilized due to the absence of ingested carbohydrates, leading to increased fatty acids and ketone bodies
in the blood. If fasting is prolonged, the production of new
protein essential to normal cellular function is disturbed, resulting in weight loss, decreased lean body mass, weakness, and
debilitation. For the arthritic patient, this means muscle atrophy, which leads to further deterioration of joint function.

In a controlled study, Sköldstam and colleagues (1979) demonstrated that fasting brings temporary relief to patients with
RA, reducing pain and stiffness. The reason why fasting tran-
sitorily relieves the symptoms of RA is not known, but the study
by Palmblad (1972) and colleagues reported that prolonged fasting in healthy young men leads to the reduction of serum substances[5] which are usually increased in any type of
inflammatory process. The effect of fasting is brief and this
approach is not justified for the treatment of any type of arthritis
because the gains are insignificant when they are put in the

[4]Lymphocytes and macrophages.
[5]Acute phase reactants.

context of the lifetime duration of the disease. However, it seems clear that the rationale for the transitory improvement observed with fasting is worth investigating, because it may contribute to our understanding of ways to control chronic inflammation.

The idea that a vegetarian diet is beneficial for patients with rheumatic diseases is widespread among patients. In the above-mentioned work of Sköldstam and colleagues, the fasting period was followed by a lactovegetarian diet. Under the conditions of the experiment there was no demonstrable beneficial effect. Their results did not eliminate the possibility that following a lactovegetarian diet over a longer time might prove beneficial. However, in a more recent study, Sköldstam (1986) clearly showed that although many patients with RA feel subjectively better, 4 months of a vegan diet, with exclusion of meat, fish, eggs, and dairy products, produced no significant suppression of rheumatoid inflammation.

The value of a low-fat diet was brought to the attention of the public by the report of Lucas and Powers in 1981. These authors used a low-fat diet in the treatment of 6 obese persons who had rheumatoid arthritis. This uncontrolled report indicated that a complete remission was induced by diet and, upon reintroducing fat into the diet, the exacerbation of symptoms within 24 to 48 hours was observed. The patients were obese and undoubtedly benefited from weight reduction. Because patients with RA may experience spontaneous remissions, a control series of patients comparable in all respects except for the diet could establish the value of a low-fat diet in the treatment of RA. This interesting hypothesis should be tested by including a large number of patients randomly assigned to the diet or to the control group, with strict rheumatological diagnostic and evaluative criteria and under double-blind conditions. Preferably, it should be a long-term study and avoid wide fluctuations in patient weight. Obviously, this would be a most difficult study to carry out.

The use of dietary manipulation in the treatment of rheumatic diseases, including caloric restriction, and changes in the proportion of protein and fat intake of both animal and vegetable origin, continues to be actively investigated. In general terms, the notion that dietary manipulation can cure any type of arthritis has not been proven; but it is likely that diet *may* prove valuable in the treatment of some types of arthritis.

The lack of present evidence establishing a "dietary cure" does not mean that nutrition is unimportant to the arthritic. Indeed, nutritional education and counseling are prominent and often neglected aspects of the treatment of patients with rheumatic diseases. Nutrition is important for patients with chronic rheumatic diseases—just as it is important for all living creatures.

CHAPTER 10

NUTRITIONAL COUNSELING FOR ARTHRITICS

The "ideal" diet does not exist, because the requirements for each individual differ. However, the fact must be accepted that self-selected mixed diets, along with improvements in hygiene and living conditions, have brought about significant gains in the life expectancy of mankind over the last two centuries.

The RDA provide a margin of safety sufficient to meet the needs of 90 to 95 percent of the healthy population. The requirements of essential and nonessential nutrients for some patients with arthritis differ in some respects from those of the general population. Your nutritional needs may be altered by disease. For example, fever, infection, or trauma will increase your caloric requirement. In order to recover, the daily requirements of an undernourished patient are greater than those necessary to maintain normal nutrition. These events are not uncommon

231

during the lifetime of many patients with the various types of chronic destructive arthritis.

You should be aware that the persistent deficiency of any essential nutrient may lead to illness; but in like manner the excessive intake may disturb body structure and function. There are several important examples of overnutrition pertinent to patients with arthritis. Probably the most common is obesity produced by an excess of calories.

There cannot be a general diet devised that would satisfy all nutritional requirements of all patients with arthritis. Age, sex, pregnancy, trauma, level of physical activity, intake of medication, or the presence of disease are among the many factors which cause individual dietary requirements to differ.

Access to water is vital for the debilitated patient. Water intake is usually not of concern to the majority of arthritics, except for those affected with very acute and destructive disease. Water intake must equal water loss that takes place through the urine, feces, respiration and, by evaporation, through the skin. When patients are unable to walk because of severe involvement of the weight-bearing joints, or because they are bedridden as a consequence of a complication of the disease, particularly in the aged, access to food and water is of major concern. In these cases dehydration may be an important factor in the rapid deterioration of body function experienced by patients as a result of damage produced by the disease.

Poverty, aging, and neglect are social factors which cannot be ignored in the progressive debilitation of some individuals. A cataclysmic event leading to hospitalization or death can be avoided in totally dependent patients by adequate dietary planning and by providing the necessary assistance at home.

Protein Requirements

Proteins are formed by a limited assortment of building blocks, the amino acids, which are essential for human life.

There is no substitute for protein in the diet as a direct or indirect source of amino acids, from which the body will produce its own proteins. Body protein comprises almost one-fifth of the body weight, 65% of which is present in the musculoskeletal system. Thus, an adequate protein intake is essential, not only to sustain body function, but also to maintain the integrity of muscle, bone, and other skeletal structures crucially affected by the arthritic process.

The many arthritics who engage in fad diets or various forms of vegetarian or macrobiotic diets should be aware of the biological value of proteins. Protein requirements are satisfied by the essential amino acids which must be supplied by the food we eat, and the nonessential amino acids which the body can form. All proteins are not nutritionally equivalent. Because they are easily digested and have a complete amino acid composition, meat, fish, milk, and egg proteins have a high biological value. Most vegetable or grain proteins are low in some of the essential amino acids. The combination of one protein with another one that contains the missing amino acids is said to be complementary. Fortunately, dietary proteins can be mutually complemented. Meals containing a variety of different vegetable proteins can supply a satisfactory amino acid mixture. This is true of the proteins from grains, vegetables, and legumes. Cereals, legumes, tubers, leaves, fruits, nuts, and yeasts contain proteins which, by themselves, are predominately of low biological value. However, some of them in combination may supply a satisfactory amino acid mixture because they complement each other.

Research in nutrition has shown that it is not absolutely necessary to eat first-class proteins such as fish, meat, eggs, or milk for maintenance of growth and good health. In combination, proteins of different biological value can provide a balanced amino acid mixture, although single proteins may be incomplete. This principle is the basis for the rational use of vegetable proteins. Well-planned vegetarian diets can sustain the growth and development of children and support the metabolic needs of adults.

Chronic tissue injury resulting from destroyed joints may increase the protein requirements of patients with destructive joint diseases. Tissue injury is usually followed by an increase in protein loss. It is thought that the minimum amount of protein required to prevent protein loss in the aged is roughly 0.5 grams per kilogram of body weight per day, which should be increased by a safety margin to overcome the effects of stress.

Protein-energy deficiencies may occur in patients with severe destructive joint disease who may suffer from lack of appetite and depression. For several reasons there is frequently a greater reduction in protein than in calories. A frequently overlooked factor leading to protein deficiency in patients with arthritis is the absence of teeth. Dietary protein is more costly than carbohydrates or fats, and animal protein is even more expensive. Therefore, people with limited resources have more difficulty in obtaining high-quality protein. High-calorie snack foods containing relatively little protein and excessive amounts of starches are frequently used because they are easier to prepare.

None of the many deleterious effects of protein deficiency on vital body functions is more devastating for a patient with a chronic disease than the impairment of the immune system. The ability of white blood cells to kill bacteria is depressed. When protein-energy-starved patients develop a common infection, the disease is more severe and the mortality is higher than in well-nourished individuals, due to impairment of the body defenses.

When carbohydrates and fats as a source of energy are deficient in the diet, the utilization of dietary amino acids is not efficient. When caloric intake is inadequate, even a diet excessive in protein cannot prevent the destruction of body protein. Thus, diets that do not provide satisfactory quantities of energy sources from carbohydrates and fats invariably lead to the destruction of body protein. For the arthritic, inadequate caloric supply means bone and muscle loss with progressive deterioration in function. This is one of the reasons you should avoid engaging in the fasting "cures" frequently thought to relieve arthritis. Although fasting may transiently alleviate your symptoms, restricted caloric intake makes it necessary to release energy by a breakdown of body protein from muscle.

Protein requirements are high in infancy, childhood, adolescence, and during pregnancy. Replacement of tissue lost as a consequence of malnutrition requires an ample supply of dietary protein. However, a diet excessive in protein fulfills no useful purpose, and it may even have a deleterious effect. Diets that are very rich in animal proteins have been shown to be detrimental to bone. These diets promote excessive elimination of calcium in the urine and stimulate the release of parathyroid hormone,[1] which encourages bone resorption.

Because protein cannot be stored in the body, dietary amino acids consumed in excess of the requirements are broken down. Excessive ingestion of protein may also lead to fluid imbalance, since protein intake above 15% of the total caloric intake can lead to an increased requirement for water to carry out the metabolic processes.

A diet excessive in protein is also frequently high in fat because some meats have a high fat content. When excessive fat intake is undesirable, it is best to choose lean meats, avoiding the visible fat, eating fish and poultry without the skin, reducing the ingestion of organ meats such as liver, kidney, or sweetbreads, and preparing meats by baking or broiling rather than frying.

An adequate diet is essential for optimal tissue repair. However, repair may still occur in spite of an inadequate diet. In such cases, simultaneous breakdown of muscle protein may provide the required amino acids for the tissue undergoing repair. In particular, starvation and those diets inadequate in calories or in protein can only lead to muscle breakdown when there is

[1]Its main function is to maintain the calcium concentration in body fluids.

severe inflammation, or during rehabilitation. The consequences of the loss of muscle mass undoubtedly constitute a major factor in the slow, progressively downhill course experienced by many patients with arthritis. It is evident that providing an adequate protein intake primarily improves the general condition by replacing the mobilized proteins in the tissues.

There are also conditions in which body protein is broken down in spite of adequate food consumption. This is true in some chronic diseases, after injuries and burns, and after surgery. Healthy, normal young adults, immobilized and kept in bed for periods of 6 to 8 weeks, can experience a loss of body protein equivalent to one-half to 2 pounds per week. This protein loss is a concern for the arthritic patient in such circumstances as obligatory bed rest due to fractures, major surgery, or severe medical complications.

The generalized loss of muscle experienced by the arthritic patient as a consequence of accidents may be devastating. In the formation of new tissue for repair, it is not the dietary surplus of amino acids, but the healing tendency of the cells, which determines the speed and extent of protein formation. When the tendency toward muscle breakdown is triggered by major surgery, it is not advisable to enforce food intake immediately after surgery, since early feeding does not appreciably alter the healing tendency. When elective surgery is anticipated, it seems more important to prepare the patient by improving the nutritional status before the surgery. A few days after the surgical event, there is usually a marked improvement in appetite. Patients with arthritis frequently ask if physical activity increases protein requirements. Surprisingly, the answer is negative.

Corticosteroid preparations, often prescribed in some forms of arthritis, promote the formation of blood sugar at the expense of tissue protein, resulting in protein loss and muscle wasting. Muscle wasting under these circumstances can be accelerated if your diet is deficient in calories and/or protein, suggesting that the diet should have protein sufficient in quantity and quality to provide for day-to-day cellular needs—and a bit more, to be on the safe side.[2]

Sugars and Fat

In the United States, carbohydrate[3] in the diet provides about 50% of the total caloric intake. Ingested carbohydrate provides the raw material for the formation of a variety of substances of great physiologic importance. Ingested carbohydrate—largely converted into glucose—is utilized to meet the energy requirements of the body.

Because certain foods high in carbohydrates are relatively inexpensive, their proportion in the diet is greater at the lower economic levels than in the most prosperous segments of society. The poorer nutritional status of the lower-income groups is not so much a reflection of their high carbohydrate intake as it is the result of the selection of the *type of foods from which they derive their carbohydrates*. Casually selected high-carbohydrate diets, containing highly refined sugars, are likely to be poor in the essential amino acids, vitamins, and minerals.

Unlike protein, fat can be stored in practically unlimited quantities. When food intake is inadequate to supply the caloric needs of the body, fat is mobilized to make up for the deficit in energy. Therefore, fat is primarily a fuel storage material.

Carbohydrate is man's primary fuel for physical exercise. The great demand for fuel accompanying physical activity may diminish or exhaust the carbohydrate stores of the body. This extreme cannot occur in arthritic patients with destructive disease, because they do not tolerate a high level of physical activ-

[2]The RDA is 0.8 g of mixed protein per kilogram of ideal weight for most healthy adults, including the elderly.

[3]Any of the substances formed by carbon, hydrogen, and oxygen, such as sugars, starches, and cellulose, most of which are formed by green plants.

ity; but it may very well occur in patients with arthritis who achieve a remission and then engage in rigorous programs of exercise.

When carbohydrate stores diminish, there is an increase in the breakdown of body proteins from muscle, as well as an accelerated breakdown of body fat. Thus, ingested carbohydrates have a protein-sparing effect when they are in ample supply in the diet. In this case, muscle tissue and fat are "spared" from being broken down into their component parts which the body needs for fuel. An adequate supply of carbohydrate is essential to maintain the integrity of skeletal and heart muscle, as well as that of the nervous system. Enough carbohydrate should be present in the diet to supply the calories necessary to maintain a stable weight.

The total fat intake is about 40% or more of the total daily caloric intake for many Americans. Fat intake in the arthritic population is equally high. Compared with the diets of humans in other parts of the world, except for that of the Eskimos, the proportion of fat in the American diet is excessively high. In the industrialized countries, there appears to be a general agreement on the desirability of lowering total caloric intake, and particularly the intake of fat. The American Heart Association recommends a diet reduced in fat content with an increased content of polyunsaturated as opposed to saturated oils in an effort to reduce the risk of atherosclerosis. This recommendation is also applicable to those arthritics who lead a sedentary existence. It is important to realize that all dietary fat is not the same. Thus, not only the quantity of fat, but also its quality may have implications for your health. Dietary fats can be animal or vegetable in origin. They have different quality and properties, depending upon the degree of unsaturation of the fatty acids. You should be aware of the meaning of saturated, unsaturated, and polyunsaturated fats, because these words are frequently used in product labels and in lay literature on the significance of fats.

As an example, at one extreme, coconut oil is largely composed of saturated fatty acids, while at the other extreme, linseed oil is mainly composed of unsaturated fatty acids. Generally, foods high in saturated fats include beef, pork, lamb, coconut and palm oils, butter, whole milk, cream, and hydrogenated fats. Those high in polyunsaturated fats include most salad or cooking oils, special margarines, and walnuts. Butter, mutton, and beef tallow, lard, olive oil, peanut oil, cottonseed oil, corn oil, and soybean oil are listed in decreasing order from highest to lowest proportion of saturation of their fatty acids.

Animal fats contain cholesterol, which is a precursor of many steroid[4] hormones, bile salts, and vitamin D. Vegetable oils have no cholesterol. In humans, cholesterol is produced in the liver and other tissues, and no more than 40% of circulating cholesterol is derived from the diet. The level of cholesterol is not exclusively dependent upon the animal fats you eat, but also upon that which your body produces.

When food in excess of caloric expenditure is ingested, the equivalent of the excess calories is deposited as fat in the adipose tissues. Because of its lower cost and its use in confections, carbohydrate is the most important precursor of fat. Essential fatty acids are those fatty acids that either cannot be produced at all or are not produced in sufficient quantity in the body to maintain growth and other physiological processes. Linoleic is the primary dietary EFA in humans. Arachidonic acid can be produced in the body from dietary linoleic acid. The proportion of unsaturated fatty acids in adipose tissue is directly related to their content in the diet. This may be important, because differences in dietary fats may, in the future, allow dietary manipulation of certain human diseases, such as atherosclerosis and, perhaps, autoimmune diseases.

EFA deficiency results in alterations in the membranes of all living cells. However, it is difficult to deplete EFA in adult humans because of the large reservoir of linoleate in adipose tissue. Even prolonged feeding of a diet deficient in EFA may not

[4]Any of the fat-soluble hormones derived from cholesterol; includes the sex hormones, and some of the adrenal hormones.

produce symptoms of deficiency in the adult. One of the most compelling reasons for you to learn about fats and EFA is that these substances are precursors of important mediators of inflammation.[5] Only 2–3% of the total calories are required as linoleic acid, a fatty acid essential for the synthesis of prostaglandins. Thus, a diet should have at least enough fat to carry the essential fatty acids and fat-soluble vitamins.

Should your diet contain a supplement of omega-3 fatty acids, in view of the action of these substances on inflammation and their reputed effects in rheumatoid arthritis? My suggestion at present is to substitute cold-water fish for red meat as much as possible. If you feel compelled to supplement your diet with omega-3 fatty acids, the daily dose probably should not be greater than 5 grams per day, which is the approximate equivalent of that in the Eskimos' diet. Eskimos have proved throughout centuries that their level of omega-3 fatty acids intake is accompanied by a potentially healthier cardiovascular profile. The effects of long-term administration of much larger doses of omega-3 fatty acids are not known.

Excessive Highly Refined Sugars

Man has experienced drastic changes in his diet over the last 20 to 30 thousand years. Refined and processed food increasingly requires less and less of the function of the alimentary tract. The function of an organ which is not called upon to perform diminishes and it often shrinks. As a consequence of the dietary changes, the mandible seems to be shrinking and the underfed bowel experiences all sorts of problems. Dentists frequently observe that we have more teeth than our mandibles can accommodate. This is, in part, a probable consequence of the slow evolutionary changes in the mandible. The man of the future has been visualized as having a large head which would

[5]Prostaglandins and leukotrienes.

accommodate a prominent brain with a very small mandible—actually an awful-looking creature, according to our present aesthetic standards.

Constipation, a frequent complaint of patients with arthritis, is usually the result of a diet rich in refined carbohydrates and low in fiber. Fiber is the part of our plant-based food that is broken down by bacteria in the colon, and is only partially digested by alimentary enzymes.

It has been proposed that people who adopt a fiber-rich, unrefined diet will reduce their chances of developing the diseases of overnutrition (such as obesity, diabetes, gallstones, and coronary artery disease), mouth diseases (dental caries and periodontal disease), and the diseases of an underfed large bowel (constipation, hemorrhoids, spastic colon, appendicitis, and cancer of the large bowel). Although strict proof for these claims is presently lacking, it is likely that some of them eventually will be established.

The frequent association of various types of arthritis and bowel disease would suggest that agents capable of influencing the microenvironment of the bowel could possibly have some influence on the course of the arthritis. It is clear that research into the effect of the composition of the diet on the microenvironment of the bowel is a potentially important area for investigation in the rheumatic diseases.

There is little argument that many patients with constipation are helped by a liberal intake of fiber-rich food. How should fiber be best introduced into the diet? An effective way is to include genuine whole-grain bread containing 100% wheat or rye, along with additional raw fruit and vegetables. Each slice of whole wheat bread contains an average of 5 grams of bran. When patients cannot eat enough bread because they cannot afford the extra calories, pure bran could be added to the diet. Coarse, raw bran is more effective than the fine variety. Fine, powdery bran is more palatable, but it contains more flour and thus more calories. Bran is more palatable if mixed with breakfast cereals, thick soups, and sauces. It is possible to enrich many foods with bran and still preserve their flavor and taste. It is advisable to begin with a small amount of bran, such as one heaping teaspoonful daily, and gradually increase the amount over a period of one week until the desired effect is obtained. When you start a fiber-rich diet, you should be aware that you may experience increased bloating and flatulence at the beginning, and that the full beneficial effect of the diet on constipation may not become evident for 3 or 4 months.

For the patient with arthritis, breakfast is a very important meal. The traditional three-meals-a-day pattern has been disturbed in the last few decades. The pattern of little or no breakfast, a light lunch, and a large evening meal containing the bulk of the day's energy supply, is frequently followed. This pattern is not adequate for most arthritics because they frequently begin their day with the oral intake of medicines that may more easily damage an empty stomach than a stomach filled with food. If any meal is omitted, too much nutritional load is put on the remaining meals. Eating breakfast has been found to be essential to maximal physical and mental efficiency during the morning hours. Skipping or slighting breakfast results in decreased output and mental alertness. In general, the patient's ability to tolerate medications is increased by taking them after breakfast. You should not take a NSAID with coffee, tea, or alcohol because the potential for harming the gastrointestinal tract is enhanced. A bulky breakfast, consisting of a whole-grain cereal such as oatmeal, with the addition of oat or wheat bran, improves the tolerance for morning medications, and is frequently beneficial for the patients with arthritis who often have constipation. The average American diet is low in fiber content compared with the diet in the developing countries. Because increased fiber intake is harmless, except in the presence of acute diseases of the bowel, it has been suggested that a prudent diet should contain at least 25 grams of fiber per day. This requires the daily consumption of some foods high in fiber, such as peas, beans, broccoli, prunes, peaches, berries, grapes, apricots, bran, almonds, or whole wheat bread.

Vitamin and Mineral Supplementation

Vitamins and minerals play important and highly specific roles in many life processes throughout the body. Fortunately, a balanced diet contains the small but crucial amounts of these nutrients and provides the energy necessary to maintain bodily function at rest and during exercise. Vitamin supplements are of no value to healthy, nonpregnant women, or men eating a balanced diet. Vitamin deficiencies may appear in those persons who go out of their way to avoid whole groups of foods, such as fresh fruit and vegetables or milk and dairy products. It follows that with proper nutrition, the consumption of vitamins and mineral supplements is unnecessarily wasteful for the healthy adult.

However, marginal deficiency of nutrients and vitamins is not uncommon in the arthritic population. Poor or erratic intake and the tendency to eat highly processed or refined foods makes deficiencies more likely. Thus, the possibility of marginal deficiencies should be covered with the routine intake of a multivitamin preparation recommended by the physician. Supplementation of vitamin B_1 may be necessary if alcohol abuse is a problem, and patients being treated with penicillamine may require a supplement of vitamin B_6. Dietary deficiency of folic acid may occur sporadically when fresh vegetables are not consumed. In these cases, as well as during pregnancy, oral contraceptive treatment or in patients abusing alcohol, a supplement of folic acid is usually prescribed. Vitamin B_{12} deficiency is seldom caused by dietary inadequacy. Even strict vegetarians may develop B_{12} deficiency only after many years of following a vegetarian diet.

Although the exact mechanism of action of vitamin C remains to be determined, it is known that it acts in the synthesis of collagen and as a co-factor in important enzymatic reactions. Patients with scurvy, the disease which results from a lack of vitamin C, may have joint pain and swelling, and are prone to develop infections. The capillary fragility responsible for the tendency to hemorrhage and poor wound healing, as well as many of the clinical findings in scurvy, result from the defect in collagen formation. The vitamin is present in milk, liver, kidneys, and fish, and is widely distributed in fruits and vegetables. Most methods of food processing partially preserve vitamin C content, and it is usually easy to fulfill the RDA of the vitamin with even a modest intake of fruits or vegetables. However, a supplement of 250 milligrams of vitamin C per day is advisable for patients with arthritis in light of the possibility of marginal deficiencies and additional requirements related to the chronicity of the disease.

Only under certain circumstances do arthritic patients require iron supplements. The anemia of RA is characteristic of chronic disease and does not respond to iron administration. Iron from vegetable sources is not as easily absorbed as that contained in meat. Frequently, dietary iron is not sufficient in patients who have had gastric surgery. True iron deficiency can occur secondary to GI bleeding or to malnutrition. Supplemental iron may be needed only if iron deficiency is present.

In the U.S. there is usually no need for concern about the adequacy of trace metal intake when a well-balanced diet is ingested. However, starvation diets and very low calorie diets may lead to trace metal deficiencies.

Phosphorus poses no special problems, because it is available in most foods, and it is usually considered to be present in adequate amounts in most diets. Good sources of protein are also good sources of phosphorus. Dietary inadequacy of magnesium is unlikely and is not seen in patients with arthritis unless they have other medical problems. Patients with arthritis do not have magnesium deficiency unless the disease is complicated by chronic alcoholism or other conditions associated with malnutrition.

Dietary inadequacy of potassium is unlikely in the absence of physical complications, but it is not uncommon when kidney disease, diabetes, vomiting, or diarrhea occur, or when diuretics are given. These conditions must be recognized and treated by the physician. Food sources of potassium are fruits, milk, meat, cereals, vegetables, and legumes.

Zinc deficiency may be seen in chronic systemic illness, in nutritionally depleted patients, and in those subjected to severe stress, such as surgery. Some patients with rheumatoid arthritis may have a marginal deficiency of zinc. The bioavailability of zinc in the diet can be reduced by substances[6] present in plant foods, which form an insoluble complex with this trace metal. In these cases a zinc supplement can be prescribed.

The study of Bigaouette and colleagues (1987) on nutritional adequacy of patients with RA showed that dietary intake of folic acid, pyridoxine, zinc, and magnesium was 60–80% of the RDA for these patients. Many individuals who do not consume a basically adequate diet are advised to take a vitamin-mineral supplement. Persons losing weight due to the arthritis, to a concomitant disease, or to voluntary restriction of food should also take these supplements.

Arthritis, Nutrition, and Pregnancy

The influence of pregnancy on the course of some rheumatic diseases is intriguing. Phillip Hench (1938) noted the beneficial effects of pregnancy on rheumatoid arthritis. It was later noted that pregnancy may also temporarily relieve the symptoms of asthma, hay fever, and psoriasis, suggesting that the effect is not specific. Several studies have shown that approximately half of the patients improve during the first trimester and an additional quarter will improve throughout the remainder of the gestation period while in the last quarter, some patients fail to improve, and some may even become worse. After delivery the symptoms of rheumatoid arthritis are known to recur in more than 90% of the patients. In general, the benefits derived from pregnancy for the rheumatoid woman are at best

[6]Phytates.

partial and temporary, which on the average last an approximate 6 weeks after delivery. The activity of the disease recurring post-partum is at least as severe as it was prior to gestation. In women with SLE, pregnancy or delivery may be associated with flare-ups of the disease, including the onset of proliferative nephritis. When severe kidney involvement is present and pregnancy occurs, the situation requires the care usually provided to a high-risk pregnancy. However, with appropriate obstetrical, pediatric, and rheumatologic care, the prognosis for the mother and baby is not as risky as previously thought.

Childbearing has definite nutritional implications for the arthritic woman as well as for the child. Rheumatoid arthritis, lupus erythematosus, as well as other inflammatory arthritides may appear in young women; thus, the question of whether or not they can have a baby is charged with emotion and is usually extremely important to a young couple. There is no easy answer to this question. Some patients have voiced the opinion that a young woman affected with severe rheumatoid arthritis should probably decide against having children because of her inability to take care of them. Although this advice may be reasonable for the woman with severe destructive disease, I believe that this is an individual decision.

You are well aware that the earning power of the arthritic woman is, on the average, quite diminished. Because many women are the heads of households and their work is the only means of support for the family, this is a primary consideration. The cost of medical care imposes an additional burden that curtails the financial potential of the family, limiting the funds available to buy food. In this respect, arthritis in the father has the same probable effect of limiting the possibilities for the children.

What does arthritis in the mother mean for the unborn fetus during pregnancy, and then for the children after they are born? What does pregnancy represent to the patient with arthritis? What do children represent to the arthritic patient and to the marriage? Some of these questions can only be answered by the individual patient after a deep soul-searching process. From the medical and obstetrical viewpoints, most arthritic women of childbearing age are able to become pregnant and to have normal deliveries. If the patient wants to avoid pregnancy, the use of female sex hormones as oral contraceptives is a good alternative, except for patients with any form of lupus erythematosus, in whom some mechanical form of contraception is preferred. This is because the use of these drugs has been shown to induce symptoms of lupus and positive ANA.

Pregnancy does change dietary requirements for the arthritic woman. The recommended allowances of some essential nutrients can be influenced by pregnancy and lactation. It is recognized that pregnant women have increased requirements for energy, and most essential nutrients per unit of body weight. During pregnancy it is not advisable to engage in dietary restriction, although care should be exercised to avoid undernutrition or overnutrition. In general, any diet containing less than 1,500 calories increases the likelihood of having a low-birth-weight infant and causes maternal protein to be used as an energy source with consequent muscle wasting. Dietary restriction or fasting, which may be used by some pregnant arthritic women to lose weight, may result in neurological damage to the offspring. A reducing diet to achieve weight loss should be delayed until after delivery or until breast feeding has been terminated. Appropriate caloric intake plus an additional 30 grams of protein per day is needed to support maternal and fetal needs for proteins during pregnancy. If limited protein intake occurs, it is often followed by decreased availability of energy which can lead to decreased birth weight and greater incidence of pre-eclampsia. On the other hand, too much protein may have a negative effect on the course and outcome of pregnancy.

The possible need for supplementary iron and folate should be considered in all pregnant women. As the maternal blood supply increases markedly during pregnancy, there is a greater demand for iron. Iron supplementation is often necessary to prevent iron-deficiency anemia. A pregnant arthritic may need an iron supplement because diet alone rarely provides enough iron to satisfy the increased demands of pregnancy. Thus, the use of 30 to 60 milligrams of supplemental iron is recommended. The need for iron during lactation is not substantially different from that of nonpregnant women, but continued supplementation of the mother for 2 to 3 weeks after delivery is advisable to replenish the iron stores depleted by pregnancy.

The current RDA for calcium during pregnancy is 1200 milligrams daily, a level 400 milligrams higher than that recommended for the nonpregnant woman. This RDA is probably insufficient for the pregnant rheumatoid woman who is treated with corticosteroids and already has osteoporotic bones or extensive joint destruction.

While reduction of the use of salt and salty foods is appropriate for all people, aggressive restriction is usually unwarranted during pregnancy. The amount of 2 to 3 grams of sodium daily can be consumed safely, unless the treatment of the arthritic requires the use of corticosteroids.

Questions frequently arise about the advisability of coffee intake during pregnancy. Recent observations support the view that its moderate consumption during pregnancy does not adversely affect its outcome. Although it is not known whether caffeine causes birth defects in humans, prudence dictates that pregnant women, and those who may become pregnant, avoid excessive consumption of caffeine-containing products, including coffee, tea, cola, and "pepper" drinks, chocolate, and some over-the-counter medications.

The advice to avoid unsupervised vitamin supplementation is reemphasized here for the pregnant arthritic woman, because she may put the infant at risk of toxicity. For instance, excess intake of vitamin A during pregnancy has been associated with central nervous system congenital malformations in the offspring. Lesions of the aortic valve, elfin face, and mental retardation have been reported in the offspring of women receiving huge doses of vitamin D during pregnancy. Infants have also been reported to develop "conditioned scurvy" some time after birth due to accelerated body disposal of vitamin C following the mother's intake of large doses of the vitamin during pregnancy. In women on massive doses of vitamin C, interruption of pregnancy can occur.

Pregnant arthritic women are vulnerable to the results of the excessive consumption of calories, use of alcohol, or cigarette smoking. Consumption of alcohol equivalent to two glasses of wine per day during pregnancy has been associated with reduced birth weight of the fetus. Drinking as little as one glass of wine or one beer per day has been found to lead to an increase in the rate of spontaneous abortion. Several studies have reported that high alcohol intake leads to birth defects, including mental retardation. The well-known effects of cigarette smoking by the pregnant arthritic woman on appetite and on bone calcium justify a brief discussion of this practice. The Surgeon General recently stressed that cigarette smoking is a major threat to the personal health of women and to their ability to bear healthy children. He noted that the death rate from lung cancer among women has tripled since the 1960s. Women who smoke are now more vulnerable to heart disease and to peptic ulcer. There are also special risks to their health and that of their offspring, because pregnant women who smoke more often experience spontaneous abortions, bleeding, and premature rupture of the amniotic membrane. Smoking during pregnancy has also been linked to lower infant birth weight. Children of parents who smoke experience more respiratory infections and more hospitalizations during the first year of life. Sleep difficulties have been reported in pregnant women as a consequence of cigarette smoking and have been noted to improve during abstinence. Though the standard recommendation to all of my patients is to avoid smoking, this is particularly stressed to arthritic women during pregnancy.

CHAPTER 11

REST AND EXERCISE

Rest and a lifelong program of exercise are two of the most important aspects of the treatment of patients with arthritis. No treatment program is adequate without the proper balance between rest and exercise and emphasis on correct habits of posture.

Our twentieth century life-style has led us into an increasingly sedentary existence which has serious implications for our health and well-being. The level of physical activity is critical for the patient who has arthritis with multiple joint involvement. Persons who eventually develop any type of arthritis engage in no more daily physical activity than does the average person. Unfortunately, this is very little. With the appearance of severe joint inflammation, patients soon discover that almost any motion increases the pain; so they have a tendency to remain even more physically inactive. We say that an inflammatory type of arthritis is active when there is inflammation in the joints or other organs. When the inflammation disappears, we say that the disease is inactive. There is no argument about the need for rest during the acute, inflammatory phase of any arthritis. An important aspect of rest which is frequently neglected is its potential to allow the patient to withdraw from psychosocial stress as well. A thorough discussion with the patient and the family about their expectations and the outcome of the disease may be very helpful at that time. Explanations and answers to their questions promote peace of mind which is required for rest. It should be made clear that a program that does not permit at least temporary relief from emotional stress is suboptimal. This may occur when the symptoms of the disease are first noticed, or during a flare-up.

Activity of rheumatoid arthritis can be recognized by the long duration of morning stiffness in the joints or in the whole body and by the presence of swollen, tender, and warm joints, which are painful on motion. Occasionally, when the activity is severe, a brief period of bed rest may be beneficial, though this must always be kept to a minimum. The period of complete rest should be brief, because prolonged physical inactivity invariably leads to muscle wasting. This is a very high price that arthritics should not have to pay. More frequently, selective immobilization of inflamed joints and general rest can provide considerable relief. Usually only acutely inflamed joints may require complete immobilization. A splint for the wrist may put this joint to rest while allowing motion of the whole extremity and fingers. Physical therapy at these times is usually limited to heat in the form of whirlpool sessions, or the use of special tanks where gentle motion of the joints can be carried out in warm water, hot wax baths for the hands, hot packs, and gentle massage. At home, a hot bath at temperatures that the body can tolerate, long hot showers on arising, and the application of hot packs to involved areas can bring about relief.

Balance between Rest and Exercise
When Inflammation Improves

Exercise is usually not a part of the treatment when the joints are severely inflamed and painful. However, gentle exercises must be prescribed early, as soon as the acute inflammation begins to subside, in the attempt to achieve a proper balance between rest and exercise. The patient seldom realizes the importance of the change in approach, from rest during the active form of the disease, to a balance of rest and exercise after the activity of the disease is controlled. It may not be readily apparent why exercise, with some few exceptions, should be done regularly for as long as you live. Unfortunately, many patients with arthritis continue to rest for life without exercising, contributing to the deterioration of their joints. I often see patients with considerable muscle wasting who have had arthritis for many years, without ever having had an exercise program. Elderly arthritics may share the common belief that their need for exercise diminishes as they grow older. Others may think that they are incapable of exercising because they are too old. The truth is that the need for exercise does *not* diminish as we become older, and that *no* patient with arthritis is too old to benefit from it.

Early in the course of any type of arthritis, an important goal of an exercise program is the prevention of muscle wasting. Even if considerable disability is present, one of the best ways to begin mobilization of the joints is through gentle exercises in warm water. This gives the patient buoyancy, both to assist movements and to diminish the necessity of weight bearing.

Patients afflicted with chronic diseases need more rest than do healthy persons. The simple act of walking a relatively short distance may rapidly produce fatigue. This reduced tolerance for physical activity is characteristic of the periods during which there is severe joint inflammation or involvement of other organs. Even in the absence of joint inflammation, any modest degree of physical activity may cause exhaustion in persons who are accustomed to an extremely sedentary life. How much physical activity each arthritic should undertake must be decided on an individual basis. Any level of physical activity leading to exhaustion is excessive. The presence of fatigue should be brought to the attention of the physician because it can often be alleviated. Initially, it is necessary to treat the disease activity, after which a gradual program of physical fitness may bring about amazing improvement. It is also essential to get enough sleep and rest between exercise periods to avoid fatigue.

An adequate night's sleep is an essential part of normal life, and extremely important for the patient with arthritis. Simple measures like avoiding alcohol at night may substantially improve night rest. The sedative effect of alcohol wears off quickly and is replaced by irritability and interruption of the sleep cycle. A nap in the afternoon can make a great difference in the lifestyle of a patient, improving tolerance for the level of physical activity that will be necessary for him to function during the remainder of the day.

One of the primary causes of irreparable loss of function leading to deformities and crippling is prolonged, unnecessary immobilization. This may create significant problems during the lifetime of many patients with arthritis, since hospitalization for many other unrelated conditions may be required. Under these circumstances, bed rest can lead to joint restriction and loss of function. When absolute bed rest is made unavoidable by a concurrent medical condition, it should be kept to a minimum, and an attempt should be made to mobilize the major joints as soon as the medical condition permits. With the aid of skilled physical therapists, this can be done while the patient is still in bed. Even if the medical condition is severe, it is usually possible to allow the major joints to be gently and passively taken through their normal range of motion. Using the upper extremities, some patients are still able to do exercises in a sitting position, even though they are bound to a wheelchair. As a general rule, passive exercises should neither produce intolerable pain at the extremes of the range of motion, nor evoke long-lasting pain in the affected joints. When a patient can perform part but not all of the movement, a therapist may provide assistance to complete the motion. This can be carried out without posing excessive demands on the heart and lungs of the patient.

Abnormal Posture

Ignorance may trigger or accelerate the development of deformities. Joint contractures can develop if the joints are not taken through their range of motion regularly. If a pillow is applied underneath the knee because this is a more comfortable position, the predictable result will be the appearance or aggravation of flexion contracture.[1] Flexion of the knees is the position of these joints in which the patient feels less pain. However, if this position is permanently adopted, stiffness sets in and the joint may become deformed. Except for special cases, the bed should be flat with a firm mattress, having no breaks and no pillows or support placed underneath the knees. During prolonged bed rest, because of the position of the feet bent downward under the weight of the sheets, flexion contractures of the ankles may also develop. After the medical condition which led to bed rest subsides, the patient may find to his dismay that the newly created deformities prevent normal ambulation.

An abnormal posture can create deformities or make them worse and is a frequent cause of pain in the back and shoulders. It may be the consequence of working in a slumped position, psychological difficulties, or chronic illness with reduced muscle tone. Abnormal posture places undue stress on the muscles of the back and the upper extremities. Correction of work or living habits, modification of posture, and exercise often produce improvement. It follows that the maintenance of normal posture and sound principles of body mechanics enhance the possibility of preventing deformities.

[1]Inability to straighten the knee completely, which is maintained in a bent position.

Your doctor frequently assumes that you understand what he means when he prescribes regular exercise. This is not necessarily the case. This usually means that you must exercise every other day or even every day, depending upon the specific problems. It also means that exercises should be done with consistency at approximately the same time and in sessions of comparable duration. However, this is not an ironclad rule. Depending upon the recurring activity of the disease and the fatigue associated with it, a flexible schedule could be adopted in which a whole day of rest may follow one day of activity, if the need arises. After discussing your postural habits with your doctor or therapist, you can examine the way you usually walk, sit, stand, or sleep. Understanding this problem is the first step in successful treatment.

Trauma, Tendonitis, Bursitis, and Fibromyalgia

Pain is not always the result of inflammation of the joints. Patients in whom the activity of the disease is arrested by treatment, or because the disease goes into spontaneous remission, may have no joint pain at all, especially if the disease has been of relatively short duration. However, after a prolonged period of disease activity, some patients will develop varying degrees of joint damage. In these patients, the pain in the joints is not due to inflammation, but is a consequence of joint destruction. Unaware of the cause of the symptoms, they may repeatedly request more potent antiarthritic medication from their physicians. They may also be reluctant to believe that they should exercise while protecting their joints, because motion may indeed produce some temporary joint discomfort. Exercise is essential to maintain joint mobility and muscle mass. Pain, stiffness, or discomfort described by patients with arthritis do not always have their origin in the inflamed or deformed joints. Faulty posture and flabbiness of the abdominal muscles are frequently responsible for low back pain. The addition of back protection and abdominal exercises to the fitness program can often relieve the back pain.

Trauma may be the underlying cause of bursitis or tendonitis causing pain in the shoulders or elbows. Trauma may not always be obvious but is a frequent contributor to pain and misery in patients with arthritis. It is frequently related to overuse of the healthier extremity when the other side is severely involved by arthritis, or simply by faulty use of crutches which may injure the hand, producing a flexor tendonitis of the fingers. Pain in the upper and lateral aspects of the thighs, often attributed to hip involvement, can be caused by trochanteric bursitis. In these conditions a combination of local corticosteroid injections, the application of heat or ultrasound, and range-of-motion exercises can be very effective. Shortening of a leg may cause pain which might be attributed to involvement of the hip. This pain may "miraculously" disappear by the adjusting of the length of the leg with a small lift applied to the shoe.

Discomfort very similar to that of primary fibrositis or fibromyalgia is not uncommon in some patients with other kinds of arthritis. These patients complain of soreness in areas of the body that appear to be normal on examination, except for marked local tenderness when pressure is applied. The pain is usually dull, but it may be quite severe, and present in multiple but predictable sites. These symptoms may incorrectly be attributed to rheumatoid arthritis, since they are worse in the morning, aggravated by fatigue, immobility, or chilling, and improved by the application of heat. Some patients who have fibromyalgia and rheumatoid arthritis have an intense personality, are perfectionistic, demanding, and have sleep disturbances. The association of fibromyalgia and RA may give rise to inappropriate treatment. These patients may experience a substantial improvement with the use of heat, the treatment of trigger points, relaxation techniques, and restoration of adequate sleep.

Many of the symptoms experienced by patients with arthritis are aggravated by psychologic stress. Muscular tension frequently reflects the person's emotional state. The psychological benefits of exercise have been known for a long time. Controlled studies have demonstrated that the exercise performed while walking 15 minutes can do as much to reduce tension as the common tranquilizing drugs. Exercise decreases tension in the muscles by improving circulation, promoting maximal contraction, resulting in maximal relaxation and increasing the production of pain-relieving chemicals by the body which help to break the pain-spasm cycle. A program of physical fitness is a viable alternative to drugs which are usually used to treat conditions characterized by tension. Cureton (1969) has suggested that personality and physical deterioration parallel each other and that improvement in physical fitness should minimize both types of deterioration. Emotional stability, self-sufficiency, and confidence have been found to be outstanding qualities of high-fitness nonarthritic groups.

Consequences of a Sedentary Existence

Many internal diseases are more frequently found in the sedentary than in the physically active. In general, arthritis with its consequent slowdown in physical activity, compounds the problem of modern men and women. Everyone who has reached his fifties, sixties, or seventies knows that we are not as tall as we were at 20. This is largely the result of actual bone loss in the bodies of the vertebrae which flatten, to some extent, in all people as we age. Bone loss is much more pronounced and accelerated in physically inactive persons, particularly those lacking weight-bearing exercise. Most arthritics are neither aware that they are much more susceptible to osteoporosis, nor do they realize that exercise has a hidden beneficial effect that helps maintain healthier bones. Mineralization of bone is a complex process dependent upon many factors; but the mechanical stress of the bone by a physically active life is one of the main promoters of bone formation. In many types of inflammatory arthritis not only are the joints and muscles involved, but bone deterioration is a major factor leading to disability in later years. Fractures occurring in osteoporotic bones can contribute to disability and impaired ambulation in patients with arthritis.

Other factors frequently contributing to osteoporosis are inadequate calcium intake, malnutrition, concomitant treatment with corticosteroids and, in women, the postmenopausal state. Disability brings about a preponderance of bone resorption over bone formation with consequent osteoporosis. A study of the relationship between the duration of the disease and the bone loss in rheumatoid arthritis has shown that the greater part of the reduction of bone mass takes place during the first 3 years of the disease. Undoubtedly, the sedentary existence of the arthritic is a major contributing factor to bone loss, and a lifelong exercise program begun early after the diagnosis is made substantially helps overcome this problem. The extreme sedentary life of many patients with arthritis as a consequence of joint disability and muscle wasting also results in poor aerobic capacity.

Thus, arthritics must plan and carry out an exercise program in the period during which the disease activity subsides if they are to have a chance to fight the disease in their later years. Programs of physical fitness for the arthritic can be an invaluable contribution to many years of independent vigorous living.

Patients must first be convinced that exercise is important. Lack of motivation is not always their fault. Some physicians may not really be convinced that exercise is necessary and they themselves lead a sedentary existence. A sedentary life reflects the same lack of respect for our bodies as does overeating, smoking, chronic alcohol abuse, or narcotic addiction. The pronouncements of physicians will not be very convincing if, with a cigarette in their hand, they tell the patient to quit smoking or recommend a relatively low-calorie diet and exercise while they themselves are fat and flabby. Consequently, a good number of patients never really take them seriously.

Decrepitude in the arthritic's later years is not a necessary consequence of aging but rather of a sedentary life which accelerates the deterioration of the body. The multiple physiological effects of sustained and vigorous exercise justify the claims that it is the cheapest available method to retard the deterioration brought about by aging.

Effects of Exercise on Muscle Mass and Strength

While attaining a reasonable level of physical fitness is a slow process, the adaptation to physical inactivity is very rapid, and for this reason sporadic or weekend exercise is not effective. One of the most devastating effects of physical inactivity is the loss of muscle mass and strength, a problem common to civilized man. Muscle mass is rapidly lost during prolonged periods of physical inactivity but it can be increased relatively quickly in a healthy person through appropriate exercise. However, the recovery of muscle mass is usually a much slower process in the arthritic patient.

There is no sound rationale to support the reluctance of many people to engage in regular exercise. Muscle conditioning is normally stimulated by muscle use and physical stress. Any condition preventing the use of the muscles, such as casting, rupture of a tendon, joint inflammation, a sedentary life, continuous bed rest, or life confined to a wheelchair rapidly leads to muscle weakness and wasting with a loss of endurance. Conversely, exercise brings about an increase in muscle mass and in muscle power. Just as the muscle responds to conditioning stress by increasing its mass and its contractile power, a sedentary life leads to the shrinking and weakness of the muscles. Some joint abnormalities require that the muscle strength be built up by the application of resistance against the motion of the desired part of the body to be strengthened. Strengthening exercises are prescribed to increase the muscle power by repetitive contractions of specified duration.

Water adds resistance to motion, therefore exercises performed in water can improve muscle strength. Isometric exercises consist of tightening the muscles without motion of the body parts. In isometric exercises the muscle makes an effort for a brief period of time against a resistance such as a wall or a bedboard. A few repetitive motions, day after day, are usually sufficient to increase the mass of muscle to some extent. These types of exercise are very useful because they permit the joints to rest while muscle strength is being built. This is highly desirable when there is inflammation of the joints. Isometric exercises can even be performed by patients who are bedridden or bound to a wheelchair. Strengthening the thigh muscles can be very helpful for patients with involvement of the knee. When these muscles are strong, the ligaments surrounding the knee and the joint capsule tighten and the joint becomes more stable. Two simple measures, the strengthening of the muscles in the anterior part of the thigh,[2] and weight reduction, if obesity is present, are probably more effective than any medication when the knees are principally involved.

The muscles make an important contribution to the function of the joints. One of the consequences of persistent joint inflammation is a decreased use of the adjacent muscles, due to pain. As a consequence, the muscles shrink and a vicious circle is established. Arthritics seldom realize that their situation makes exercise imperative. A continuous program of exercise is not considered to be fun by most individuals. That which interferes even more, buried in the mind of every patient with arthritis, whether his disease is of recent onset or he has been battling it over a long period of time, is an obsessive thought that perhaps when he wakes up tomorrow the arthritis will be gone—so why go through all this pain of exercise? In reality, the arthritis is probably not going to "go away," not today, not to-

[2]Quadriceps.

morrow, or next year, and it is this fact with which he must learn to cope before he can succeed in managing his disease. If he wants to function to the fullest extent of his capabilities, he must make his exercise program another habit like brushing his teeth, taking a bath, or combing his hair.

Although, under certain circumstances, some degree of discomfort must be tolerated to achieve fitness and optimal function, in the majority of cases conditioning can be achieved with pleasure rather than with pain or discomfort.

Physical Fitness with Joint Protection

Of course you now wonder what benefit you can obtain from exercise. With the help of your doctor and therapist you should try to identify your strengths and limitations to determine a rationale for your exercise program. What are your goals when you begin an exercise program? At any time during the course of arthritis some important goals of exercise are to maintain or increase joint motion and muscle strength or to improve function. Exercise can help you to prevent deformities and allow you to become more independent. When joint damage has already occurred, preservation or restoration of function are very important objectives. If you have lost muscle mass and strength, an obvious objective is to build muscle strength, which is critical to improving the function of your joints. Self-inflicted injury to your ailing joints and muscles is the most common obstacle that may prevent you from achieving these goals. The risk of self-inflicted damage to the musculoskeletal system is increased when you begin to exercise. There are many possibilities for the arthritic to sustain injuries as a consequence of performing physical activities that are automatic and almost effortless for normal individuals.

Contraction of the muscles surrounding the joints is a major shock-absorbing mechanism; therefore, strengthening the muscles surrounding weight-bearing joints will best protect the joints. An adequate exercise program not only increases the stability of the joints but also may improve their range of motion. Improvement in strength can be easily and quickly noticed, but a substantial gain in muscle mass will take much longer.

During the implementation of a program of physical fitness, setbacks are to be expected; but this should not discourage you. Unfortunately, many patients abandon a program of exercise after the *first* setback. If you achieve a certain level of physical activity and you experience a complication such as pneumonia or you need surgery, the process of physical conditioning is interrupted and ground is rapidly lost. After the setback, it is a mistake to attempt to continue the fitness program at the level at which it was interrupted. Muscles weaken and rapidly shrink if they are not used. Resumption of exercise should be slow and progressive. In most cases, a modest beginning and increasing the activity in gradual increments will enable you to avoid the disappointment of excessive discomfort. Programs of physical fitness must be tailored to your particular needs. That a general program cannot be designed to serve the specific needs of all patients will soon become clear.

While exercising, the joints should be protected from further damage. There are many ways to perform the same function in the activities of our daily lives, and some of these may tax the joints more than others, thereby producing further discomfort and damage. Skillful physical and occupational therapists can teach you the principles of joint protection to help you prevent joint damage while you exercise.

Joints can be abused through ignorance. If inflammation is present in the knee, fluid often accumulates. In this case, aspiration of the fluid followed by an intra-articular injection of corticosteroids may produce relief. During the period immediately following this treatment, the joint should be protected by avoiding an inordinate amount of walking and by the use of a cane, if necessary, in the hand opposite the affected joint. If the joint is not adequately protected, its overuse may lead to the rapid collapse of articular cartilage with irreparable destruction of the joint. Similarly, any program of exercise should take into consideration the particular disabilities of the patient. For example, exercise involving impact loading of weight-bearing joints, such as jogging, should be avoided when the knees have been damaged. The program often must concentrate on treating specific weaknesses which will help to protect the joints during their normal function.

Slight discomfort or muscle soreness after the completion of exercise is often a normal reaction and is to be expected. This soreness is not in the joints but occurs around the joints and may increase if pressure is applied to the belly muscles. However, a major drawback of some programs of physical fitness prescribed for patients with arthritis is that the exercises may be painful. It may be discouraging for an arthritic patient to enthusiastically begin a program of physical activity only to discover very soon after the first session that all his joints hurt, and that he becomes exhausted and is barely able to do anything else for the rest of the day. This problem is not peculiar only to the arthritic. "Normal" urban dwellers or suburbanites who have played ball at a summer picnic may find themselves very uncomfortable the following day, having difficulty in finding a comfortable sitting position, and experiencing aches and pains which may require several days to dissipate. Weekend tennis players who are not physically fit often find that their shoulders hurt and that aches and pains appear in other areas of the body which slowly abate before the next game. To them it may not be obvious that pain is the consequence of poor physical conditioning. When this happens to patients with arthritis they may not realize that the pain or discomfort experienced after exercise is not due to the arthritis but the result of being in poor physical condition.

Several studies have suggested a rationale for conditioning exercise in the treatment of RA. It has been proposed that a program of physical fitness can improve aerobic function without detrimental effects on the joints. In the study by Harkcom and colleagues, women with rheumatoid arthritis performed one of three low-intensity aerobic exercise protocols 3 times per week for 12 weeks. The authors reported that all exercise groups improved their aerobic capacity and endurance, and described improvement in activities of daily living with reduced joint pain and fatigue. They showed that exercise in the duration of up to 35 minutes can be of value, and as little as 15 minutes of exercise 3 times per week is sufficient to improve aerobic capacity even when patients have severe limitations.

With a modest beginning, which assumes a total lack of physical fitness, the arthritic must gradually increase the level of activity, leading to one that will adequately maintain the muscle mass and contribute to the best possible function of the joints. It should be stressed that programs available at private spas or other community organizations are usually not adequately prepared to meet the needs of a patient with arthritis. The exercises used in the program for the arthritic must take into account the particular pattern of joint involvement of the individual and incorporate the techniques of joint protection.

If deformities are to be prevented, you must understand that it is highly beneficial to keep your joints functional in spite of some discomfort. This problem perpetuates itself because pain may prevent function and physical inactivity then leads in turn to further loss of motion of the joints. This cycle can be interrupted by the treatment of inflammation prescribed by your doctor and by maintaining limited function in spite of some level of discomfort. Why you must tolerate some discomfort is a fine point which may be confusing and difficult to understand, because it is clear that pain and discomfort are usually the signals to cease physical activity. In some patients the interruption of the pain-inactivity-decreased-function-pain cycle requires that he tolerate some discomfort during the exercise and after it is over. When exercise induces any amount of pain or prolonged periods of discomfort, the physician should be consulted. The decision to continue with the exercise program despite this mild discomfort should never be the patient's alone, but should be supported by the attending physician and supervised by the therapist.

That which is tolerable and that which is excessive discomfort may not be the same for all individuals. Even the same exercise may not bring up the same sensation of pain in the same individual under differing circumstances. There is one simple guideline. Exercise or activity that produces discomfort or pain that persists one hour or longer after physical activity has ended is probably excessive, and an activity that is lighter or of shorter duration should be tried. This problem is an excellent one to discuss with your doctor or therapist. The program of exercise can be supervised by either a physical or an occupational therapist, so long as the exercises are performed as prescribed, the joints are protected, and the condition is not worsened by injuries. Periodic supervision is a must because your needs are continually changing.

Fatigue, Exercise, and Cardiovascular Fitness

Physical activity provides an outlet for the relief of tension and mental fatigue, aids in weight control, improves posture, and enhances one's self-image. Endurance and a sense of well-being are mainly dependent upon circulatory fitness. Exercise must be continued as a lifetime habit, since its benefits rapidly disappear once it has been discontinued.

Patients with inflammatory types of arthritis frequently experience fatigue, often wake up with stiffness, and have difficulty getting started in the morning. As morning stiffness wears off, the patient usually functions relatively well for a few hours, but then becomes increasingly tired in the afternoon and is sometimes unable to perform even minor tasks. The activity of the disease may be largely responsible for the fatigue. Consequently, when the activity of the disease subsides, the fatigue improves. Less frequently recognized is the fact that a lack of physical fitness may also significantly contribute to the fatigue. In some cases the appearance or worsening of fatigue does not necessarily mean that the exercise is excessive. It may mean that you simply need to allow for a generous period of rest after exercise. Any sedentary person would feel tired after exercise, and in this respect arthritics do not differ from other people. In addition to the joint damage inflicted by arthritis and the lack of physical fitness, patients may have other physical impairments such as heart disease or neurological deficits which also may limit the level of exercise they are able to tolerate.

Thus, exercise should be performed *to tolerance*. Tolerance refers not only to the joints but also implies adequate cardio-vascular function. It is important to have your doctor's clearance of your cardiovascular status before engaging in a program of physical activity. Even patients with cardiovascular problems can engage in limited but extremely important programs of ex-ercise with careful monitoring of the cardiovascular function. Symptoms of cardiovascular or pulmonary problems may not appear in a patient who is engaged in very limited physical activity. Even though the cardiovascular function is found to be normal in the pre-exercise physical examination, the use of saunas, steambaths, or whirlpools with high temperatures after exercising is not advisable for the severely disabled or elderly arthritic.

Dynamic exercise like jogging, rope skipping, swimming, bicycling, rowing, dancing, calisthenics, or brisk walking pro-motes cardiovascular fitness by increasing the capacity of the heart and lungs to perform work. For some arthritics such exer-cise may be possible and quite beneficial, while for others this type of exercise may not be possible or may even be contraindi-cated, depending upon the specific pattern of joint involvement. Endurance is an attribute well known to athletes. Though it takes longer to lose muscle mass and strength, just one or two weeks of physical inactivity are sufficient to produce a measur-able loss of endurance which is the first indication of the decline in fitness. Endurance is built through the regular repetition of exercise which not only strengthens the group of muscles performing the function but also forces the heart and lungs to work harder. When these exercises are performed consistently, they stimulate circulatory fitness by increasing the capacity of the heart and lungs to do work. Consequently, the patient is often able to perform a function like walking or normal work with progressively less fatigue.

The availability of swimming facilities offers a unique opportunity to patients with arthritis if they have a minimal command of swimming techniques. In order to be able to experience maximal benefit from these facilities, the patient should at least be able to swim one whole length of the pool independently. Lap swimming is an excellent method of achieving optimal fitness, allowing you to progressively build your strength and endurance. This is ideal for patients with involvement of weight-bearing joints, because the body weight is supported by the buoyancy of the water. The backstroke is probably the easiest style for many patients with arthritis, allowing the individual to be relaxed on his back, which is frequently possible when the lower spinal articulations are not involved. Swimming is particularly helpful when the shoulders are involved.

It is not necessary to know how to swim in order to benefit from exercise performed in water. The severely disabled patient or those patients with less destructive disease but lacking command of swimming techniques still can perform water exercise in therapeutic pools under the supervision of a physical therapist. Warm water exercise may be very effective in relieving pain related to muscle spasm. Similar motions which produce pain when performed in the gym may cause almost no discomfort if they are performed in water. Depending upon the circumstances, many exercises prescribed by the physician or therapist can also be done in the pool. Patients unable to swim can use swimming aids that increase their buoyancy and allow them to exercise without being afraid of drowning. Swimming belts, for instance, may make a substantial difference in what a disabled patient can do in the water. Even if the activities in water are carried out independently, these exercises, along with swimming, should be done in supervised pools.

Repetitive exercises or those performed in water should not be carried to the point of fatigue or pain. The end point of exercise is often a state of pleasant relaxation but not exhaustion. Many patients have indicated that they find it more pleasant to perform their exercises in the water rather than in the gym. Swimming may be much easier than land exercises for overweight persons because the buoyancy helps support their weight. The water temperature is an important consideration. In particular, the arthritic with severe destructive disease who cannot move easily in the water should avoid pools with temperatures lower than that of the body, because cold water stiffens the muscles and reduces peripheral circulation. Equally important, floor exercises should not be performed in chilling temperatures since these conditions favor cramping and spasm and make exercise unpleasant.

Planning the Exercise Program

A detailed description of specific exercises for the arthritic is not helpful because the exercise program is always highly individualized and should be prescribed by your doctor or therapist. However, it can be very useful for you to know some principles behind planning the exercise program.

When the joint inflammation is under control, a deliberate effort should be made to strengthen the corresponding muscles, because they are essential to the protection of the joints. Before a fitness program is initiated, the capacity of the patient to engage in the program has to be assessed. The treating physician should be involved in planning the exercise program because the information from a complete physical examination should be available to the therapist. Your physician will assess your cardiovascular capacity and prescribe the program. Alternatively, he will work in conjunction with a physical therapist who has experience and interest in arthritic problems. There may also be medical problems which preclude certain exercises or make the use of a pool undesirable or contraindicated without supervision. Patients with arthritis having symptoms or a history of cardiovascular abnormalities may need careful study of their cardiovascular performance during exercise to assess their tolerance. It is clear that the therapist should be aware of the diagnosis, specific patterns of joint disability, presence of inflammation, or other types of organ involvement which would lead to restrictions in the program or require emphasis on certain aspects of therapy.

For example, some patients in whom the hands and other joints of the upper extremities are predominantly involved may not understand why they should exercise their legs. Muscular movement is the main force propelling the blood returning to the heart. Therefore, the use of the legs in exercise significantly expedites the efficient return flow of blood to the heart. This is an excellent reason for including leg exercises in a physical fitness program. The program may frequently have to be modified according to the gains or losses experienced by the patient. The exercise plan should provide for progression. Within the tolerance level, the program should provide for moderate overloading of the muscles to develop strength and increase demands on the cardiorespiratory system. Progression should be effected by gradually increasing the intensity or duration of the exercise, or both. For these reasons I believe it to be very beneficial for the patient to have a long-lasting relationship with a qualified physical or occupational therapist. Continuity in both medical management and in the rehabilitation program are highly desirable to bring about the optimal outcome for the individual.

It is evident that the fitness program may begin at completely different levels for different individuals. A cardinal rule is to begin slowly and to build gradually. The initial sessions are generally brief, usually lasting no more than 10 to 15 minutes.

There are many types of fitness programs which can be adopted by patients with arthritis, depending upon the stage of the disease and their ability to function. Primary activities promoting endurance, such as walking or bicycling, may be particularly suitable for some arthritics, while they may be undesirable or impossible for others, depending upon their particular disabilities. What is beneficial to one patient may be contraindicated in the treatment of another patient. This should be continually emphasized and no decisions should be made without thoroughly discussing them with the physician. For instance, vigorous exercises such as jogging, bicycling, or calisthenics have often been prohibited to patients with rheumatoid arthritis. The reason for this recommendation of caution is that stress has been shown to aggravate the inflammatory process. Exercise which is contraindicated during a period of active inflammation may actually become of great value once control of inflammation has been achieved. I do not encourage arthritics to engage in jogging unless they have already been joggers for years and the joints of their lower extremities are normal. Although jogging is an excellent conditioning method, arthritics with involvement of weight-bearing joints should be cautioned that running may lead to foot and leg disorders which may aggravate stable joint deformities. Even though it takes longer to achieve the same aerobic effect, the benefit from brisk walking is nearly equivalent to that of jogging when long-term comparisons are made. Simulated rowing on a rowing machine can also lead to significant conditioning improvement in cardiovascular fitness. The patient who has experienced a remission with little or no permanent residual damage has the capacity to engage in several different methods of enhancing physical fitness such as swimming, walking, calisthenics, or dancing. Variety can be invaluable in a fitness program to sustain the person's interest. Walking is much safer and generally more enjoyable for older arthritic people. Bicycling rates high in promoting fitness in a normal individual. The slumped posture one has to adopt to ride on a bicycle with racing handlebars poses undue stress to the cervical spine. In addition to the problem encountered by those with involvement of joints in the lower extremities, the wrists can be traumatized by pressure and sustained abnormal position. Very debilitated patients with reduced muscle mass may find it difficult to maintain balance. Many arthritics can perform this exercise in the comfort and safety of the home using an indoor stationary bicycle, or outdoors on a touring bicycle. However, even this exercise can be harmful to some patients with severe involvement of the knees or hips. Since stationary bikes are widely advertised and available without prescription, patients with arthritis will be well advised to consult their physicians prior to their use.

Because swimming is a non-weight-bearing exercise, it is ideal for overweight individuals and for patients with arthritis with involvement of the joints of the lower extremities. Calisthenics is usually a valuable part of the exercise program because it promotes aerobic fitness. Therapeutic dance, combining many elements of walking and calisthenics can also be an important part of a fitness program. Recreational sports such as bowling or golf should not be confused with sports or activities that have fitness value. Neither bowling nor golf have a major role in a program of physical fitness for the arthritic, although both may be outlets for relaxation, enjoyment, and some modest physical activity.

Patients with arthritis of the hips, knees, and joints of the feet should avoid physical activities producing pain in these joints. Sports producing impact type stress in these joints, or excessive twisting and bending of the knees, are not advisable for these patients. As a general rule, if a sport or activity produces pain, it should be carried out at a modest pace and, if it still produces discomfort, it should not be done at all. In healthy individuals a program of exercise may prevent the development of sports-related injuries. I believe that physically fit arthritic individuals are likely to sustain considerably fewer injuries, given the same mechanical or physical stress, than arthritic subjects who have led sedentary lives.

When to do the exercise is always a personal decision. Arthritics seldom enjoy early morning activities. To loosen up, mild exercises are recommended on arising, along with a whirlpool session or a long, hot shower. However, stretching as well as strengthening exercises should be done after the morning stiffness has subsided, except in those patients in whom stiffness lasts all day long. Sometimes, relief from pain experienced about one hour after taking pain-relieving medication makes the exercise session easier. In any case, exercise immediately after eating is to be discouraged. Particularly for the more disabled patient, several mini-sessions of 10 to 15 minutes during the day may be better than one long session of exercise. However, one or two daily sessions of 20 to 30 minutes each may be sufficient, and this schedule is often successfully followed. The degree of inflammation present is the major determinant of how much and how long a joint will be mobilized during the exercise session. However, it is clear that how much exercise you can do, that is, your tolerance for exercise, also depends upon your level of physical fitness, muscle mass, and cardiorespiratory status.

Psychological intolerance for exercise may be reached well before physical exhaustion. A patient may experience slight aches, breathlessness, or other mildly distressful feelings which halt exercise before appreciable overloading has occurred. One should look for such factors as anxiety, boredom, and fear of physical injury which may be behind a greatly reduced tolerance for exercise. The patient should gradually learn his true limits by a slowly progressive and mild overloading of the muscles. A lifelong program of exercise promotes a sensation of well-being, increases the endurance of the individual, and allows him to perform better both mentally and physically. Those who exercise regularly have a more elegant posture and walk more swiftly than those leading a sedentary existence. Their performance at work is apt to improve if they are physically fit. A person's general learning potential for a given level of intelligence increases or decreases in accordance with the degree of his physical activity. There is considerable evidence to support the concept that the quality of life is improved by a well-tolerated program of increased physical activity.

Advanced technology has drastically transformed the society of the developed nations. Basically, our ancestors were physically active, hard-working men and women, living in rural areas, while we have been transformed into a population of sedentary, anxious city-dwellers and suburbanites. We may think that we engage in a great deal of physical activity, and we may even be tired at the end of the day; but this type of activity does not do much toward keeping our bodies physically fit. Many people have a vague idea of the value of a program of exercise. When asked if he exercises, the patient may claim that his daily work is exhausting and he therefore does not need any additional exercise. Others may retort that they are constantly "on the run" and that they "have no time left for anything else." This reaction is commonplace when patients hear that exercise is prescribed as a part of their treatment. In this respect, I have heard all kinds of excuses—"I have no time," "I don't have transportation," "Insurance doesn't cover the fees of the therapist," "I get enough exercise at work."

The truth is that there is always time if you set your priorities, that anyone can find transportation for one or two sessions with a therapist, and that most of the time it is up to you to continue the program on your own. Because you do it yourself, it is one of the least expensive aspects of the treatment of arthritis. Exercise performed during most types of work or during routine activities confers little fitness. Moreover, repetitive exercise performed during work can even be traumatic to certain joints and groups of muscles, while other parts of the body remain inactive. The muscles ignored by daily routine become weaker. The main problem is that patients do not think exercise is important enough to be worth the effort. Indeed, city-dwellers seldom walk except for short distances, avoid climbing stairs, and would rather sit, ride an elevator, drive a car, or watch television, than pursue active recreational activity. Everything is done for us, mechanically or automatically; consequently we have very little opportunity to use our own muscles and tax our cardiovascular systems. Industry of the developed world has worked hard to make life easier through automation which requires us to expend ever less physical effort.

However, there is increasing evidence that a sedentary life endangers the overall function of our bodies and a variety of medical problems have been found to be directly or indirectly related to this lack of physical activity. Modern man, especially when he lives in urban and suburban areas, has become an increasingly sedentary person. Conservative statistics indicate that more than half of all Americans do not exercise regularly. It is very common to see young individuals with deplorable levels of physical fitness. There are studies suggesting that exercise may even add years to the life of the individual. Between 1950 and 1970 the mortality from heart disease in the United States decreased. Among other factors which have been suggested to explain this declining mortality, decreased smoking, decreased dietary intake of saturated fats, and more widespread use of programs of physical fitness are of particular interest to patients with arthritis. It has been shown that regular physical activity does not invariably prevent a heart attack, but that it does make its occurrence less likely. The attacks also tend to be less severe and the chance of survival is greater among the physically fit. According to the President's Council on Physical Fitness and Sports, the conclusions of a 10-year study were that regular exercise, in combination with other good living habits, can help increase life expectancy by as much as 11 years for men and 7 years for women. There is no doubt that everyone, without exception, could benefit from a lifelong program of physical fitness.

Functional Adaptation

It is my opinion that the effort to achieve physical fitness is even more important to a patient afflicted with arthritis than for most persons. The adaptation of the body to function in spite of joint deformities is greatly aided by fitness. This adaptation does not take place if, in addition to the deformities produced by the arthritis, the muscles are flabby and the body generally unfit. The changes that are the result of a physically fit body do not happen by chance or by sporadic effort. They are accomplished only by the daily activity of the self-disciplined person making a conscious effort to achieve physical fitness. Prolonged inflammation and pain in the joints force the patient into an even more sedentary life-style with many lamentable consequences which can be prevented or lessened by a program of physical exercise. A home program of physical fitness is obviously vital to a patient afflicted with a chronic arthritis.

The major benefits attributed to regular exercise in both medical and lay literature are improved cardiovascular function, the prevention of anxiety, depression, low back pain, bone loss, and other problems associated with old age. Exercise alleviates stiffness, muscle spasm, and weakness and, in most people, it can improve respiratory function. It has been shown to produce a modest decrease in serum cholesterol levels and to contribute to a reduction in body weight. Exercise may possibly be beneficial to diabetics who may require less insulin, and may help prevent the formation of blood clots.

Inflammation of the small joints of the spine and the sacroiliac joints is a feature of the spondyloarthropathies such as ankylosing spondylitis, Reiter's syndrome, some forms of inflammatory bowel disease, and psoriatic arthritis. The main problem of these patients is that articulations of the spine tend to fuse, and if the posture is not adequate, fusion occurs, with a marked curvature of the spine. This can be prevented by postural exercises that permit fusion of the spine in an erect position which allows function. Although low back pain is not a feature of other types of arthritis, many patients may complain of low back pain due to poor conditioning, faulty posture, and abnormal biomechanical action. Weak abdominal muscles impose considerable stress upon the back. This problem is often corrected with an exercise program of gradual progression and instruction in proper posture and back protection. The strengthening of abdominal muscles can be extremely helpful for patients with backache. Swimming offers particular advantages for strengthening the back and abdominal muscles.

The progressive joint damage and disability experienced by many patients with arthritis is responsible for social isolation and dependency. Social mobility and the ability to independently seek new social experiences is severely compromised in the arthritic patient. Perhaps the greatest benefit from maintaining physical fitness is the degree of independence that it provides. The ability to plan and do things without depending on relatives, friends, or needing assistance is a significant advantage for the arthritic.

Exercise and Flexion Contractures

One of the most important goals of the treatment of a patient with arthritis is to prevent the development of contractures or to reduce them when they are present. If the components of muscles, tendons, and joints are not stretched, they become tighter. Most of the contractures commonly found in patients with arthritis are flexion deformities, which can be the consequence of changes in the joint capsule, the synovial membrane, the ligaments, or the muscles powering the joints. The extent to which these structures participate in the contracture varies with the different stages of the arthritis. When inflammation of the joint predominates, pain triggering the adjacent muscle spasm is an important factor in early contracture. At this stage, the treatment of the contracture is the treatment of the inflammation, and little is gained by the use of muscle relaxants. When inflammation is controlled and pain subsides, the contracture often improves or disappears. Removal of synovia can have a definite influence in alleviating the contracture. Later on, in a more chronic stage, changes in the articular capsule, ligaments, and tendons are not inflammatory in nature, and depend upon the presence of scar tissue. In these cases, the stretching of the joint can be accomplished by stretching exercises, wedge casting, splinting, or by traction, which allows the gradual stretching of the scar tissue through the application of prolonged, gentle force.

Stretching exercises may have a beneficial effect by relieving the tightness secondary to prolonged disuse or to being inactive in the same position. An example is the shortening of hip flexors that frequently occurs when a person sits for a long time. Prolonged sitting while watching television is a frequent cause of restriction of the motion of the hip in sedentary individuals. The purpose of stretching exercises is to prevent contractures or to increase range of motion when contracture has occurred. These exercises should always be performed very gently. They are not very useful in the presence of severe destruction of the joint and they are contraindicated if the decreased range of motion of the joint is due to fusion of the bone ends with the actual disappearance of the joint space.

Functional Exercise for a Better Life

The primary purpose of the exercise program is to help you function independently in your activities of daily life. A patient able to move all four extremities is instructed to do active exercises independently. Functional exercise is what you do in real life, such as walking, getting dressed, cooking, shaving, driving, and the many activities of daily living. They are taken for granted when you are healthy but eventually become very arduous tasks if you are stricken by arthritis. The appearance of arthritis in young persons who are artistically inclined, such as a talented musician, may demand that the individual make painful career decisions. Many inflammatory arthritides frequently involve the small joints of the hands; therefore, these patients may experience great difficulties in pursuing a professional career in music or in art. However, many patients may go into remission and the lesions may become stabilized. In these patients there is no evidence that the continuation of an activity such as playing the piano or drawing in moderation does harm to the arthritic hand. Although some young arthritics can be discouraged, some of my patients have continued a successful career in show business, the concert hall, and teaching piano, violin, cello and other instruments. These activities can, of course, be tremendous sources of enjoyment and personal fulfillment. Unfortunately, relatively few people have the option of engaging in creative expression, and with the exception of those with the most severe deformities, those having talent and the desire should not be prohibited from engaging in such activity.

Alert and educated patients can evaluate the beneficial effect of the exercise program by assessing their ability to function. They can easily see that they can walk longer distances, perform tasks which they were unable to do before, and engage in physical activities with little or no fatigue.

Improvement due to a program of exercise is not seen in a short time. This is a relative disadvantage when we compare the effects of exercise to the rapid relief the patient can sometimes experience with a new medication. As a consequence, many patients may not see the need for continuing with the exercises as prescribed and frequently stop doing them regularly. The patient must realize that time is an important factor in the improvement produced by exercise. Though minor improvement can be noted within a few weeks, major improvement can often be seen only after months of daily exercise.

After the initial acute stage is over and the activity of the disease is controlled, it is important to complement the exercise with activities that the individual may like and may be willing to pursue. Occupational therapists may be invaluable in helping plan this aspect of the exercise program. When the arthritis is in remission, the need for a regular program of exercise is frequently ignored. Many patients will try to substitute games and recreational activities for a program of exercise. While fun activities are useful, they are not substitutes for a lifelong program of physical activity. It is far better to become physically fit before engaging in a given sport than to attempt to use the sport as a means of getting in shape. Some of my rheumatoid patients play golf, swim, ski, bowl, or ride a bicycle and some in complete remission with normal joints in their lower extremities are avid joggers. Two of my patients, one man and one woman, have finished a local marathon. Of course, both were in complete remission and had no involvement of the lower extremities. The level of exercise performed may be more or less vigorous, depending upon their existing disabilities. Many patients with arthritis frequently live in loneliness or isolation. The practice of exercise affords an excellent opportunity for social interaction.

Knowing how other patients have reacted to a prescribed exercise program is seldom helpful to a new patient about to begin the experience. Not only are there different types of arthritis, but the problems of each person differ significantly, even if both individuals have been diagnosed as having the same type of arthritis. No two patients with arthritis are affected in exactly the same manner. Their needs in all areas of treatment may be completely dissimilar. Treatment indicated for one patient may not be helpful or may even be contraindicated for another patient. Whatever individual program is finally developed, it should be followed with perseverance, and with the understanding that this aspect of the treatment is no less important than any other of the concomitant parts of the comprehensive treatment of the disease.

REFERENCES

Adams, R. D. 1983. Approach to the patient with nervous system disease. In *Harrison's Principles of Internal Medicine*. R. G. Petersdorf, R. D. Adams, E. Braunwald, K. J. Isselbacher, J. B. Martin, and J. D. Wilson (eds.). New York: McGraw-Hill.

Adams, R. 1977. *Miracle Medicine Foods*. West Nyack, NY: Parker.

Airola, P. O. 1968. *There Is a Cure for Arthritis*. West Nyack, NY: Parker.

Alexander, D. D. 1956. *Arthritis and Common Sense*. Hartford, CT: Witcover Press.

Altman, R. D., Schultz, D. R., Collins-Yudiskas, B., Aldrich, J., Arnold, P. I., Brown, H. E. 1984. The effects of a partially purified fraction of ant venom in rheumatoid arthritis. *Arthritis Rheum* 27:277–284.

Arnett, F. C. 1987. Seronegative spondyloarthropathies. *Bull Rheum Dis* 37(1), 1–12.

Living and Loving. 1982. Atlanta, GA: Arthritis Foundation.

Arthritis Foundation Medical Information Series on Rheumatoid Arthritis.

Arthritis: The Basic Facts. 1978. Atlanta, GA: Arthritis Foundation.

Avioli, L. V., Krane, S. M. 1977. *Metabolic Bone Disease*. New York: Academic Press.

Bardana, E. J., Jr., Manilow, M. R., Houghton, D. C., *et al.* 1982. Diet-induced systemic lupus erythematosus (SLE) in primates. *Am J Kidney Dis* 1:345–352.

Barnes, L. A. 1975. Safety considerations with high ascorbic acid dosage. *Ann NY Acad Sci* 258:523.

Bauer, J., Figley, Banwell, A. 1981. Psychological and sexual health in rheumatic diseases. In: *Textbook of Rheumatology*. W. N. Kelly, E. D. Harris, S. Ruddy, C. B. Sledge (eds.). Philadelphia: W. B. Saunders. pp. 501–510.

Bauer, W. 1935. What should a patient with arthritis eat? *JAMA* 104:1–6.

Bayles, T. B., Palmer, R. J., Massad, M. F., Judd, E. H. 1950. Vitamin B excretion studies in patients with rheumatoid arthritis. *New Engl J Med* 242:249–257.

Bayles, T.B., Richardson, M., Hall, F.C. 1943. Nutritional background of patients with rheumatoid arthritis. *New Engl J Med* 299:319–324.

Beck, B. F. 1935. *Bee Venom Therapy: Bee Venom, Its Nature and Its Effects on Arthritis and Rheumatic Conditions*. New York: Appleton-Century-Crofts.

Biegel, L. 1984. *Physical Fitness and the Older Person*. L. Biegel (ed.). Rockville, MD: Aspen Publishing Co. pp. 13–26.

Bigaouette, J., Timchalk, M. A., Kremer, J. 1987. Nutritional adequacy of diet and supplements in patients with rheumatoid arthritis who take medications. *J Amer Diet Assoc* 87:1687–1688.

Blankenhorn, D. H. 1985. Two new diet-heart studies. (Editorial). *New Engl J Med* 312:851–852.

Bradlow, A., Mowat, A. G. 1985. Alcohol consumption in arthritic patients: Clinical and laboratory studies. *Ann Rheum Dis* 44:163–168.

Briggs, M. H. 1973. Side effects of vitamin C. *Lancet* 2:1439.

Briggs, M. H. 1974. Vitamin E supplements and fatigue. *New Engl J Med* 290:579.

Brobyn, R. D. 1975. The human toxicology of dimethylsulfoxide. *Ann NY Acad Sci* 243:500–509.

Carr, C. J. 1982. Food and drug interactions. *Ann Rev Pharmacol Toxicol* 22:19–29.

Carston, R. 1978. *Devil's Claw Root and Other Natural Remedies for Arthritis*. 2nd ed. Vancouver: Alive Books.

Carter, M. 1969. *Helping Yourself with Foot Reflexology*. West Nyack, NY: Parker.

Chandra, R. K., Newberne, P. M. 1983. In Nutrition, Immunity and

Infection: Present knowledge and future directions. *Lancet* 1:688–691.

Chang, Y. H., Bliven, N. L. 1979. Anti-arthritic effects of bee venom. *Agents Actions* 9:205.

Charaka Samhita. Trans. A. Ch. Kaviratna. Calcutta.

Clark, L. 1971. *Get Well Naturally*. New York: Arc Books.

Consensus Conference: Osteoporosis. 1984. *JAMA* 252:799–802.

Cramp, A. J. 1921. *Nostrums and Quackery*. Chicago: American Medical Association Press.

Crout, R. J. Hearing before the Select Committee on Aging. 96th Congress, 2nd Session, 24 March 1980. Pub. No. 96–232.

Cureton, T. K. 1969. *The Physiological Effects of Exercise Programs on Adults*. Springfield, IL: Charles Thomas. pp. 15–22.

Czajka-Narins, D. M. 1984. Minerals. In: *Food, Nutrition and Diet Therapy*. M. V. Krause, L. K. Mahan (eds.). Philadelphia: W. B. Saunders. pp. 144–180.

Damboriena, P. 1969. *Tongues as of Fire: Pentecostalism in Contemporary Christianity*. Washington: Corpus Books.

Dong, C. H., Banks, J. 1975. New Hope for the Arthritic. New York: T. Y. Crowell.

Dornton, R. 1968. *Mesmerism*. Cambridge, MA: Harvard University Press.

Edwards, Harry. 1963. (repr. 1978) *The Power of Spiritual Healing*. Burrows Lea: Anchor Press.

Ekblon, B., Lovgren, O., Alderin, M., Friedstrom, M., Satterstrom, G. 1975. Effect of short term physical training in patients with rheumatoid arthritis. *Scand J Rheumatol* 4:80–86.

Fabio, A. D. *Rheumatoid Diseases Cured at Last*: Franklin, TN: The Rheumatoid Disease Foundation.

Fenz, E. 1941. Kupfer ein neues mittel gegen chronischen und subacuten gelenkrheumatismus. *Munch Med Woschr* 18:1101–1105.

Food and Nutrition Board, National Research Council: Recommended dietary allowances. 9th ed. Washington, D.C.: National Academy of Sciences. 1980.

Friedman, C. D., Siegelaub, A. B., Selzer, C. C. 1974. Cigarettes, alcohol, coffee and peptic ulcer. *N Engl J Med* 290:469.

Gibson, R. G., Gibson, L. M., MacNeill, A. D. *et al.*: Homeopathic therapy in rheumatoid arthritis: Evaluation by double-blind clinical therapeutic trial. *Br. J. Clin Pharmacol* 1980. 9:453–59

Glauber, H., Wallace, P., Griver, K., and Brechtel, G. 1988. Adverse metabolic effect of omega-3 fatty acids in non-insulin dependent diabetes mellitus. *Ann Int Med*. 108:663–668.

Glymour, C., Stalker, D. 1983. Engineers, Cranks, Physicians, Magicians. *New Eng J Med* 308:960–964.

Goldin, R. H., McAdam, L., Louie, J. S., Gold, R., Bluestone, R. 1976. Clinical and radiological survey of the incidence of osteoarthritis among obese patients. *Ann Rheum Dis* 35:359–363.

Good, R. A., Fernandes, G., West, A. 1984. Nutrition and immunity. In: *Nutrition Reviews: Present Knowledge in Nutrition*, 5th Ed. Washington, D.C.: Nutrition Foundation.

Gordon, B. L. 1949. *Medicine Throughout Antiquity*. Philadelphia: F. A. Davis Co.

Harkcom, T. M., Lampman, R. M., Figley Banwell, B., Banwell, B., Castor, C. W. 1985. Therapeutic value of gradual aerobic exercise training in rheumatoid arthritis. *Arthritis Rheum* 28:32–39.

Harkness, J. A. L., Griffin, A. J., Heinrich, I., Gibson, T., Grahame, R. 1982. A double-blind comparison study of metronidazole and placebo in rheumatoid arthritis. *Rheum Rehab* 21:231–234.

Harris, E. D., Jr., 1981. Pathogenesis of rheumatoid arthritis. In: *Textbook of Rheumatology*. W. Kelly, E. D. Harris, Jr., S. Ruddy, C. Sledge (eds.). Philadelphia: W. B. Saunders.

Harris, E. D., Jr., 1981. Rheumatoid arthritis: The clinical spectrum. In: *Textbook of Rheumatology*, Vol. 1. W. Kelly, E. D. Harris, Jr., S. Ruddy, C. Sledge (eds.). Philadelphia: W. B. Saunders. pp. 928–963.

Hathcock, J. N. 1982. Nutritional toxicology: Definition and scope. In: *Nutritional Toxicology*, Vol. I. J. N. Hathcock (ed.). New York: Academic Press. pp. 1–15.

Hayes, K. C., Hegsted, D. M. 1973. Toxicity of the vitamins. In: *Toxicants Occurring Naturally in Foods*. National Research Council (eds.). Washington, D.C.: National Academy of Sciences.

H. B. 63 Introduced to the 117th General Assembly of the State of Ohio, 1987–1988.

Hench, B. S., Bauer, W., Dawson, M. H., Hall, F., Holbrook, W. P., Key, J. A., McEwen, C. The problem of rheumatism and arthritis. Review of American and English Literature. 1938. (Sixth Rheumatism Review) *Ann Int Med* 13:1838–1990, 1940.

Hench, B. S., Bauer, W., Boland, E., Dawson, M. H., Freyberg, R. H., Holbrook, W. P., Key, J. A., Locke, C. N., McEwen, C. Rheumatism and Arthritis. Review of the American and English Literature. 1940. (Eighth Rheumatism Review) *Ann Int Med* 15:1002–1108, 1941.

Hench, P. S., Kendall, E. C., Slocum, C. H., Polley, H. F. 1949. The effects of a hormone of the adrenal cortex [hydroxy-11-dehydrocortico-sterone: compound E] and of pituitary adrenocorticotropic hormone on rheumatoid arthritis. Preliminary report. *Proc Staff Meet Mayo Clin* 24:181–197.

Hiscoe, H. B. 1983. Does being natural make it good? *New Eng J Med* 308:1474–75.

Hitchcock, J., Bednorski, Sr. G. 1980. *Charismatics*. Chicago, IL: Thomas Moore Press.

Hoffer, C. J., Bistrian, B. R., Young, V. R., Blockburn, G. L., Mathews, D. E. 1984. Metabolic effects of very low calorie weight reduction diets. *J Clin Invest* 73:750–758.

Hoffman, A. 1974. Psychological factors associated with rheumatoid arthritis. *Nurs Res* 23:218.

Holden, C. 1980. Flurry over venom. *Science* 207:161.

Huang Ti Nei Ching Su Wên. (Translation 1949.) I. Veith. Baltimore: Williams and Wilkins.

Hutchins, P., Walker-Smith, J. A. 1982. Food allergy: Gastrointestinal system. *Clin Immunol Allergy* 2:43–76.

Jacob, S. W., Herschler, R. 1983. Introductory remarks: Dimethyl-sulfoxide after twenty years. In: Biological Actions and Medical Applications of Dimethylsulfoxide [DMSO]. J. C. de la Torre (ed.). *Ann NY Acad Sci* 411.

Jaffe, J. A. 1985. Penicillamine. In: *Arthritis and Allied Conditions*, 10th Ed. D. J. McCarty (ed). Philadelphia: Lea and Febiger. pp. 502–511.

Jaffe, R. M., Kasten, B., Young, D. S., MacLowry, J. D. 1975. False negative stool occult blood tests caused by ingestion of ascorbic acid (vitamin C) *Ann Int Med* 83:824.

Jarvis, D. C. 1960. *Arthritis and Folk Medicine*. Greenwich, CT: Fawcett.

Joyce, C. R. B., Welldon, R. M. C. 1965. The objective efficacy of prayer. A double blind clinical trial. *J Chron Dis* 18:367–97.

Katch, F. I., McArdle, W. D. 1977. *Nutrition, Weight Control and Exercise*. Boston: Houghton-Mifflin.

Kaufman, W. 1981. Niacinamide: A most neglected vitamin. *Prev Med* 6:1–48.

Kelley, V. E., Ferretti, A., Izui, S., Strom, T. B. 1985. A fish oil diet rich in eicosapentaenoic acid reduces cyclooxygenase metabolites, and suppresses lupus in MRL-lpr mice. *J Immunol* 134:1914–1919.

Kellgren, J. H., Lawrence, J. S., and Bier, F. 1963. Genetic factors in general osteoarthritis. *Ann Rheum Dis* 22:239–255.

Kowsari, B., Finnie, S. K., Carter, R. L., Love, J., Katz, P., Laongley, S., Panush, R. S. 1983. Assessment of diet of patients with rheumatoid arthritis and osteoarthritis. *J Am Diet Assoc* 82:657–659.

Krane, S. M., Potts, J. T. 1983. Skeletal remodeling and factors influencing bone and bone mineral metabolism. In: Harrison's *Principles of Internal Medicine*. New York: McGraw-Hill. p. 1921.

Kremer, J. M., Bigaouette, J., Michalec, A. U., Timchalk, M. A., Lininger, L., Rynes, R. I., Huyck, C., Zieminski, J. and

Bartholomew, L. E. 1985. Effects of manipulation of dietary fatty acids on clinical manifestations of rheumatoid arthritis. *Lancet* 8422:184–187.

Krieger, D. 1979. *The Therapeutic Touch*. Englewood Cliffs, NJ: Prentice Hall.

Leach, W. A., Baumgard, S., Bromme, J. 1973. Obesity: Its relationship to osteoarthritis of the knee. *Clin Orthop* 93:271–273.

Ledit, S. 1969. *Therapeutic Exercise*. Ballentine, MD: Waverly Press.

Levy, M. 1974. Aspirin use in patients with major upper gastrointestinal bleeding and peptic ulcer disease. *New Engl J Med* 290:1158.

Lewis, I. M. 1977. *Ecstatic Religion: An Anthropological Study of Spirit Possession and Shamanism*. Harmondsworth, Middlesex: Penguin.

Lightfoot, R. W. 1985. Treatment of rheumatoid arthritis In: Arthritis and Allied Conditions, 10th Ed. D. J. McCarty, (ed). Philadelphia: Lea and Febiger.

Linn, R., Stuart, S. L. 1979. *The Last Chance Diet*. Secaucus, NJ: Lyle Stuart, Inc.

Lipsky, P. E., Ziff, M. 1980. Inhibition of human T-cell function in vitro by D-penicillamine and $CuSO_4$. *J Clin Invest* 65:1068–1076.

Lockshin, M. D. 1981. Unproven remedies committee. *Arthritis Rheum* 24:1188–1190.

Lucas, C. P., Powers, L. 1981. Dietary fat aggravates active rheumatoid arthritis. *Clin Res*. 29:754A.

Lucas, R. 1969. *Common and Uncommon Uses of Herbs for Healthful Living*. New York: Arc Books.

Luukkainan, R., Isomaki, N., Kajander, A. 1983. Prognostic value of the type of onset of rheumatoid arthritis. *Ann Rheum Dis* 42:274–275.

Mabenly, F. H. 1910. Brief notes on the treatment of rheumatism by bee stings. *Lancet* 2:235.

Malinow, M. R., Bardana, E. J., Jr., Pirofsky, B. *et al*. 1982. Systemic lupus erythematosus-like syndrome in monkeys fed alfalfa sprouts: Role of a nonprotein amino acid. *Science*. 216:415–17.

Manjo, G. 1975. *The Healing Hand. Man and Wound in the Ancient World*. Cambridge, MA: Harvard University Press.

Masi, T. A., Maldonado-Cocco, J. A., Kaplan, S. B., Feigenbaum, S. L., Chandler, R. W. 1976. Prospective study of the early course of rheumatoid arthritis in young adults: Comparison of patients with and without rheumatoid factor positivity at entry and identification of variables correlating with outcome. *Seminars in Arthritis Rheum* 5:299–326.

Masi, A. T., Medger, T. A., Jr. 1979. Epidemiology of the rheumatic diseases. In: *Arthritis and Allied Conditions*, 9th Ed. D. J. McCarty, (ed.). Philadelphia: Lea and Febiger. pp. 11–35.

McCarty, D. J., (ed). 1985. *Arthritis and Allied Conditions* 10th Ed. Philadelphia: Lea and Febiger.

McCarty, D. J., O'Duffy, J. D., Pearson, L., Hunter, J. B. 1985. Remitting seronegative symmetrical synovitis with pitting edema RS₃PE syndrome. *JAMA* 254:2763–2767.

McCay, C. M., Maynard, L. A., Sperling, G., Barnes, L. L. 1939. Retarded growth, lifespan, ultimate body size and age changes in albino rat after feeding diets restricted in calories. *J Nutr* 18:1013.

McGraw, D. B. Summer 1980. Meaning and belonging in a charismatic congregation: An investigation into sources of neo-pentecostal success. *Review of Religious Research*, Vol. 21., No. 3. pp. 294–301.

McNutt, Francis, O. P. 1974. *Healing*. Notre Dame, IN: Ave Maria Press.

Miller, D. R., Hayes, K. C. 1982. Vitamin excess and toxicity. In: *Nutritional Toxicology: Definition and Scope*, Vol I. J. N. Hathcock (ed.). New York: Academic Press. pp. 81–133.

Modolfsky, N., Chester, W. J. 1970. Pain and mood patterns in patients with rheumatoid arthritis. *Psychosom Med* 32:309–318.

Moss, A. J. 1985. Caution: Very low calorie diets can be deadly. (Editorial.) *Ann Int Med* 102:121–122.

Murphy, B. F. 1974. Hypervitaminosis E. *JAMA* 227:1381.

National Center for Health Statistics, PHS Publication No. 1000, Series 11, No. 17. 1966. Washington, D.C.: United States Government Printing Office.

Nelson, R. A., Jr. 1966. A new concept of immunosuppression in hypersensitivity reactions and in transplantation immunity. *Surv Opthalmol* 11:498–505.

Neuberger, M. 1910. *History of Medicine*. London: Oxford Medical Publications.

Nordemar, R. 1981. Physical training in rheumatoid arthritis: A control long term study. *Scand J Rheumatol* 10:23–30.

Oberleas, D. 1973. Phytates. In: *Toxicants Occurring Naturally in Foods*. Washington, D.C.: National Academy of Science. pp. 363–371.

O'Conner, E. D. 1971. *The Pentecostal Movement in the Catholic Church*. Notre Dame, IN: Ave Maria Press.

Olefsky, J. M. 1983. Obesity. In: *Harrison's Principles of Internal Medicine*. 10th Ed. R. G. Petersdorf, R. D. Adams, E. Braunwald, K. J. Isselbacher, J. B. Martin, J. D. Wilson (eds.). New York: McGraw-Hill. pp. 440–46.

Ott, J. 1958. *My Ivory Cellar*. Chicago: Twentieth Century Press.

Palmblad, J., Contell, I., Hohn, G., Norberg, R., Strauder, H., Sundblat, I. 1972. Acute energy deprivation in man. Effect of serum immunoglobulin antibody response. Complement factor 3 and 4, acute phase reactants and interferon-producing capacity of blood lymphocytes. *Clin Exp Immunol* 30:50–55.

Panush, R. S. 1984. Controversial arthritis remedies. *Bull Rheum Dis* 34(5):1–8.

Panush, R. S., Carter, R. L., Katz, P., Kowarsi, B., Longley, S., Finnie, S. 1983. Diet therapy for rheumatoid arthritis. *Arthritis Rheum* 26:462–471.

Panush, R. S., Webster, E. M. 1985. Food allergies and other adverse reactions to foods. *Med Clin North Am* 69:533–546.

Parke, A. L., Hughes, G. R. V. 1981. Rheumatoid arthritis and food: A case study. *Br Med J* 282:2027–2029.

Pathak, M. A., Fitzpatrick, T. B., Parrish, J. A. 1983. Photosensitivity and other reactions to light. In: *Harrison's Principles of Internal Medicine*. R. G. Petersdorf, R. D. Adams, E. Braunwald, K. J. Isselbacher, J. B. Martin, J. D. Wilson (eds.). New York: McGraw-Hill.

Pearson, D., Shaw, S. 1982. *Life Extension: A Practical Scientific Approach*. New York: Warner Books.

Phillips, P. E., Christian, C. 1985. Infectious agents in clinical rheumatic disease. In: *Arthritis and Allied Conditions*. 10th Ed. D. J. McCarty (ed.). Philadelphia: Lea and Febiger. pp. 431–449.

Pinals, R. S., Dalakos, T. B., Streeten, D. H. P. 1979. Idiopathic edema as a cause of nonarticular rheumatism. *Arthritis Rheum* 22:396–399.

The President's Council on Physical Fitness and Sports, Publication No. OS-77-50013. 1978. Washington, D.C.: U.S. Department of Health, Education and Welfare.

Prickett, J. D., Robinson, D. R., Steinberg, A. D. 1983. Effects of dietary enrichment with eicosapentaenoic acid upon autoimmune nephritis in female NZB/NZW F_1 mice. *Arthritis Rheum* 266:133–39.

Prickett, J. D., Trentham, D. E., Robinson, D. R. 1984. Dietary fish oil augments the induction of arthritis in rats immunized with type II collagen. *J Immunol* 132:725.

Richardson, J. 1980. *The Herb Encyclopedia*. Springfield, UT: Thorn Books.

Ritter, E. K. 1965. Magical Expert(= Assipu) and Physician(Asu). Notes on two complementary professions in Babylonian medicine. *Assyriological Studies*, No. 16, The Oriental Institute of the University of Chicago. Chicago, IL: University of Chicago Press.

Roberts, J. L., Hayashi, J. A. 1983. Exacerbation of SLE associated with alfalfa ingestion. *New Engl J Med* 308:1361.

Rodman, G. P., Schumaker, H. R., Zvaifler, N. J. (eds.). 1983. *Primer on the Rheumatic Diseases*. Atlanta, GA: The Arthritis Foundation.

Ruddy, S. The management of rheumatoid arthritis: The clinical spectrum. In: *Textbook of Rheumatology*. W. N. Kelly, E. D. Harris, S. Ruddy, C. B. Sledge (eds.). Philadelphia: W. B. Saunders. p. 928.

Rudman, D., Bleier, J. C. Nutrition and nutritional requirements. In: *Harrison's Principles of Internal Medicine*, 10th Ed. R. G. Petersdorf, R. D. Adams, E. Braunwald, K. J. Isselbacher, J. B. Martin, J. D. Wilson (eds.). New York: McGraw-Hill. pp. 426–443.

Saville, P. D., Dickson, J. 1968. Age and weight in osteoarthritis of the hip. *Arthritis Rheum* 11:635–644.

Schaffner, R. M. 1977. Current regulations and future activities of the Food and Drug Administration for regulating colors. In: *Current Aspects of Food Colorants*. T. E. Furia (ed.). Boca Raton, FL: CRC Press. pp. 85–90.

Schrauzer, G. N., Rhead, W. J. 1973. Ascorbic acid abuse: Effects of long term ingestion of excessive amounts on blood levels and urinary excretion. *Int J Nutr Res* 43:201.

Schultz, D. R., Arnold, P. I. 1979. Venom of the ant pseudomyrmex sp: Further characterizations of two factors that affect human complement protein. *J Immunol* 119:1690–1699.

Shaw, J. H., Sweeney, E. A. 1973. Nutrition in relation to dental medicine. In: *Modern Nutrition in Health and Disease*. R. S. Goodheart, M. E. Shils (eds.). Philadelphia: Lea and Febiger. pp. 733–769.

Shelton, H. M. 1978. *Fasting for Renewal of Life*. Tampa, FL: Natural Hygiene Press.

Shkendirov, S., Koburova, K. 1982. Adolapin: A newly isolated analgetic and anti-inflammatory polypeptide from bee venom. *Toxicon* 20:317–321.

Simkin, P. 1982. In *Inflammatory Diseases and Copper* J. R. J. Sorenson (ed.). Clifton, NJ: Humana Press.

Skinner, M., Cathcart, E. S., Mills, Pinals, R. S. 1971. Tetracycline in the treatment of rheumatoid arthritis: A double blind controlled study. *Arthritis Rheum* 14:727–732.

Sköldstam, L. 1986. Fasting and vegan diet in rheumatoid arthritis. *Scand J. Rheum* 15:219–223.

Sköldstam, L., Larsson, L., Lindstrom, F. D. 1979. Effects of fasting and lacto-vegetarian diet on rheumatoid arthritis. *Scand J. Rheumatol* 6:249–255.

Smith, H. D. 1965. *The Secret of Instantaneous Healing*. West Nyack, NY: Parker.

Smyth, H. A. 1985. Nonarticular rheumatism and psychogenic musculoskeletal syndrome. In: *Arthritis and Allied Conditions*, 10th Ed. D. J. McCarty (ed.). Philadelphia: Lea and Febiger. pp. 1083–1094.

Sorenson, J. R. J. 1982. *Inflammatory Diseases and Copper*. Clifton, NJ: Humana Press.

Stamler, J. 1978. Lifestyle, major risk factors, proof and public policy. *Circulation* 58:3–19.

Steere, A. C., Malawista, S. E., Snydman, D. R., Shope, R. E., Andiman, W. A., Ross, M. R., Steele, F. M. 1977. Lyme arthritis. An epidemic of oligocarticular arthritis in children and adults in three Connecticut communities. *Arthritis Rheum* 20:7–17.

Sushruta Samhita. II. (Translated by K. L. Bhishagratua. 1907–1911.) Varanasi, India: Chowkhamba Sanskrit Series Office.

Swezey, R. L. 1978. *Arthritis, Rational Therapy and Rehabilitation*. Philadelphia: W. B. Saunders.

Thompson, R. C. 1903–1904. *The Devil and Evil Spirit of Babylonia and Assyria*, Vol. IV. London.

U.S. Senate Select Committee on Nutrition and Human Needs. February 1977. Dietary Goals for the United States. Washington, D. C.: U. S. Government Printing Office.

Vandenbroucke, J. P., Hazevoet, H. M., Cats, A. 1984. Survival and cause of death in rheumatoid arthritis: A 25 year prospective follow-up. *J Rheumatol* 11:158–16.

Vetrano, V. 1978. In: *Fasting for Renewal of Life*. H. M. Shelton (ed.). Tampa, FL: Natural Hygiene Press.

Wade, C. 1972. Natural Hormones: *The Secret of Youthful Health*. West Nyack, NY: Parker.

Walker, W. R., Beveridge, S. J., Whitehouse, M. W. 1981. Dermal copper drugs: The copper bracelet and Cu(II) salicylate complexes. *Agents Actions* [suppl] 8:359–367.

Walker, W. R. 1982. The results of a copper bracelet clinical trial and subsequent studies. An investigation of the therapeutic value of the 'copper bracelet' dermal assimilation of copper in arthritic/rheumatoid conditions. In: *Inflammatory Diseases and Copper*. J. R. J. Sorenson (ed.). Clifton, NJ: Humana Press.

Warmbrand, M. 1962. *The Encyclopedia of Health and Nutrition*. New York: Pyramid Communications, Inc.

Webb, R. B. 1980. Prolonged mild nutritional deficiencies: Significance for health maintenance. *J Nutr Elderly* 1:3–22.

Willer, J. C., Dehen, H., Cambier, J. 1981. Stress-induced analgesia in humans: Endogenous opioids and nalaxone-reversible depression of pain reflexes. *Science* 212:689–690.

Williams, E. R., Caliendo, M. A. 1984. *Nutrition. Principles, Issues and Applications*. New York: McGraw-Hill.

Williams, R. C., McCarty, D. J. Clinical picture of rheumatoid arthritis.

In: *Arthritis and Allied Conditions*, 10th Ed. D. J. McCarty (ed.). Philadelphia: Lea and Febiger. pp. 605–619.

Williams, R. J. 1971. *Nutrition Against Disease*. New York: Pitman.

Wojtulewski, J. A., Gow, P. J., Walter, J., Grahme, R., Gibson, T., Panayi, G. S., Mason, J. 1980. Clotrimazole in rheumatoid arthritis. *Ann Rheum Dis* 39:469–472.

Wolff, B. B. 1971–72. Current psychosocial concepts in rheumatoid arthritis. *Bull Rheum Dis* 22:656a.

Wood, A. A. J., Oates, J. A. Adverse reactions to drugs. In: *Harrison's Principles of Internal Medicine*, 10th Ed. R. G. Petersdorf, R. D. Adams, E. Braunwald, K. J. Isselbacher, J. B. Martin, J. D. Wilson (eds.). New York: McGraw-Hill.

Wyburn-Mason, R. *Lancet*. 1976. i. 489: The free-living amoebic causation of rheumatoid and autoimmune diseases. *International Medicine* 1979. 1:20–25.

Zeman, F. J. 1983. Clinical Nutrition and Dietetics. Lexington, MA: The Collamore Press, D. C. Heath and Co.

Ziff, M. 1983. Diet in the treatment of rheumatoid arthritis. *Arthritis Rheum* 26:457–461.

Zurier, R. B., Mitnick, H., Bloomgarden, D., Weissman, G. Effect of bee venom on experimental arthritis. 1973. *Ann Rheum Dis* 32:466–470.

Zvaifler, N. J. 1985. Etiology and pathogenesis of rheumatoid arthritis. In: *Arthritis and Allied Conditions*. D. J. McCarty, (ed.). Philadelphia: Lea and Febiger.

INDEX